Lone Pine Publishing

Tree & Shrub
Gardening
for
Minnesota
and
Wisconsin

Don Engebretson
Don Williamson

© 2005 by Lone Pine Publishing
First printed in 2005   10 9 8 7 6 5 4 3 2
Printed in China

The Publisher: Lone Pine Publishing

10145 – 81 Avenue   1808 – B Street NW, Suite 140
Edmonton, AB, Canada T6E 1W9   Auburn, WA, USA 98001

Website: www.lonepinepublishing.com

Library and Archives Canada Cataloguing in Publication

Engebretson, Don, 1955–
   Tree & shrub gardening for Minnesota and Wisconsin / Don Engebretson, Don Williamson.

   Includes index.
   ISBN 13: 978-1-55105-483-4
   ISBN 10: 1-55105-483-3

   1. Ornamental trees—Minnesota. 2. Ornamental shrubs—Minnesota.
3. Ornamental trees—Wisconsin. 4. Ornamental shrubs—Wisconsin.
I. Williamson, Don, 1962– II. Title. III. Title: Tree and shrub gardening
for Minnesota and Wisconsin.
SB435.52.M6E53 2005   635.9'77'09775   C2005–901644–2

Editorial Director: Nancy Foulds
Project Editor: Sandra Bit
Editorial: Lee Craig, Volker Bodegom, Audrey McClellan, Nancy Foulds
Illustrations Coordinator: Carol Woo
Production Support: Elliot Engley, Trina Koscie
Photo Coordinator: Don Williamson
Production Manager: Gene Longson
Book Design: Heather Markham
Layout & Production: Curtis Pillipow, Heather Markham
Cover Design: Gerry Dotto
Illustrations: Ian Sheldon
Scanning & Digital Film: Elite Lithographers Co.

All photos by Tamara Eder, Tim Matheson, Laura Peters, Allison Penko and Tim Wood, except:
AAFC 76, 86a, 87b, 165a, 172b; Sandra Bit 246; Chicagoland Grows Inc. 153, 155a&b; Janet Davis 77a&b; Dean Didur 154b; Don Doucette 18a, 145a, 213a, 326, 328b; Derek Fell 102b, 103a&b, 192b, 219a, 315a; Erika Flatt 26a, 28b, 105c, 231b, 330, 333b; Anne Gordon 218, 219b, 275a; Lynne Harrison 169a, 184b; Linda Kershaw 104; Dawn Loewen 13a, 83a, 124b, 170, 237a, 238b; Janet Loughrey 265b; Heather Markham 284b; Steve Nikkila 168b, 289a&b, 293c; Kim Patrick O'Leary 33, 56a&c; Mark Turner 88, 101, 102a, 118a, 233a; Robert Ritchie 22b, 42a, 67a, 70, 72, 98b, 99a, 110, 111b, 120, 121a, 173b, 180b, 183b, 184a, 201a, 223a, 257a&b, 281a, 337a; USDA-US National Arboretum 154a; Don Williamson 275b.

Cover photos by Tim Matheson except where noted. *Clockwise from top left:* thornless honeylocust, maple (Laura Peters), maple, redbud, eunonymus, aralia, maple, maple (Laura Peters), viburnum berries (Tamara Eder)

Map: based on USDA plant hardiness zones map (1990)

This book is not intended to be a 'how-to' guide on eating garden plants. No plant or plant extract should be consumed unless you are certain of its identity and toxicity and of your potential for allergic reactions.

We acknowledge the financial support of the Government of Canada through the Book Publishing Industry Development Program (BPIDP) for our publishing activities.

PC: P16

CONTENTS

ACKNOWLEDGMENTS

My father knows his trees, and his shrubs, too, and when I was a child he would patiently teach me the names of the many varieties of trees and shrubs that grew in our large yard and the surrounding woods of Deephaven, Minnesota. During our summer vacations, he would identify the trees on our travels, always quick to point out the particular attributes of a hemlock, tamarack, balsam or poplar, and the differences between jack, red, white and scotch pines.

It all fell on deaf ears, of course. What little boy is the least bit interested in trees and shrubs? But little boys grow up, and if they're lucky, they will have had a father who instilled in them a kernel of appreciation for the wonderful plants that surround us. If they are extra lucky, they will also have had a mother who encouraged them to read and write and think for themselves. So this book is for my parents, and is the direct result of two things they told me as a child: "Know your trees and shrubs," and, "Turn off that stupid TV, and read a book!" —*Don Engebretson*

Don Williamson thanks the Creator.

Both authors gratefully acknowledge the many people who provided photographs for this project and the gardeners who allowed them to photograph their private gardens.

THE TREES & SHRUBS AT A GLANCE

A Pictorial Guide in Alphabetical Order, by Common Name

American Bittersweet
p. 76

Aralia
p. 78

Arborvitae
p. 80

Barberry
p. 88

Bog Rosemary
p. 104

Beech
p. 92

Birch
p. 96

Blueberry
p. 100

Boxwood
p. 106

Bush Honeysuckle
p. 110

Cotoneaster
p. 122

Butterfly Bush
p. 112

Cherry
p. 114

Chokeberry
p. 120

Crabapple
p. 126

Currant
p. 132

Deutzia
p. 138

Daphne
p. 134

Dogwood
p. 140

Douglas-Fir
p. 146

Elderberry
p. 148

Euonymus
p. 156

False Spirea
p. 164

Elm
p. 152

False Cypress
p. 160

Fir
p. 166

Forsythia
p. 170

Fringe Tree
p. 174

Hazelnut
p. 182

Ginkgo
p. 176

Hawthorn
p. 178

Heather
p. 186

Hemlock
p. 188

Holly
p. 190

Honeylocust
p. 192

Honeysuckle
p. 196

Hornbeam
p. 200

Horsechestnut
p. 202

Hydrangea
p. 206

Juniper
p. 212

Kentucky Coffee Tree
p. 218

Kerria
p. 220

Kiwi
p. 222

Lilac
p. 224

Linden
p. 230

Maackia
p. 234

Magnolia
p. 236

Maple
p. 240

Mountain Ash
p. 248

Ninebark
p. 252

Oak
p. 254

Pearl Bush
p. 258

Peashrub
p. 260

Persian Parrotia
p. 264

Pine
p. 266

Poplar and Aspen
p. 272

Potentilla
p. 276

Redbud
p. 280

Rhododendron
p. 282

Russian Cypress
p. 288

Serviceberry
p. 290

Smokebush
p. 294

Spirea
p. 298

Spruce
p. 304

Sumac
p. 308

Summersweet Clethra
p. 312

Tree Peony
p. 314

Trumpetcreeper
p. 316

Viburnum
p. 318

Virginia Creeper
p. 324

Witchhazel
p. 334

Weigela
p. 326

Willow
p. 330

Yew
p. 338

INTRODUCTION

Those of us fortunate enough to live in Minnesota and Wisconsin hardly need reminding of the importance of trees and shrubs to the landscape. From the majestic wilderness areas of our two great states to the attractive yards and parks in our cities and suburbs, trees and shrubs contribute a beauty and value to our land and lives that many of us perhaps take for granted.

First-time visitors traveling our states are often overheard to remark, "I can't get over how many trees there are!" Frequent flyers who regularly view our country from 30,000 feet can attest that our two 'Superior States' are covered by a richer, greener carpet than most of America. Our region's relatively cool climate, vast stretches of rich soil, and ample rainfall have proven to be one of nature's preferred growing ranges for vast varieties of deciduous and evergreen trees and shrubs. Incorporating both into our residential landscapes is an essential task that brings great reward.

Trees and shrubs are woody perennials that live for three or more years. They normally maintain a permanent live structure above ground all year, but in cold climates a few shrubs die back to the ground each winter. The root system, protected by the soil over the winter, sends up new shoots in spring; shrubs that form flowers on new wood will bloom that same year. Such plants act like herbaceous perennials, but because they are woody in their native climates, they are still classified as shrubs. Buddleia (butterfly bush) is one such perennial-like shrub.

In general, a tree is defined as a woody plant having a single trunk and growing over 15' tall, whereas a shrub is multi-stemmed and no taller than 15'. These definitions are not absolute, because some tall trees are multi-stemmed, and some short shrubs have single trunks. Even the height definitions are open to interpretation. For example, some Japanese maple cultivars may be multi-stemmed and grow only about 10' tall, but they are still usually referred to as trees. Furthermore, a given species may grow as a tree in favorable conditions but be reduced to a shrub on harsher sites. It is always best to judge the suitability of a tree or shrub for your garden by its expected mature size.

Some vines are also included in this guide. Like trees and shrubs, these plants maintain living woody stems above ground over winter. They generally require a supporting

Red horsechesnut
'Crimson King' maple

structure to climb upon, but many can also be grown as trailing ground-covers. Again, the definition is not absolute. With proper pruning, some vines can be trained to form free-standing shrubs, and, conversely, some shrubs can be trained to grow up and over walls and other structures.

Woody plants are characterized by leaf type—whether deciduous or evergreen and needled or broad-leaved. Deciduous plants lose all their leaves each fall or winter. They can have needles, like dawn redwood and larch, or broad leaves, like maple and dogwood. Evergreen trees and shrubs do not lose their leaves in winter. They can also be needled or broad-leaved, like pine and rhododendron, respectively. Semi-evergreen plants are generally ever-greens that in cold climates lose some or all of their leaves—for example, some types of viburnum.

The climate of Wisconsin and Minnesota is conducive to growing a wide variety of trees and shrubs. Cold winters bring the dormancy that woody plants need to renew their growth cycle. Summers are warm enough to stimulate strong growth, a woody plant's primary defense against disease and insect attack.

Woody plants prefer gradual cooling to send them into dormancy. When cold Canadian air, which tends to blow across our states from the northwest to the southeast, brings far-below-freezing temperatures within hours of warm 'Indian summer' conditions in mid-fall, woody plants can be harmed.

Once winter arrives, woody plants can be stressed—and young plants even killed—if snow is scarce and the freeze line extends too far into the root zone. Winter winds can also test the mettle of woody plants. Some plants are susceptible to too much sun in winter; one side of the plant may be warmed enough to start the sap flowing, only to have nighttime temperatures freeze it again. Injurious cracks in the bark (sunscald) can then develop.

You can provide winter protection by installing a burlap wall. Before the ground freezes, take wooden stakes that are taller than the plant (think about winter sun angle) and pound them into the ground on the plant's south side. Use two stakes for a flat screen or three if you want a mild 'V' shape. Staple burlap to the stakes; it should be four to six inches away from branch tips.

Although both Minnesota and Wisconsin receive enough natural moisture to allow many woody plants to survive, the timing of that moisture can be questionable. Supplemental watering is nearly always needed during summer and fall for young woody plants and for all evergreens, even when the amount of rainfall is average. Fall is an important time to continue watering evergreens. Evergreens continue to transpire throughout winter, losing moisture to the atmosphere at a time when their frozen roots are unable to replace it.

Hardiness zones listed for a plant are useful to help you decide what to place in the landscape as well as where to place it. Don't, however, be put off because a catalog or book says a plant is hardy only to a certain zone. Local topography in the yard creates microclimates, small areas that may be more or less favorable for growing different plants.

Colorado blue spruce
Rosemary willow

'Betty' magnolia
Ponderosa pine

Daphne

Buildings, hills, low spots, drainage patterns and prevailing winds all influence your garden and its micro-climates (see Getting Started, p. 24, for more information on assessing conditions in your garden and growing out-of-zone plants). Pick the right spot in your garden for that tender shrub, and you may be surprised at how well it does.

Wisconsin and Minnesota soils are influenced by various factors, some dating back to the glacial eras. Many soil types can be found in a small geographical area, so you will need to become familiar with your yard and garden's particular soil profile. One influential factor is how recently your home was built and whether it has a basement. Contractors digging for foundations often unearth dense clay subsoil that becomes the top layer of your garden soil. This nearly impermeable layer creates an inhospitable environment for many trees or shrubs you may want to plant. You will notice how often in this book the ideal soil for a plant is described as loose, deep, well drained and slightly acidic.

No matter what challenges you face in your garden, you will discover a tree, shrub or vine that thrives in your space. A trip to a nearby park, arboretum or botanical garden, where trees are labeled and unusual specimens grown, is invaluable for showing you trees, shrubs and vines that thrive in your area. Also, keep your eyes open when walking through your neighborhood. You may see a tree or shrub that you hadn't noticed before or that you were told wouldn't grow in your area. What is actually growing is the best guide.

HARDINESS ZONES MAPS

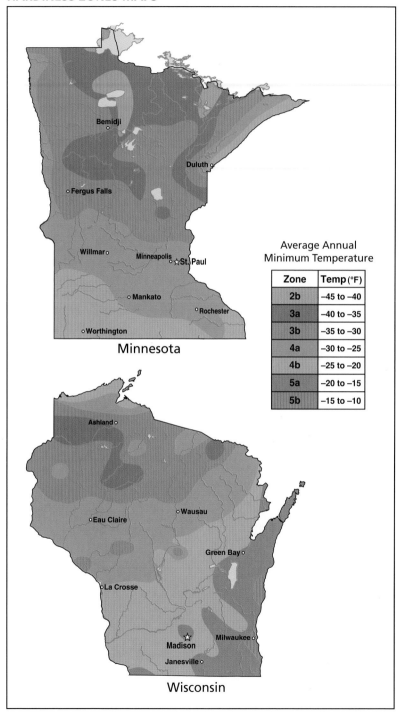

Minnesota

Average Annual
Minimum Temperature

Zone	Temp (°F)
2b	−45 to −40
3a	−40 to −35
3b	−35 to −30
4a	−30 to −25
4b	−25 to −20
5a	−20 to −15
5b	−15 to −10

Wisconsin

Many enthusiastic and creative people garden in Minnesota and Wisconsin. Individuals, growers, societies, schools and publications located throughout our two great states provide information, encouragement and fruitful debate for the novice or experienced gardener. Wisconsin and Minnesota gardeners are passionate about their plants and will gladly share their knowledge and opinions about what is best for any little patch of ground.

Outstanding garden shows, public gardens, arboretums and display gardens in our two states attract gardeners and growers from all over the world. Seek them out as sources of inspiration and information. Open yourself to the possibilities—you'll be surprised by the diversity of woody plants that thrive in our area. Initially you may want to plant mostly tried and true, dependable varieties, but don't be afraid to try something different or new. Gardening with trees and shrubs is fun and can be a great adventure if you're willing to take up the challenge.

Virginia creeper

Butterfly bush

Rhododendron

Woody Plants in the Garden

Trees and shrubs create a framework around which to design a garden. These long-lasting features anchor the landscape; in a well-designed garden they create interest all year. In spring and summer, woody plants provide shade and beauty with foliage and flowers. In fall, the leaves of many tree and shrub species change color, and brightly colored fruit attracts attention and birds. In winter, the true backbone of the garden is revealed; the sculpture-like branches of deciduous trees and shrubs are laid bare, perhaps dusted with snow or frost, and evergreens take precedence in keeping the garden colorful.

Carefully selected and placed, woody plants are a vital and vibrant element of any landscape, from the smallest city lot to the largest country acreage. They can provide privacy and hide unattractive views. Conversely, they can frame an attractive view and draw attention to particular features or garden areas. Trees and shrubs soften the hard lines of such structures as buildings, fences, walls and driveways. Well-positioned woody plants create an attractive background against which other plants can shine. Used in groups, trees and shrubs can give spectacular flower or fall color shows, and a truly exceptional species with year-round appeal will stand alone as a specimen plant in a prime location.

In addition, woody plants help moderate the climate in your home

Birds and squirrels are frequent garden visitors.

American beech (below) is a great shade provider.

and garden. As windbreaks, they provide shelter from winter cold, reducing heating costs and protecting tender garden plants. A well-placed deciduous tree keeps the house cool and shaded in summer but allows much-appreciated warmth and light from the sun through in winter. Woody plants also prevent soil erosion, retain soil moisture, reduce noise and filter the air.

Attracting wildlife is an often overlooked advantage of gardening. As cities expand, our living space encroaches on more and more wildlife habitat. By choosing plants, particularly native plants, that are beneficial to local wildlife, we provide food and shelter to birds and other animals, thereby helping fulfill our obligation as stewards of the environment. We can bring nature closer to home. The only difficulty is that the local wildlife may so enjoy a garden that they consume it! It is possible, though, to find a balance and attract wildlife while protecting the garden from ruin.

When the time comes to select woody plants, think carefully about the various physical constraints of your garden and the purposes you want the plants to serve. First and foremost, consider the size of your garden in relation to the mature sizes of the plants in question. Very large plants are always a bad idea in a small garden. Remember, too, that trees and shrubs grow not only up, but also out. Within a few years, what started as a small plant may become a large, spreading tree. Spruces are often sold as small trees, but many eventually grow too wide for small garden. Always learn the mature width of the woody plants you select—and plant accordingly.

Another consideration that relates to size is placement. Don't plant trees and shrubs too close to buildings, walkways, entryways or driveways. A tree planted right next to a house may hit the overhang of the roof, and trying to fix the problem by pruning will often spoil the tree's natural appearance. Plants placed too close to paths, doors and driveways may eventually block access completely and give the property an unkempt appearance.

Consider, too, the various features (outstanding elements that attract you to a plant) of tree and shrub species. Many plants have more than one feature, thereby providing interest over a longer period. Decide which features (described below) are most important to you, and which will best enhance your garden. A carefully selected group of woody plants can add beauty to the garden all year. Whether you are looking for showy flowers, fall color, fast growth, unusual bark or a beautiful fragrance, you can find trees or shrubs with features to suit your design. Consult the individual plant entries and the Quick Reference Chart at the back of the book.

Form is the general shape and growth habit of the plant. Trees come in a variety of shapes, from tall and columnar to wide and gracefully weeping. Similarly, shrubs may be rounded and bushy or low and ground hugging. Form can also vary as the year progresses and leaves are developed and lost. A unique winter growth habit can make a tree or shrub truly outstanding.

Swedish columnar aspen has a fastigiate form.
Dwarf Alberta spruce has a dwarf form.

White fir

'Blue Chip' juniper is a prostrate plant.

'Tricolor' beech

You should be familiar with some growth-form terminology when considering a purchase. A *shade tree* is commonly a large deciduous tree, but it can be any tree that provides shade. An *upright, fastigiate* or *columnar* plant has main branches and stems pointing upward and is often quite narrow. *Dwarf* properly refers to any variety, cultivar or hybrid that is smaller than the species, but the term is sometimes mistakenly used to mean a small, slow-growing plant. The crucial statistic is the expected size at maturity. If a species grows to 100', then a 30–50' variety would be a dwarf but might still be too big for your garden. *Prostrate* and *procumbent* plants are low growing, bearing branches and stems that spread horizontally across the ground. These forms are sometimes grafted onto upright stems to create lovely, weeping plant forms.

Foliage is one of a plant's most enduring and important features. Leaves come in a variety of colors, shapes, sizes, textures and arrangements. You can find shades of green, blue, red, purple, yellow, white or silver. *Variegated* types have two or more colors combined on a single leaf. *Rugose* refers to leaves that are tightly wrinkled. The variety of shapes is even more astounding, from short, sharply pointed needles to broad, rounded leaves the size of dinner plates. Leaf margins can be smooth, like those of many rhododendrons, or so finely divided that the foliage appears lacy or fern-like, as with some elderberry and sumac cultivars. Foliage often varies seasonally, progressing from tiny, pale green spring buds to the vibrant colors of fall. Evergreens provide welcome greenery even in the snowiest, coldest depths of winter.

Growing plants with different leaf sizes, textures and colors creates contrast and makes your garden more interesting and appealing. An entire garden can be designed based on varied foliage. Whether it forms a neutral backdrop or stands out in sharp contrast to the plants around it, foliage is a vital consideration in any garden.

Flowers are so influential that their beauty may be enough reason to grow a tree or shrub that is otherwise dull or even unattractive, such as forsythia. Keep in mind that flowering generally lasts just a few weeks or occasionally a month; only a few woody plants flower all summer. You can achieve different but equally striking effects if you group plants that flower at the same time or distribute them around the garden. To always have something in bloom, choose species with staggered flowering periods. An easy, effective way to create a season-long progression of blooms is to visit your garden center regularly. People who shop for plants only in spring often have gardens dominated by spring bloomers.

Fruit comes in many forms, including winged maple samaras, dangling birch catkins, spiny horsechestnut capsules and the more obviously 'fruity' serviceberry and crabapple pomes. Fruit can be a double-edged sword. It is often attractive and provides interest in the garden in late summer and fall, when most plants are past their prime. When

Forsythia flowers announce spring's arrival.

Nanking cherry

Paper birch

Many honeysuckles have fragrant flowers.
Corkscrew hazelnut in flower

it drops, however, it can attract pests and create a mess and even a foul odor if allowed to rot on the ground. Choose the location of your fruiting tree carefully. If you know the fruit can be messy, don't plant it near a patio or a sidewalk. Most fruit isn't terribly troublesome, but consider that some seasonal cleanup may be required.

Bark is one of the most overlooked features. Species with interesting bark will greatly enhance your landscape, particularly in winter. Bark can be furrowed, smooth, ridged, papery, scaly, exfoliating (peeling) or colorful. A few species valued for their bark are birch, ninebark, cherry, paperbark maple, beech and hornbeam.

Fragrance, although usually associated with flowers, is also a potential feature of the leaves, fruit and even wood of trees and shrubs. Summersweet clethra, witchhazel, arborvitae, viburnum and lilac are examples of plants with appealing scents. Situate fragrant plants near your home, where the scent can waft into an open window, or over pathways.

Branches as a feature combine elements of form and bark and, like those two features, can become an important winter garden attribute. Branches may have an unusual gnarled or twisted shape (corkscrew hazelnut), bear protective spines or thorns (barberry and hawthorn) or be brightly colored (red-osier dogwood and kerria).

Growth rate and **life span,** although not aesthetic features of woody plants, are nonetheless important aspects to consider. A fast-growing tree or shrub that grows 24" or more a year will mature quickly and can be used to fill in space in a new garden. A slow-growing species that grows less than 12" a year may be more suitable in a space-limited garden.

Short-lived plants are usually quick to mature and reach flowering age, and they often appeal to people who enjoy changing their garden design or who aren't sure exactly what they want. Long-lived trees, on the other hand, are an investment in time. Some trees can take a human lifetime to reach their mature size, and some may not flower until 10 years after planting. You can enjoy a long-lived tree as it develops, and you will also leave a legacy for future generations—your tree may well outlive you.

Red elderberry

Blue holly

Fast-Growing Trees & Shrubs
- Ash
- Birch
- Butterfly bush
- Elderberry
- Forsythia
- Honeylocust
- Hydrangea
- Lilac
- Linden
- Poplar
- Red-twig dogwood
- Silver maple
- Staghorn sumac
- Virginia creeper

Slow-Growing Trees & Shrubs
- Beech
- Boxwood
- Chokeberry
- Daphne
- Euonymus
- Fir
- Fringe tree
- Ginkgo
- Holly
- Hornbeam
- Paperbark maple
- Rhododendron
- Russian cypress
- Yew

Getting Started

Before you fall in love with the idea of having a certain plant in your garden, it's important to consider the growing conditions it needs and if any areas of your garden are suitable. Your tree or shrub will need to not only survive, but thrive, in order for its flowers or other features to reach their full potential.

All plants are adapted to do best under certain growing conditions. Choosing plants to match your garden is far more practical than trying to alter your garden to match the plants. Yet it is through the use of trees and shrubs that we can best alter a garden's conditions. Over time, a tree can change a sunny, exposed garden into a shaded one, and a hedge can turn a windswept area into a sheltered one. The woody plants you choose must be able to thrive in the garden as it exists now, or they may not live long enough to produce these changes.

Light, soil conditions and exposure are important factors to guide your selection. As you plan, look at your garden as it exists now, but keep in mind the changes trees and shrubs will bring.

LIGHT

Buildings, trees, fences, the time of day and the time of year influence the amount of light in your garden. Light levels are often divided into four categories for gardening purposes: full sun, partial shade (partial sun), light shade and full shade. Some plants can adapt to a wide range of light levels, but most have narrower preferences.

Full sun locations receive direct sunlight most of the day—for instance, an open location along a south-facing wall. Heat from the sun may be more intense in one spot than another, depending on, for example, the degree of shelter from wind.

Partial shade locations receive direct sun for part of the day and shade for the rest. An unobstructed east- or west-facing wall gets partial shade. **Light shade** locations receive shade most or all of the day, but with some sun getting through to ground level, such as when a small-leaved tree allows dappled light onto the ground beneath it. **Full shade** locations receive no direct sunlight. The north wall of a house is often in full shade.

SOIL

Plants have a vital relationship with the soil in which they grow. Many important plant functions take place underground. Soil holds air, water, nutrients, organic matter and various organisms. Plant roots depend upon these resources for growth and use the soil to anchor the plant body. In turn, plants influence soil development by, for example, breaking down large clods with their roots and by increasing soil fertility when they die and decompose.

Soil particles come in various sizes. Sand particles are the largest. Water drains quickly from a sandy soil, and nutrients can be rapidly washed away. Sand has lots of air spaces and doesn't compact easily. Clay particles are the smallest, visible only through a microscope. Water penetrates clay very slowly and drains away even more slowly. Clay holds the most nutrients but has little room for air, and it compacts easily. Silt particles are smaller than sand particles and larger than clay particles. Most soils are loams, made up of a combination of different particle sizes.

Slope also affects the ground's drainage and moisture-holding properties. Knowing how quickly

Hemlock grows well in full sun or full shade. False cypress prefers full sun.

Potentilla adapts well to clay soil.

Bog rosemary does well in wet soil.

Smokebush is very tolerant of gravely, alkaline soil.

the water drains out of your soil will help you decide whether you should plant moisture-loving or drought-tolerant plants. Rocky soil on a hillside will probably drain quickly and is best for plants that prefer a well-drained soil. Low-lying areas tend to retain water longer, and some areas may rarely drain at all. Moist areas suit plants that require a consistent water supply; constantly wet areas should be reserved for plants that are adapted to boggy conditions.

In very wet areas, drainage can be improved by adding organic matter to the soil, by installing some form of drainage tile or by building raised beds. Consult with nursery professionals before adding sand to heavy clay soils, or you may create something much like concrete. Working some gypsum into a clay soil along with organic matter will help break it up and allow water to penetrate and drain more easily. Water retention in sandy soil can be improved by adding organic matter.

Another important consideration is the soil's pH—its acidity or alkalinity. Soil pH influences the availability of nutrients for plants. A pH of 7 is neutral; lower values (down to 0) indicate acidic conditions, and higher values (up to 14) indicate alkaline conditions. Most plants prefer a neutral soil pH of 6.5 to 7.5. Ask your Minnesota or Wisconsin cooperative extension agent about your local soils. The agent can make general recommendations or will tell you how to have your soil tested. Highly recommended, a soil test is useful for indicating the exact pH and other conditions of your particular soil.

If a soil test reveals a pH problem, you can make your soil more acidic by adding horticultural sulfur or more alkaline by adding horticultural lime. The test results should include recommendations for additive quantities.

It is much easier to amend soil in a small area than in an entire garden. The soil in a raised bed or planter can be adjusted easily to suit a few plants whose soil requirements vary greatly from the conditions in your garden.

Heather requires acidic soil.

Ninebark thrives in alkaline soil.

EXPOSURE

Exposure is an important consideration in all gardens that include woody plants. Wind, heat, cold, rain and snow are the elements to which your plants may be exposed, and some are more susceptible to injury by these forces than others. Buildings, walls, fences, hills and hedges or other woody plants can all influence your garden's exposure.

Hedges make excellent windbreaks.

Wind can cause extensive damage to plants, particularly to evergreens in winter. Plants in windy locations become dehydrated if they can't replace water lost through the leaves fast enough, or can't replace it at all because the ground is frozen. Although the standard recommendation is to keep plants well watered in fall until the ground freezes, it is just as important to prevent drought stress during the heat of summer. Tests have shown that a plant deprived of water in summer suffers greater winter windburn. The goal is to avert plant stresses throughout the growing season. Broad-leaved evergreens, such as rhododendron and holly, are most at risk from winter dehydration, so grow them in a sheltered site.

Daphne is worth trying in zone 3.

Young barberry in mulched bed

Strong winds can cause physical damage by breaking weak branches or by blowing entire trees over. However, woody plants often make excellent windbreaks to shelter other plants. Hedges and trees temper the wind's effect without the turbulence found on the leeward side of more solid structures, such as walls or fences. Windbreak trees should be species that can flex in the wind or should be planted far enough from buildings to avoid extensive property damage if they or their branches fall.

Hardiness zones (see map, p. 15, and Quick Reference Chart, p. 342)

give an indication of whether a species can tolerate the conditions in your area, but they are only guidelines. Daphne is generally listed as a Zone 4 plant but often thrives in sheltered spots in Zone 3. Don't be afraid to try species that are not listed as hardy for your area. Plants are incredibly adaptable and just might surprise you.

Here are some tips for growing out-of-zone plants:

• Before planting, observe your garden on a frosty morning. Do some areas escape frost? They are potential sites for tender plants. Keep in mind that cold air tends to collect in low spots and can run downhill, through breaks in plantings and structures, much as water does.

• Provide shelter from the prevailing wind.

• Plant in groups to create windbreaks and microclimates. Rhododendrons, for instance, grow better if they are planted in small groups or grouped with plants that have similar growing requirements.

• Mulch young plants in fall, at least for their first two years, with a thick layer of clean organic mulch, such as bark chips, composted woodchips, composted leaves or compost mixed with peat moss. Good winter protection requires a minimum depth of 6–8".

• Water thoroughly before the ground freezes in winter.

• Cover or screen frost-tender shrubs with a layer of burlap or horticultural cloth, or use special insulating blankets available at garden centers. Plants in containers can be dug into the vegetable garden or placed under shelter or against a building for protection.

Purchasing Trees & Shrubs

Having considered the features you like and the range of growing conditions your garden offers, you can select the plants. Any reputable garden center should have a good selection of popular woody plants. Finding unusual specimens could require a few phone calls and a trip to a specialized nursery. Mail-order nurseries can be a great source of the newest and most unusual plants.

You'll also find many of the newest and hardiest varieties of trees and shrubs close to home. For over 150 years, the University of Minnesota has been a world leader in the research and development of hardy woody plants. Often the most highly recommended variety of apple, apricot, cherry, pear or plum will be a U of M introduction. Varieties of crab-apples, dogwoods, blueberries, azaleas, maples and many other kinds of woody trees and shrubs that thrive in northern conditions have also been developed in the research facilities of the U of M, at the University of Wisconsin and in private nurseries in both states.

Many garden centers and nurseries offer a one-year warranty on trees and shrubs, but because trees take a long time to mature, always choose the healthiest plants regardless. Never purchase weak, damaged or diseased plants, even if they cost less. Examine the bark and avoid plants with visible damage. Check that the growth is even and appropriate for the species. A shrub should be bushy and branched right to the ground, and a tree should have a

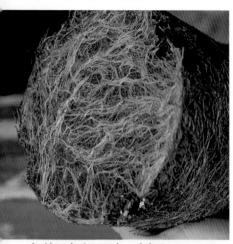

Avoid purchasing root-bound plants.
Purchasing plants in fall lets you see the fall color.

strong leader. Observe the leaf and flower buds. If they are dry and fall off easily, the plant has been deprived of moisture. The stem or stems should be strong, supple and unbroken. The rootball should be soft and moist when touched. Do not buy a plant with a dry rootball.

Woody plants are available for purchase in three forms:

Bare-root stock has roots surrounded only by moist sawdust or peat moss and a plastic wrapping. Reject stock that appears to have dried out during shipping. Keep the roots moist and cool, and plant as soon as possible in spring (see p. 35).

Balled-and-burlapped (B & B) stock comes with the roots surrounded by soil and wrapped in burlap, often secured with a wire cage for larger plants. The plants are usually field grown and then dug up, balled and burlapped the year they are sold. Large trees are available in this form, but be aware that the soil and rootball can be very heavy, and extra expenses for delivery and planting may apply. It is essential that the rootball remain moist. You can plant almost anytime during the growing season (see p. 35).

Container plants are most common at garden centers and nurseries. They are grown in pots filled with potting soil and have established root systems. Container stock is easy to plant, establishes quickly after planting and can be planted almost anytime during the growing season (see p. 37).

When choosing a plant, make sure it hasn't been in the container

Temporary winter storage for container plants.

too long. If the roots densely encircle the inside of the pot, then the plant has become root-bound. A root-bound tree or shrub will not establish well, and as the roots mature and thicken, they can choke and kill the plant. Note that sometimes field-grown stock is dug and sold in containers instead of burlap; ask if you aren't sure. Such plants must be treated like balled-and-burlapped stock when planting.

Bigger is not always better when it comes to choosing woody plants. Smaller plants of a given species often grow up healthier and more robust than larger stock, particularly in the case of field-grown (as opposed to container-grown) plants. When a plant is dug up out of the field, the roots are severely cut back. The smaller the plant, the more quickly it can recover from the shock of being uprooted.

Improper handling can damage woody plants. You can lift bare-root stock by the stem, but do not lift any other trees or shrubs by the trunk or branches. Rather, lift by the rootball or container, or, if the plant is too large to lift, place it on a tarp or mat and drag it.

Care during transport is also critical. Even a short trip home from the nursery can be traumatic for a plant. The heat produced inside a car can quickly dehydrate a tree or shrub. If you are using an open vehicle for transport, lay the plant down or cover it to shield it from the wind. Avoid mechanical damage such as rubbing or breaking branches during transport.

Once home, water the plant if it is dry and keep it in a sheltered location until you plant it. Remove damaged growth and broken branches but do no other pruning. Plant your tree or shrub as soon as possible. A bare-root tree or shrub should be planted in a large container of potting soil if it will not be planted outdoors immediately. If you must store a container plant over a cold winter before planting, bury the entire container until spring.

Planting Trees & Shrubs

Before you pick up a shovel and start digging, be certain to call either the Minnesota or Wisconsin one-call service that will prompt all utility companies to mark the gas, electric, phone and any other underground utility lines. Your local government or county offices will usually have the phone number handy if you can't locate it. Be careful when digging around underground electric or gas lines, and don't plant trees or shrubs within three feet of them. Even if you don't damage anything by digging, the roots may cause trouble in the future, or the plant may have to be cut down if the pipes or wires ever need servicing.

Check the mature plant size as well. The plant you have in front of you is likely pretty small. Once it reaches its mature height and spread, will it still fit the space you have chosen? Is it far enough away from the house, the driveway and walkways? Will it hit the overhang of the house or any overhead power lines?

If you're planting several shrubs, make sure that they won't grow too close together once they are mature. Normally, to determine the spacing, add the mature spreads and then divide by two. For example, when planting a shrub with an expected spread of 4' next to one with an expected spread of 6', you would plant them 5' apart. To avoid gaps in hedges and windbreaks on maturity, the spacing should be just one-half to two-thirds the spread of the mature plant.

Finally, double-check the conditions. Will the soil drainage be adequate? Will the plant get the right amount of light? Is the site very windy? It's important to start with the plant in the right spot and in the best conditions you can give it.

WHEN TO PLANT

For the most part, trees and shrubs can be planted at any time of year, but some seasons are better for the plants and more convenient than others. Preferred planting times are given at the beginning of each plant entry in this book.

Spring is a great time to plant shrubs and some trees, such as redbud and magnolia. It gives the tree or shrub an entire growing season to become established before winter and get started before the weather turns really hot. Avoid planting during the hottest and driest part of summer, when plants suffer the immediate effects of transplant shock combined with the stress of blistering sun and heat. For most trees, planting in early fall is best, avoiding all the heat of summer and giving them at least three months to establish root systems before slipping into winter dormancy.

Begonias surrounded by boxwood hedge

Bare-root stock is generally available only in spring and must be planted as soon as possible to avoid moisture loss.

Balled-and-burlapped and container stock can be planted at any time with satisfactory results, but it is always wise to avoid planting in the heat of summer.

The time of day to plant is also a consideration. Avoid planting in the heat of the day. Planting in the morning or evening—or on a cloudy, calm day—will be easier on both you and the plant.

It's a good idea to plant as soon as possible after you bring your specimen home. If you have to store the tree or shrub for a short time before planting, keep it out of direct sunlight and ensure the rootball remains moist.

PREPARING THE HOLE

Trees and shrubs should always be planted at the depth at which they were growing, or just above the roots if you are unsure of the depth for bare-root stock. The depth in the center of the hole should equal the depth of the rootball or container, but it is usually helpful to dig deeper around the edge. This hole shape prevents the plant from sinking as the soil settles and encourages excess water to drain away from the new plant.

Sizing up the hole (above), digging the hole (below)

Be sure that the plant is not set too deeply. Planting even 2–4" too deep can cause problems. Most potted, field-grown trees are planted deeply in the pot in order to keep the freshly dug tree from tipping over, and there may be mulch on top of the soil as well. In this case it is generally best to scrape off the soil until you find the root mass and then plant to just above it.

Make the hole for bare-root stock wide enough to completely contain the expanded roots, with a bit of extra room on the sides. Make the hole for balled-and-burlapped or container stock about twice the width of the rootball or container.

The soil around the rootball or in the container is not likely to be the same composition as the soil you just removed from the hole. The extra room in the hole allows the new roots an easier medium (backfill) to grow into than undisturbed soil, providing a transition zone from the rootball soil to the existing on-site soil. It is good practice to rough up the sides and bottom of the hole to aid in root transition and water flow. It is also good practice to loosen the soil for a distance beyond the hole with a garden fork or power tiller.

PLANTING BARE-ROOT STOCK

Remove the plastic and sawdust from the roots. Soak the entire root system of bare-root trees and shrubs in a bucket of water for 12 hours prior to planting. Make sure the hole is big enough to allow the roots to fully extend. Fan out the roots and center the plant over the hole's central mound—which is often made cone shaped and larger than for burlapped or container plants—using it to help spread out and support the roots.

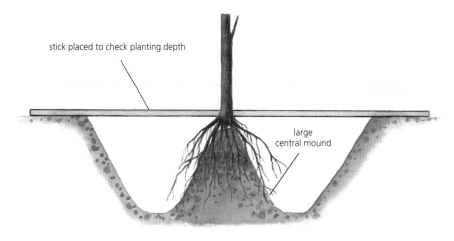

stick placed to check planting depth

large
central mound

Planting bare-root stock

PLANTING BALLED-AND-BURLAPPED STOCK

Burlap was originally made out of natural fibers. It could be loosened and left wrapped around the rootball to eventually decompose. Modern burlap may or may not be made of natural fibers, and it can be difficult to tell the difference. Synthetic fibers will not decompose and will eventually choke the roots. It is always best to remove any burlap from around the rootball to prevent girdling and to maximize contact between the roots and the soil. If roots are already growing through the burlap, remove as much burlap as you can while avoiding damage to these new roots. If you know the burlap is natural and decide to leave it on, loosen it from the rootball and tuck it below the soil line so it won't wick water into the air away from the roots.

If a wire basket holds the burlap in place, it should be removed as well. You may need strong wire cutters to get the basket off. If the tree is very heavy, it may not be possible to remove the base of the basket, but cut away at least the sides, where most of the important roots will be growing.

With the basket removed, set the still-burlapped plant on the center mound in the hole. Lean the plant over to one side and roll the upper part of the burlap down to the ground. When you lean the plant in the opposite direction, you can often pull the burlap out from under the roots. If the tree is difficult to move once it's in the hole, you may need to cut away as much burlap as you can instead.

Past horticultural wisdom suggested removing some top branches when planting to make up for roots lost when the plant was dug out of the field. The theory was that the roots could not provide enough water to the leaves, so top growth should be removed to achieve 'balance.' We now know that the top growth—where photosynthesis occurs and thus where energy is produced—is necessary for root development. The new tree or shrub might drop some leaves, but don't be alarmed; the plant is doing its own balancing. A light pruning will not adversely affect the plant, but remove only those branches that have been damaged during transport and planting. Leave your new plant to settle in for a year or two before you start any formative pruning.

PLANTING CONTAINER STOCK

Containers are usually made of plastic or pressed fiber. Both kinds should be removed before planting. Although some containers appear to be made of peat moss, they do not decompose well. The roots may have difficulty penetrating the pot sides, and the fiber will wick moisture away from the roots.

Container stock is very easy to plant (see photos, p. 37). Gently remove or cut off the container and observe the root mass to see whether the plant is root-bound. If roots are circling around the inside of the container, they should be loosened or sliced. Any large roots encircling the soil or growing into the center of the root mass instead of outward should be removed before planting. A sharp pair of hand pruners or a pocketknife will work well for this task.

BACKFILLING

With your bare-root, balled-and-burlapped or container plant in the hole and standing straight up, it is time to replace the soil. A small amount of organic matter, well mixed into the backfill, will

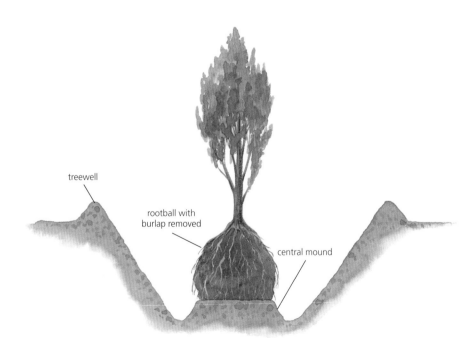

treewell

rootball with
burlap removed

central mound

Planting balled-and-burlapped stock

1. Gently remove container.

2. Ensure proper planting depth.

3. Backfill with amended soil.

4. Settle backfilled soil with water.

5. Ensure newly planted shrub is well watered.

6. Add a layer of mulch.

Young tree in its new home

Adding organic matter to backfill soil

be more vulnerable to blowdown in a strong wind.

Backfill should generally reach the same depth the plant was grown at previously, or just above the rootball. If planting into a heavy soil, raise the plant about 1" to help improve surface drainage away from the crown and roots. The graft unions of grafted stock are generally kept above ground to make it easy to spot and remove suckers sprouting from the rootstock.

When backfilling, it is important to have good root-to-soil contact for initial stability and good establishment. If large air pockets remain after backfilling, the result could be excessive settling and root drying. Use water to settle the soil gently around the roots and in the hole, being careful not to drown the plant. It is a good idea to backfill in small amounts rather than all at once. Add some soil, then water it down, repeating until the hole is full. Stockpile any soil that remains after backfilling and use it to top up the soil around the plant as the backfill settles.

If you are working with a heavy clay soil, ensure that the surface drainage slopes away from your new transplant. With other soil types, build a temporary 2–4" high, doughnut-like mound of soil around the perimeter of the hole to capture extra water. Water into this reservoir for at least the whole first season. Doing so ensures that water will percolate down through the new root mass. The ring of soil, called a **treewell,** is an excellent tool for conserving water, especially during dry spells. In periods of heavy rain you may need to breach the treewell to prevent the roots from becoming waterlogged. The treewell can be

encourage the plant to become established, but too much creates a pocket of rich soil that the roots may be reluctant to move beyond. If the roots do not venture beyond the immediate area of the hole, the tree or shrub will be weaker and much more susceptible to problems, and the encircling roots could eventually choke the plant. Such a tree will also

rebuilt when drier conditions resume. In a year or two, once the tree or shrub has become established, the treewell will no longer be needed and should be permanently removed.

To conserve water, mulch around the new planting. Composted wood chips or shredded bark will stay where placed, unlike pebble bark or peat moss. Do not use too much (2–4" is adequate) and avoid mulching directly against the trunk or base of the plant, which can encourage disease problems.

STAKING

Some trees may need to be staked in order to provide support while the roots establish. Staking is recommended only for bare-root trees, top-heavy trees over 5' tall or trees planted in windy locations (particularly evergreens, which tend to catch winter winds). The stakes should be removed as soon as the roots have had a chance to become established, which normally takes about a year.

Growing trees and shrubs without stakes is preferable because unstaked trees develop more roots

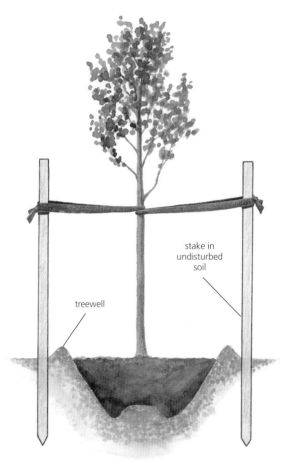

stake in
undisturbed
soil

treewell

Two-stake method

and stronger trunks. Most newly planted trees can stand on their own without staking. You can always stake later if you find it's needed.

Two common methods are used for staking newly planted trees. Wood or metal stakes can be used.

The **two-stake** method is suitable for small trees (about 5–6' tall) and for trees in low-wind areas. Drive two tall, sturdy stakes into the soil on directly opposite sides of the tree, in line with the prevailing wind and just outside the planting hole.

Driving the stakes near the tree can damage the roots and will not provide adequate support. Tie strong cord, rope, cable or wire to the stakes. The end that goes around the trunk should be a wide, belt-like strap of material that will not injure the trunk. Your local garden center should have ties designed for this purpose, or you can cushion the rope or wire with a section of rubber hose. Attach the straps to the tree about 3–4' above the ground.

treewell

Three-stake method

The **three-stake** method is used for larger trees and for trees in areas subject to strong or shifting winds. This technique is much the same as the two-stake method, but with three short, sturdy stakes evenly spaced around the tree. Attach heavy wire or cable to each stake, again with wide strapping or padding on the end that goes around the trunk. To keep the straps in place, position them just above the lower branches.

Here are a few points to keep in mind, regardless of the staking method used:
- Never wrap rope, wire or cable directly around a tree trunk. Always use non-damaging material. Reposition the strapping every two to three months to prevent any rubbing or girdling injury.
- Never tie trees so firmly that they can't move. Young trees need to be able to move in the wind to produce strong trunks and to develop roots more thickly in appropriate places to compensate for the prevailing wind.
- Don't leave the stakes in place too long. One year is sufficient for almost all trees. The stakes should be there only long enough to give the roots some time to grow and establish. The tree will actually be weaker if the stakes are left for too long, and over time the ties can damage the trunk and weaken or kill the tree.

TRANSPLANTING
If you plan your garden carefully, you should rarely need to move trees or shrubs. Some woody plants (see the individual species entries) resent being moved once established, and you should avoid transplanting them whenever possible.

When it is necessary, you can generally transplant evergreens in spring before growth starts, or later in the season after it stops, as long as it is not during a spell of hot weather. Deciduous plants should be transplanted only while dormant—when the branches are bare of leaves in spring, fall or early winter. The younger the tree or shrub, the more likely it is to reestablish successfully when moved to a new location. For every inch of trunk diameter, it typically takes one year for a tree to become well established after transplanting.

When woody plants are transplanted, they inevitably lose most of their root mass. Take care to dig a rootball of an appropriate size. The size of the tree or shrub will determine the minimum size of the rootball that must be dug out in order for the plant to survive. As a general guideline, for every 1" of main stem width, which is measured 6–12" above ground, you need to excavate a rootball at least 12" wide, and preferably larger.

Rootballs are heavy, and a 24" rootball is probably the most the average gardener can manage without heavy equipment. Therefore, trees with trunks more than 2" in diameter should be moved only by professionals. Shrubs cannot always be measured as easily as trees, so you will need to use your best judgment. Because shrubs mature fairly quickly, it may be easier to start with a new one rather than try to move a very large specimen.

Plant only young specimens of redbud (above) or magnolia (below), because they dislike being transplanted when older.

If it is necessary and feasible to transplant a shrub or small tree, follow these steps:

1) Calculate the size of the rootball to be removed, as described above.
2) Water the rootball area to a depth of 12" and allow excess water to drain away. The moist soil will help hold the rootball together.
3) Wrap or tie the branches to minimize branch damage and to ease transport from the old site to the new one.
4) Slice a long spade or shovel into the soil vertically, cutting a circle the size of the calculated rootball around the plant. Cut down to about 12". This depth should contain most of the roots for the size of tree or shrub that can be transplanted manually.
5) At this point, most small, densely rooted trees and shrubs can be carefully removed from the hole by leaning on the spade or shovel and prying the plant up and out. If you encounter resistance, you may have missed some roots and should repeat step 4. Once the plant has been freed, place it on a tarp and continue with step 10.

Larger trees and shrubs will require additional steps; continue with step 6.

6) Cut another circle one shovel-width outside the first circle, to the same depth.
7) Excavate the soil between the two cut circles.
8) When the appropriate rootball depth is reached, carefully cut horizontally under the rootball. When you encounter a root, cut it with a pair of hand pruners or

Spruces also dislike being transplanted when older.

loppers. The goal is to sculpt out a rootball that is standing on a pedestal of undisturbed earth.

9) Spread a tarp in one side of the hole. Gently remove the pedestal and lean the rootball over onto the tarp. Carefully cut any remaining roots in the pedestal. Lift the tree and rootball out of the hole with the tarp, not by the stem or branches.

10) Lift or drag the tarp to the new location and plant immediately. See planting instructions given in preceding sections for information on when to plant, how to plant, staking, etc. Transplanted trees and shrubs can be treated as balled-and-burlapped stock.

Caring for Trees & Shrubs

The care you give your new tree or shrub in the first two years after planting is the most important. During this period of establishment, it is critical to remove competing weeds, to keep the plant well watered and to avoid all mechanical damage. Be careful with lawn mowers and string trimmers, which can quickly girdle the base of the plant. Whatever you do to the top of the plant affects the roots, and vice versa.

Once established, woody plants generally require minimal care. A few basic maintenance tasks, performed regularly, save time and trouble in the long run.

WEEDING

Weeds can rob young plants of water, light and nutrients, so keep weeds under control to encourage optimal growth of your trees and shrubs. Avoid deep hoeing around woody plants because it may damage shallow-rooted species. A layer of mulch is a good way to suppress weeds. If you believe that you must use commercial weed killers, consult your local nursery or extension agent for advice, and follow the label directions carefully.

MULCHING

Mulch is an important gardening tool. It helps soil retain moisture, it buffers soil temperatures and it prevents soil erosion during heavy rain or strong winds. Mulch prevents weed seeds from germinating by blocking out the light, and it can deter pests and help prevent diseases. It keeps lawn mowers and line trimmers away from plants, reducing the chance of damage. Mulch can also add aesthetic value to a planting.

Organic mulches, such as compost, composted wood chips, bark chips, shredded bark, composted leaves and dry grass clippings, add beneficial nutrients to the soil as they break down over time, but they must be replenished on a regular basis.

Inorganic mulches, such as stones, crushed brick or gravel, do not break down and so do not have to be replenished. These types of mulches don't provide nutrients, and they can also adversely increase soil temperatures. Some books recommend using black plastic or ground cloth under the mulch, but doing so can disrupt the microbial balance of the soil, prevent worms and other important soil organisms from moving freely to the surface and restrict the movement of oxygen and water into the soil.

For good weed suppression, the mulch layer should be 2–4" thick. Try to maintain a mulch-free zone immediately around the trunk or stem bases. Piling mulch up around the base of a plant may encourage fungal decay and rot.

Keep mulch from the base of your tree or shrub.

WATERING

The weather, type of plant, type of soil and time of year all influence the amount of watering needed. Pay attention to the wind; like hot, dry weather, it can dry out your soil and plants quickly and necessitate more frequent watering. Different plants require different amounts of water; some, such as willow and some birch, will grow in temporarily waterlogged soil, whereas others, such as pine, prefer dry, sandy soil. Sandy soils and slopes retain less water than heavy clay soils and flat or low areas. More water is needed when plants are getting established in a new location, flowering or producing fruit.

SOIL PROBE

You can make a soil probe from a ⅜" to ½" diameter wooden dowel. Carve one end into a point, then cut a groove or paint a mark 12" up from that end. Do not finish the wood, because you want it to discolor as it absorbs the soil moisture. Push the rod into the soil 12" deep, leave it for up to a minute then remove the stick. If it has darkened with moisture, you don't need to water. If it is still dry, water immediately. It is quite possible for our heavy clay soils to be dry down to 3" but plenty wet enough farther down. I have seen many a plant saved from drowning through the use of this simple probe.

Plants are good at letting us know when they are thirsty. Wilted, flagging leaves and twigs are a sign of water deprivation, but excessive water can also cause a plant to wilt. Test for soil moisture by checking at least 2" down with your fingers or with a soil probe. If you detect moisture, you don't need to water.

Make sure your young trees and shrubs are well watered in fall. Continue to water as needed until the ground freezes. Fall watering is important for all evergreen plants because once the ground has frozen, the roots can no longer draw moisture from it, leaving the foliage susceptible to drying out.

Once established, trees and shrubs usually need watering only during periods of excessive drought. To keep water use to a minimum and reduce evaporation losses, avoid watering in the heat of the day. Work organic matter into the soil to help the soil absorb and retain water, and apply mulch to help prevent water loss. Collect and use rainwater whenever possible.

FERTILIZING

Most garden soils provide all the nutrients plants need, particularly if you use an organic mulch and mix compost into the soil before planting your garden. Simply allowing leaf litter to remain on the ground after the leaves drop in autumn promotes natural nutrient cycling of nitrogen and other elements in the soil.

Not all plants have the same nutritional requirements, however. Some plants are heavy feeders, whereas others thrive in poor soils. Pay attention to the leaf color of your plants as an indicator of nutritional status. Yellowing leaves, for example, may indicate nutrient deficiency.

When you do fertilize, use only the recommended quantity; too much can be harmful. Roots are easily burned by fertilizer applied in too high a concentration. Synthetic fertilizers are more concentrated than organic fertilizers and therefore have the potential to cause more problems.

Granular fertilizers consist of small, dry particles that can be spread with a fertilizer spreader or by hand. Consider using a slow-release type of granular fertilizer. It may cost a bit more but will save you time and reduce the risk of burn by releasing the nutrients gradually over the growing season. One application per year is normally sufficient. Applying the fertilizer in early spring provides nutrients for spring growth.

Tree spikes are slow-release fertilizers that are quick and easy to use. Pound the spikes into the ground around the dripline of the tree or shrub (see diagram, p. 47). These spikes work well for fertilizing trees in lawns because the grass tends to consume most of the nutrients released from surface applications.

Fertilizing should be done only to correct a visible nutrient deficiency, to correct a deficiency identified by a soil and tissue test, to increase vegetative, flower or fruit growth or to increase the vigor of a plant that is flagging.

Applying fertilizer incorrectly or in excess will not benefit your plants. In fact, it will make a tree or shrub more susceptible to some pests and diseases and can accelerate a plant's decline.

Do not fertilize trees or shrubs
- when a soil and tissue test indicates sufficient soil nutrients
- if your plants are growing and appear healthy
- if your plants are sufficiently large and you want to reduce pruning and shearing
- during times of drought, when the roots will not absorb nutrients, and when excess, partially wetted fertilizer can burn root hairs.

If you do not want to encourage fast growth, do not fertilize. Remember that most trees and shrubs do not need fertilizer and that fast growth may make plants more susceptible to problems. In particular, fall fertilizing with chemical fertilizers is not recommended—the resulting late-season new growth is easily damaged in winter. Organic fertilizers are activated by soil organisms that are not as active in cool weather and can be applied in fall.

Unnecessary or excessive fertilizer pollutes our local lakes, streams and groundwater. Many homes in Minnesota and Wisconsin obtain their drinking water from wells, which can be contaminated by fertilizers. Use fertilizers wisely, and both your plants and our environment will benefit.

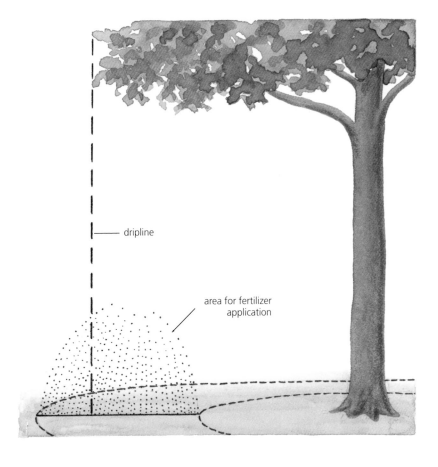

dripline

area for fertilizer application

Pruning

Pruning helps to maintain the health and attractive shape of a woody plant. It also increases the quality and yield of fruit, controls and directs growth, and creates interesting plant forms, such as topiary, espalier and bonsai. Pruning is perhaps the most important maintenance task when growing trees and shrubs—and the easiest to mess up. Fortunately for new gardeners, it is not difficult to learn and can even be enjoyable if done correctly from the beginning and continued on a regular basis.

Proper pruning combines knowledge and skill. General knowledge about how woody plants grow, and specific knowledge about the growth habits of your particular plant, will help you avoid pruning mistakes that can ruin a plant's shape or make it prone to disease and insect damage.

If you are unsure about pruning, take a pruning course. Courses may be offered by a local garden center, botanical garden, community college or master gardener program. Excellent books are also available on the subject.

Another option is to hire a professional, such as an arborist certified by the International Society of Arboriculture (ISA). Certified professionals understand the plants and have the special pruning training and equipment to do a proper job. They might even be willing to show you some pruning basics. *Always* call a professional to prune trees growing near power lines or other hazardous areas or to prune or cut down large branches and trees that could damage buildings, fences or cars or hurt pedestrians. Many gardeners have injured themselves or others, or caused significant property damage, simply because they didn't have the equipment or the know-how to remove a large branch or tree.

Plants will always try to grow to their genetically programmed potential size. If you are doing a lot of pruning to keep a tree or shrub in check, the plant may be too large for the site. We cannot emphasize enough how important it is to consider the mature size of a plant before you put it into the ground.

WHEN & HOW MUCH TO PRUNE

Aside from removing damaged growth, do not prune for the first year after planting a tree or shrub. After that time, the first pruning should develop the plant's structure. For a strong framework, do not prune branches that have a wide angle at the crotch (where the branch meets another branch or the trunk), because these branch intersections are the strongest. Prune out branches with narrower crotches while ensuring an even distribution of the main (scaffold) branches. These branches will support all future top growth.

Trees and shrubs vary greatly in their pruning needs. Some plants, such as boxwood, tolerate or even thrive on heavy pruning and shearing, but other plants, such as cherry, may be killed if given the same treatment. Pruning guidelines are given in each species entry in this book.

The amount of pruning also depends on your motivation. Much less work is involved in simply tidying the growth, for example, than in creating intricate topiary.

Many gardeners are unsure about what time of year they should prune. Knowing when a plant flowers is the easiest way to know when to prune. (See p. 54 for information on pruning conifers.)

Trees and shrubs that flower before about July, such as rhododendron and forsythia, should be pruned after they finish flowering. These plants form next year's flower buds

Proper hand pruner orientation

in summer and fall. Pruning just after the current year's flowers fade allows plenty of time for the next year's flowers to develop and avoids taking away any of the current year's blooms.

Late-flowering species, such as peegee hydrangea, can be pruned early in the year instead. These plants form flower buds on new stems as the season progresses, and pruning in spring just before or as the new growth begins to develop encourages the best growth and flowering.

Some plants, such as maple, have a heavy spring flow of sap. As long as proper pruning cuts are made, these trees can still be pruned in spring. If the excessive bleeding is aesthetically unappealing or is dripping on something inappropriately, wait until these species are in full leaf before pruning.

Take care when pruning any trees in early spring, when many canker-causing organisms are active, or in fall, when many wood-rotting fungi release their spores. At these times of cool weather, the plants are fairly inactive and less able to fight off invasion.

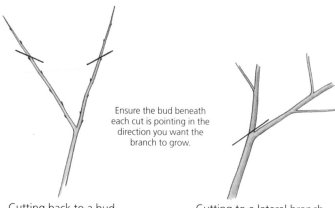

Ensure the bud beneath each cut is pointing in the direction you want the branch to grow.

Cutting back to a bud   Cutting to a lateral branch

Inspect trees and shrubs annually for any dead, damaged, diseased or awkwardly growing branches and to determine what other pruning, if any, is needed. Always remove dead, diseased and damaged branches as soon as you discover them, at any time of year.

THE KINDEST CUT

Trees and shrubs have a remarkable ability to repair their wounds, but it is critical to make proper pruning cuts. A proper pruning cut, although still a wound, minimizes the area where insect and disease attack can occur and takes advantage of the areas on a plant where it can best deal with wounds. The tree or shrub can then heal as quickly as possible, preventing disease and insect damage.

Using the right tools makes pruning easier and more effective. The size of the branch being cut determines the type of tool to use.

Hand pruners should be used for cutting branches up to ³/₄" in diameter. Using hand pruners for larger stems increases the risk of damage, and it can be physically strenuous.

Loppers are long-handled pruners used for branches up to 1½" in diameter. Loppers are good for removing old stems. Hand pruners and loppers must be properly oriented when making a cut (see photo, p. 49). The blade should be to the plant side of the cut and the hook to the side being removed. If the cut is made with the hook toward the plant, the cut will be ragged and slow to heal.

Pruning saws have teeth specially designed to cut through green wood. They can be used to cut branches up to 6" in diameter and sometimes larger. Pruning saws are easier to use and much safer than chainsaws.

Hedge clippers, or shears, are intended only for shearing and shaping hedges.

Make sure your tools are sharp and clean before you begin any pruning task. If the branch you are cutting is diseased, sterilize the tool before using it again. Use denatured alcohol or a solution of 1 part bleach to 10 parts water for cleaning and sterilizing.

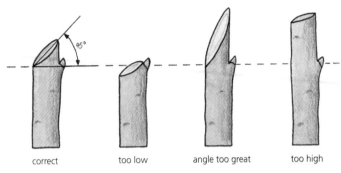

correct   too low   angle too great   too high

Cutting back to a bud

TYPES OF PRUNING CUTS

You should be familiar with the following types of pruning cuts.

Cutting back to a bud is used for shortening a branch, redirecting growth or maintaining the size of a tree or shrub. Each cut should be made slightly less than ¼" above a bud (see diagrams). If the cut is too far away from, or too close to, the bud, the wound will not heal properly. Cut back to buds that are pointing in the direction you want the new growth to grow in.

Cutting to a lateral branch is used to shorten limbs and redirect growth. The diameter of the branch to which you are cutting back must be at least one-third of the diameter of the branch you are cutting. As with cutting back to a bud, cut slightly less than ¼" above the lateral branch and line up the cut with the angle of the branch that is to remain (see diagrams). Whenever possible, make cuts at an angle so that rain won't seep into the open wound.

Removing limbs can be a complicated operation. Because the wound is large, it is critical to cut in the correct place—at the branch collar—to ensure quick healing. The cut must be done in steps (see diagram below) to avoid damaging the bark.

The first cut is on the bottom of the branch to be removed. This cut should be 12–18" up from the branch

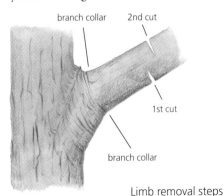

branch collar   2nd cut

1st cut

branch collar

3rd cut at branch collar

Limb removal steps

diseases. Do not make flush cuts and do not leave stubs; both can be slow to heal.

The use of pruning paint or paste has been much debated. The current consensus is that these substances do more harm than good. Trees and shrubs have a natural ability to create a barrier between living wood and dead or decaying sections. An unpainted cut will eventually heal over, but a cut that has been treated with paint or paste may never heal properly.

Shearing is used to trim and shape hedges. Because some of the normal pruning rules (such as being careful where you cut in relation to buds) are disregarded in shearing, only plants that can handle heavy pruning should be sheared.

Informal hedges take advantage of the natural shape of the plant and require only minimal trimming. These hedges generally take up more room than formal hedges, which are trimmed more severely to assume a neat, even appearance. Formal hedges are generally sheared at least twice per growing season.

collar and should extend one-third of the way through the branch. The purpose of the first cut is to prevent bark from peeling down the tree when the second cut causes the main part of the branch to fall. The second cut is made a bit farther along the branch from the first cut and is made from the top of the branch. This cut removes most of the branch. The final cut should be made just above the branch collar. The plant tissues at the branch collar quickly create a barrier against insects and

incorrect

correct

Hedge shape

For any hedge, make sure all sides are trimmed to encourage even growth. The base of your hedge should always be wider than the top to allow light to reach the entire hedge and to prevent it from thinning out at the base. A hedge will gradually increase in size despite shearing, so allow room for this expansion when planting.

Thinning, or renewal pruning, is a rejuvenation process that maintains the shape, health and productivity of shrubs. It opens up space for air and light to penetrate and provides room for young, healthy branches and selected suckers to grow. Thinning often combines the first two cuts discussed above, and it is the most frequently performed pruning practice. Plants that produce new growth from ground level (either from the crown or by suckers) can be pruned this way.

A shrub that is thinned annually should have one-quarter to one-third of the growth removed. Cutting the oldest stems encourages new growth without causing excessive stress from loss of top growth. Although some plants can be completely cut back to the ground and seem to suffer no ill effects, it is generally better to remove no more than one-third of the growth.

Follow these four steps to thin most multi-stemmed shrubs:
1) Remove all dead, diseased, damaged, rubbing and crossing branches to branch junctions, buds or ground level.
2) Remove up to one-third of the growth each year, leaving a mix of old and new growth, and

Thinning cuts

cutting unwanted stems at or close to the base. Do not cut stems below ground level, because many disease organisms are present in soil.
3) Thin the top of the shrub to allow air and light penetration and to balance the shape.

BRANCH COLLARS
To learn to identify branch collars, look at the branch intersections of an apple or pear tree. There will be a slight swelling at the base of each branch. This swelling is actually trunk tissue and must be protected to ensure quick and complete wound closure. Once you see and feel this collar on an apple or pear, you'll have an easier time finding it on other trees. If you aren't sure where a collar ends, err on the side of caution and cut slightly farther out from the trunk.

Sheared arborvitae

Because removing the oldest stems generally thins out the top as well, this step is not always necessary.

4) Repeat the process each year on established, mature shrubs. Regular pruning of shrubs will keep them healthy and productive for many years.

Fully extended mugo pine candles

PRUNING CONIFERS

Coniferous trees and shrubs, such as spruce, pine and juniper, require little or no pruning other than to fix damage or correct wayward growth. Proper pruning procedures do differ, however, for different conifers.

Spruce trees have buds all along their stems and can be pruned at almost any time of year. Branches can be pruned back into the last two or three years of growth.

Pines, on the other hand, must be shaped and directed in mid- to late spring, after the danger of frost has passed. At this time, the new growth, called candles, should have almost fully extended but should still be pliable. Pinch the candles by up to half their length before they are fully extended. Pines do not have side buds along their stems, but when the candles are pinched at the proper time, new buds will set near the pinched end. For bushy, dense growth, pinch all candles by half. Pinching should be done by hand and not with shears or hand pruners. This technique can be time-consuming and has a limited effect. It is best to choose a cultivar with a naturally dense, bushy habit that is expected to reach an appropriate size for the space you have.

Yews, junipers and arborvitae can be lightly sheared for hedging. It is best to begin training hedge plants when they are very young. Yews can be pruned heavily during dormancy, but it is better to shear them on an ongoing basis. As specimens, yews can be heavily hand pruned at almost any time to keep their natural shape.

When removing a branch on a conifer, cut it back to the branch collar at the trunk. Before you start cutting, take a good look at a few branches because the collar can be difficult to find on a conifer. Cutting a branch back partway is usually pointless because most conifers, including pine and fir, will not regenerate from old wood. Juniper can regenerate from old wood, but slowly, and it may result in an oddly shaped plant. To avoid disfiguring the plant, make sure you really need to remove a branch before you do so. This is another reason to think about mature size before you plant any tree or shrub.

If the central leader on a young conifer is broken or damaged, cleanly remove it and train a new leader in its place. In doing so you reduce the chance of infection and prevent many opportunistic leaders from competing. Gently place a straight stake next to the main trunk. Do not insert the stake into the ground. Tie the stake to the main trunk, being careful not to girdle the tree by tying it too tightly. Bend the chosen new leader as uprightly as possible and tie it to the stake. Remove the stake when the new leader is growing strongly upright. Remove or cut the tips of any other leaders that attempt to form.

Older, larger trees may be irreparably damaged by the loss of a leader.

TREE TOPPING

One pruning practice that should never be performed is tree topping. Topping is done in an attempt to control height or size, to prevent trees from growing into overhead power lines, to allow more light

Topping disfigures and stresses trees.

onto a property or to prevent a tall tree from potentially toppling onto a building.

Topped trees are ugly, weak and potentially hazardous. A tree can be killed by the stress of losing so much of its live growth, or by the gaping, slow-to-heal wounds that are vulnerable to attack by insects and wood-rotting fungi. The heartwood of a topped tree rots out quickly, resulting in a weak trunk. The crotches on new growth also tend to be weak. Topped trees, therefore, are susceptible to storm damage and blowdown. Hazards aside, topping a tree spoils its aesthetic value and that of the surrounding landscape.

It is much better to completely remove a tree, and start again with one that will grow to a more appropriate size, than to attempt to reduce the size of a large, mature specimen.

True topiary made of boxwood

Apple espalier

Spruce and juniper bonsai

SPECIALTY PRUNING

Custom pruning methods are used to create interesting plant shapes.

Topiary is the shaping of plants into animal, abstract or geometric forms. True topiary uses hedge plants sheared into the desired shape. Species that can handle heavy pruning, such as boxwood, are chosen. A simpler form of topiary involves growing vines or other trailing plants over a wire frame to achieve the desired form. Small-leaved ivy and other flexible, climbing or trailing plants work well for this kind of topiary.

Espalier involves training a tree or shrub to grow in two dimensions instead of three, with the aid of a solid wire or other framework. The plant is commonly trained against a wall or fence, but it can also be freestanding. This method is popularly applied to fruit trees, such as apple, when space is at a premium. Many gardeners consider the forms attractive and unusual, and you may want to try your hand at espalier even if you have lots of space.

Bonsai is the art of developing miniature versions of large trees and landscapes. A gardener prunes the top growth and roots and uses wire to train the plant to the desired form. The severe pruning creates a dwarfed form. Many books are available on the subject, and courses may be offered at colleges or by horticultural or bonsai societies.

Propagating Trees & Shrubs

Many gardeners enjoy the art and science of starting new plants. Although some gardeners are willing to try growing annuals from seeds and perennials from seeds, cuttings or divisions, they may be unsure how to go about propagating their own trees and shrubs. Many woody plants can be propagated with ease, however, allowing the gardener to buy a single specimen and then clone it, rather than buying additional plants.

Do-it-yourself propagating does more than cut costs. It can become an enjoyable part of gardening and an interesting hobby in itself. As well, it allows gardeners to add to their landscapes species that may be hard to find at nurseries.

A number of methods can be used to propagate trees and shrubs. Many species can be started from seed, which can be a long, slow process, but some gardeners enjoy the variable and sometimes unusual results. Simpler techniques include cuttings, ground layering and mound layering.

CUTTINGS

Cut segments of stems can be encouraged to develop their own roots and form new plants. Cuttings are treated differently depending on the maturity of the growth.

Hydrangea
Willow

Cuttings taken in spring or early summer from new growth are called **greenwood** or **softwood** cuttings. They can actually be the most difficult cuttings to start because they require warm, humid conditions that are as likely to cause the cuttings to rot as to root.

Cuttings taken in fall from mature, woody growth are called **hardwood** or **ripe** cuttings. In order to root, these cuttings require a coarse, gritty, moist and preferably warm soil mix and low, but not freezing, air temperatures. They may take all winter to root. These special conditions make it difficult to start hardwood cuttings unless you have a cold frame, heated greenhouse or propagator.

The easiest cuttings to start are those taken in late summer or early fall from new (but mature) growth that has not yet become completely woody. They are called **semi-ripe, semi-mature** or **semi-hardwood** cuttings.

Follow these steps to take and plant semi-ripe cuttings:

1) Take cuttings about 2–4" long from the tip of a stem, cutting just below a leaf node (the node is the place where a leaf meets the stem). There should be at least two nodes on the cutting. The tip of each cutting will be soft, but the base will be starting to harden.
2) Remove the leaves from the lower half of each cutting. Moisten the stripped end and dust it lightly with rooting hormone powder (consult your local garden center for the appropriate kind).

pebble to keep slit open

rock for
extra
weight

wire to hold branch

Ground layering

3) Plant the cuttings directly in the garden, in a cold frame or in pots. The soil mix should be well drained but moist. Firm the cuttings into the soil to ensure that no air spaces will dry out the emerging roots.
4) Keep the cuttings out of direct sunlight and keep the soil moist.
5) Make sure the roots are well established before transplanting. The plants should root by the time winter begins.
6) Protect new plants from extreme cold for the first winter. Plants in pots should be kept in a cold but frost-free location.

Plants for Semi-Ripe Cuttings
Butterfly Bush
Cotoneaster
False cypress
Forsythia
Hydrangea
Potentilla
Russian cypress
Willow

GROUND LAYERING
Layering—ground layering in particular—is the easiest propagation method and the one most likely to produce successful results. Layering allows future cuttings to form their own roots before being detached from the parent plant. In ground layering, a section of a flexible branch is buried until it produces roots. The method is quite simple.

1) Choose a branch or shoot growing low enough on the plant to reach the ground. Remove the leaves from the section of at least four nodes that will be underground. At least another four should protrude above ground at the new growth end.
2) Twist the leafless section of the branch, or make a small cut on the underside near a leaf node. This damage will stimulate root growth. Use a toothpick or small pebble to hold the cut open.

Chokeberry
Dogwood

Euonymus

3) Bend the branch down to see where it will touch the ground and dig a shallow trench (about 4" deep) there. The end of the trench nearest the shrub can slope gradually upward, but the end where the branch tip will be should be vertical to force the tip up.

4) Use a peg or bent wire to hold the branch in place. Fill the soil back into the trench, and water well. A rock or brick on top of the soil will help keep the branch in place.

5) Keep the soil moist but not soggy. Roots may take a year or more to develop. Once roots are well established, the new plant can be severed from the parent and planted in a permanent location.

The best shrubs for layering have low, flexible branches. Spring and fall are the best times to start the layer. Many species respond better in one season or the other, but some, such as rhododendron, respond equally well in either.

Plants to Layer in Spring
Chokeberry
Daphne
Dogwood
Lilac
Magnolia
Smokebush
Virginia creeper
Witchhazel

Plants to Layer in Fall
Arborvitae
Blueberry
Euonymus
Forsythia
Hazelnut
Honeysuckle
Serviceberry
Viburnum

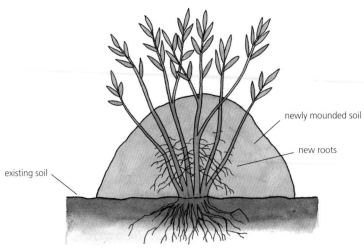

existing soil

newly mounded soil

new roots

Mound layering

MOUND LAYERING

Mound layering is a simple way to propagate low, shrubby plants. With this technique, the shrub is partially buried in a mound of well-drained soil mix. The buried stems will then sprout roots along their lengths. This method can provide many new plants with little effort.

Mound layering should be initiated in spring, once new shoots begin to grow. Make a mound from a mixture of sand, peat moss and soil over half or more of the plant. Leave the branch tips exposed. More soil can be mounded up over the course of summer. Keep the mound moist but not soggy.

At the end of summer (or, for large plants, the following season), gently wash the mound away and detach the rooted branches. Plant them out either directly where you want them or in a protected, temporary spot if you want to shelter them for the first winter.

Plants to Mound Layer

Cotoneaster
Dogwood
Euonymus
Forsythia
Heather
Lilac
Potentilla

Cotoneaster

Problems & Pests

Tree and shrub plantings can be both assets and liabilities when it comes to pests and diseases. Many insects and diseases attack only one plant species. Mixed plantings can make it difficult for pests and diseases to find their preferred hosts and establish a population. At the same time, because woody plants are in the same spot for many years, any problems can become permanent. The advantage is that beneficial birds, insects and other pest-devouring organisms can also develop permanent populations. The plants selected for this book, which include some native plants that have survived the conditions in Minnesota and Wisconsin for millennia, are generally less susceptible to problems.

For many years, pest control meant spraying or dusting, with the goal to eliminate every pest in the landscape. A more moderate approach advocated today is known as IPM (Integrated Pest Management or Integrated Plant Management). The goal of IPM is to reduce pest problems to levels of damage that you can accept.

Consider whether a pest's damage is localized or covers the entire plant. Will the damage kill the plant or is it only affecting the outward appearance? Are there methods of controlling the pest without chemicals? For an interesting overview of IPM, consult the University of Minnesota website (http://ipmworld.umn.edu/) or the University of Wisconsin website (http://ipcm.wisc.edu/programs/school/default.htm).

IPM is an interactive system in which observation, identification and assessment are the primary tools. Observing your plants on a regular basis will allow you to assess the severity of any infestation. It will also let you catch problems early, when they are easier to control with minimal effort. Seeing an insect does not mean you have a problem, though. Most insects do no harm at all, and many are beneficial to your garden as pollinators or predators. Take immediate action against the well-known garden pests you are already familiar with, but wait until you have identified any other insects as harmful before attempting to control them. You may find that an insect you are concerned about is actually eating the ones you don't want.

A good IPM program includes learning what conditions your particular plants need for healthy growth, what pests might affect them, where and when to look for those pests, and how and when to best control them. Keep records of pest damage; your observations can reveal patterns useful in spotting recurring problems and in planning your maintenance regime. Most problems strike at about the same time each year.

An effective, responsible pest management program has four steps. Cultural controls are the most important. Physical controls should be attempted next, followed by biological controls. Resort to chemical controls only when the first three possibilities have been exhausted. Chemicals can endanger gardeners and their families and pets, and they kill as many good organisms as bad ones, leaving the whole garden vulnerable to even worse attacks.

Cultural controls are the gardening techniques you use in the day-to-day care of your garden. Perhaps the best defense against pests and diseases is to grow your woody plants in the conditions for which they are adapted. It is also important to keep your soil healthy, with plenty of organic matter added.

Other cultural controls are equally straightforward. Choose resistant varieties of trees and shrubs that are not prone to problems. Space your plants so they have good air circulation in and around them and are not stressed by competing for light, nutrients and space. Remove plants that are decimated by the same pests every year. Dispose of diseased foliage and branches by burning the material or by taking it to a permitted dump site. Prevent the spread of disease by keeping your gardening tools clean and by tidying up dead plant matter every fall.

Sticky trap

Frogs eat many insect pests.

Predatory ground beetle

to pests. Garden centers offer a wide array of such devices. Physical control of diseases usually involves removing the infected plant or plant parts in order to keep the problem from spreading.

Biological controls make use of predators that eat pests. Animals such as birds, snakes, frogs, spiders, ladybird beetles, bats and certain bacteria can play an important role in keeping pest populations manageable. Encourage these creatures to take up permanent residence in your garden. A birdbath and bird-feeder will encourage birds to enjoy your yard and feed on a wide variety of insect pests. Beneficial insects are probably already living in your landscape, and you can encourage them to stay by planting appropriate alternate food sources. Many beneficial insects eat nectar from plants such as yarrow and daisies. In many cases it is the young and not the adult insects that are predatory.

Another form of biological control is the naturally occurring soil bacterium *Bacillus thuringiensis* (Bt for short; Btk for *B.t.* var. *kurstaki*), which breaks down the gut lining of certain insect pests. It is commonly available in garden centers.

Physical controls are generally used to combat insect and mammal problems. An example of such a control is picking insects off shrubs by hand, which is not a daunting task if you catch the problem when it is just beginning. Simply drop the offenders into a bucket of soapy water (soap prevents them from floating and climbing out and may suffocate them).

Other physical controls for insects and mammals include traps, barriers, scarecrows and natural repellents that make a plant taste or smell bad

Chemical controls should rarely be necessary, but if you must use them, many less-toxic organic options and more precisely targeted pesticides are becoming available because consumers are demanding effective pest-control products that do not harm the environment. One drawback to using any chemical, however, is that it may also kill the beneficial insects that you have been trying to attract.

Organic chemicals are now available at most garden centers. Follow the manufacturer's instructions carefully. A larger amount or concentration of the insecticide is not any more effective in controlling insect pests than the recommended dosage. Many people think that because a pesticide is organic, they can use however much they want. Although organic sprays are made from natural sources and will more readily break down into harmless compounds, they can be as dangerous as synthetic chemical sprays. An organic spray kills because it contains a lethal toxin. NEVER overuse any pesticide. Always practice target application or 'spot spraying'; rarely does the whole area or even the whole plant need to be sprayed.

Note that if a particular pest is not listed on the package, it will not be controlled by that product. It is also important to find out at what stage in an insect's life cycle you will get the best control. Some pests can be controlled only at certain stages. Proper and early identification of pests is vital for finding a quick solution.

Alternatives to commercial chemical pesticides are available or can easily be made at home; horticultural oils and insecticidal soaps, for example, are effective and safer to use for pest control (see p. 73).

Whether it's organic or synthetic, the authors strongly believe that any pesticide we apply disrupts the balance of microorganisms in the soil profile (containers with sterile planting mix excluded), kills many beneficial insects and sets gardeners on the vicious circle of having to use those products to control their problems. We would like to see all forms of pesticides used on plants eliminated, or at least severely reduced, and people willing to accept some pest damage.

Cultural, physical, biological and chemical controls are all possible defenses against insect pests. Many diseases, however, can be dealt with only culturally. Often it is the weakened plants that succumb to diseases, although some diseases can infect plants regardless of their level of health. Some diseases, such as powdery mildew, are largely a cosmetic concern, but they may weaken a plant enough to make it susceptible to other diseases and pests. Prevention is often the only hope. Once a plant has been infected, it (or the infected parts) should be destroyed in order to prevent the disease from spreading.

Ladybird beetle
Ladybird larvae are voracious predators of garden pests.

GLOSSARY OF PESTS & DISEASES

Anthracnose

Fungus. Yellow or brown spots on leaves; sunken lesions and blisters on stems; can kill plant.

What to Do. Choose resistant varieties and cultivars; keep soil well drained; thin out stems to improve air circulation; avoid handling wet foliage. Remove and destroy infected plant parts; clean up and destroy debris from infected plants in fall. Applying liquid copper fungicide can minimize damage.

Aphids

Tiny, pear-shaped insects, winged or wingless, in green, black, brown, red or gray. They cluster along stems and on buds and leaves and suck sap from plants, causing distorted or stunted growth. Sticky honeydew forms on surfaces, encouraging

Green aphids

sooty mold. Example: woolly aphids.

What to Do. Squish small colonies by hand; dislodge with brisk water spray from hose. Predatory insects and birds feed on aphids. Spray serious infestations with insecticidal soap (see p. 73) or neem oil according to directions.

Woolly aphids

Beetles

Many types and sizes; usually rounded, with hard, shell-like outer wings covering membranous inner wings. Some are beneficial (e.g., ladybird beetles or 'ladybugs'); others are not (e.g., Japanese beetles, leaf skeletonizers, bark beetles, weevils). Wide range of possible chewing damage: small or large holes in or around margins of leaves or can consume entire leaves or areas between

Beetle damage

leaf veins ('skeletonize'); may also chew holes in flowers and eat through root bark. Some bark beetles carry deadly plant diseases. Larvae: see Borers, Grubs.

What to Do. Pick beetles off shrubs at night and drop them in soapy water; spread an old sheet under small trees and shrubs and shake off beetles to collect and dispose of them, using a broom to reach tall branches.

Leaf skeletonizer damage

Hot Pepper Wax™ brand insect repellent discourages beetles and may also repel rabbits and deer.

Japanese beetles

Blight

Many types of fungal or bacterial diseases (e.g., leaf blight, needle blight, petal blight, snow blight, twig blight). Leaves, stems and flowers blacken, rot and die. See also Fire Blight, Gray Mold.

What to Do. Thin out stems to improve air circulation; keep mulch away from base of plants; remove debris from garden at end of growing season. Remove and destroy infected plant parts. Sterilize equipment after each cut to avoid reinfecting plant and spreading fungus.

Borers

Variably sized, worm-like larvae of some moths, wasps and beetles; among the most damaging of plant pests. Burrow into plant stems, leaves or roots, under bark and sometimes into heartwood, destroying conducting tissue and structural strength. Burrows are sites for infection and decomposition to begin; some borers carry infection.

What to Do. Site tree or shrub properly and keep as healthy as possible with proper fertilizing and watering. May be able to squish borers within leaves. Remove and destroy bored parts; may need to remove entire plant.

Bugs (True Bugs)

Small insects up to $1/2$" long; green, brown, black or brightly colored and patterned. Many are beneficial; a few pests, such as lace bugs, pierce plants to suck out sap. Toxins may be injected that deform plants; pierced tissues result in sunken areas, leaves that rip as they grow and dwarfed or deformed leaves, buds and new growth.

What to Do. Remove debris and weeds from around plants in fall to destroy overwintering sites. Spray plants with insecticidal soap (see p. 73)

or neem oil according to directions.

Canker

Swollen or sunken lesions on stems or branches, surrounded by living tissue. Caused by many different bacterial and fungal diseases; most enter through wounded wood, sometimes after woodpecker activity.

What to Do. Maintain vigor of plants; avoid wounding or injuring trees (e.g., string trimmer damage), especially in spring when canker-causing organisms are most active; control borers and other bark-dwelling insects. Prune out and destroy infected material. Sterilize pruning tools before, during and after use on infected plants.

Case Bearers
see Caterpillars

Caterpillars
Larvae of butterflies, moths and sawflies

Caterpillar on hawthorn flowers

(e.g., bagworm, budworm, case bearers, cutworm, leaf rollers, leaf tiers, loopers, webworm). Chew foliage and buds; severe infestations can completely defoliate plants.

What to Do. Removal from plant is best control; use high-pressure water and soap or pick caterpillars off by hand if plant is small enough; cut off and burn large tents or webs of larvae. Control biologically using Bt (see p. 64). Apply horticultural oil in spring. Slippery or sticky barrier bands on trunks prevent caterpillars from climbing trees to reach leaves.

Dieback

Plant slowly wilts, browns and dies, starting at branch tips. Caused by wide range of disease organisms, cultural problems and nutrient deficiencies.

What to Do. Keep plants healthy by providing optimal growing conditions. Cut off dead tips below dead sections.

Fire Blight

Highly destructive bacterial disease of the rose family, which includes crabapple, cherry, pear, cotoneaster, hawthorn, kerria and serviceberry. Infected areas appear to have been burned. Look for bent twig tips (resembling a shepherd's hook), branches that retain leaves over winter and cankers on plant's lower parts. Disease usually starts at young tips and kills its way down stems.

What to Do. Choose resistant plant varieties. Remove and burn infected parts, making cuts at least 24" below infected areas. Sterilize tools after each cut on infected plant. Pollinating birds and insects may reinfect plants through flowers. Remove and burn wholly infected plants.

Galls

Unusual swellings of plant tissues (leaves, buds, flowers, fruit, stems or trunks) caused by insects or diseases. Often a specific gall affects a single genus or species.

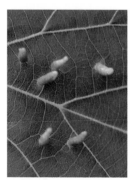

Poplar galls

What to Do. Cut out and destroy galls. Insect galls, which usually contain eggs and juvenile forms, are more unsightly than damaging to plant. Control insects before they lay eggs; otherwise, remove and destroy galls before young insects emerge. Galls caused by disease often require destruction of plant. Avoid placing other susceptible plants in same location.

Fuzzy oak galls

Gray Mold (*Botrytis* Blight)

Fungal disease. Gray fuzz coats affected surfaces; leaves, flowers or fruit may blacken, rot and die. Common on dead plant matter and on damaged or stressed plants in cool, damp, poorly ventilated areas.

What to Do. Thin out stems for better air circulation; keep mulch away from base of plant, particularly in spring when plant starts to sprout; remove debris from garden in fall; do not overwater. Remove and destroy infected plant parts.

Grubs

Larvae of various beetles, commonly found underground, usually curled in 'C' shape. White or gray body with white, gray, brown or reddish head. Problematic in lawns; may feed on roots of shallow-rooted trees and shrubs. Plant wilts despite regular watering; may pull easily out of ground in severe cases.

What to Do. Throw any grubs found while digging onto a stone path or patio for birds to devour; apply para- sitic nematodes or milky disease spore to infested soil (ask at garden center).

Leafhoppers & Treehoppers

Small, wedge-shaped, green, brown, gray or multi-colored insects; jump around franti- cally when disturbed. Suck juice from plant leaves; cause distorted growth; carry diseases such as aster yellows. Treehoppers damage bark when they slit it to lay eggs.

What to Do. Encourage predators by growing nectar-rich species such as yarrow. Wash insects off with strong spray of water; spray insecticidal soap (see p. 73) or neem oil according to directions.

Leaf Miners

Tiny, stubby, yellow or green larvae of some butterflies and moths. Tunnel within foliage, leaving winding trails; tunneled areas are lighter in color than rest of leaf. Unsightly rather than health risk to plant.

What to Do. Remove debris from area in fall to destroy overwintering sites; attract parasitic wasps with nectar plants such as yarrow. Remove and destroy infected foliage.

Leaf miner damage

Leaf Rollers

see Caterpillars

Leaf Scorch

Yellowing or browning of leaves begins at tips or edges. Most often caused by drought or heat stress, but some- times by bacteria.

What to Do. Water susceptible plants dur- ing droughts and avoid planting them where excessive heat reflects from pavement or buildings. For bacterial leaf scorch, remove plant and replace with resistant species. To help prevent or ameliorate bacterial leaf scorch: control the insect carriers (leafhoppers and spittlebugs) of scorch bacteria; prune out scorched shoots as soon as symptoms appear; inject bacteri- cide into the trunk of lightly damaged specimens; fertilize and irrigate as appropriate.

Leaf Spot

Bacterial: small brown or purple speckles grow to encompass entire leaves (may drop). *Fungal:* black, brown or yellow spots and withering leaves (e.g., black spot, scab, tar spot).

What to Do. Bacte- rial infection is more

severe—must remove entire plant. For fungal infection, remove and destroy infected plant parts; sterilize removal tools; avoid wetting foliage or touching it when wet; remove and destroy debris at end of growing season; spray compost tea (see p. 73) on leaves.

Mealybugs

Tiny crawling insects related to aphids; appear covered with white fuzz or flour. Sucking damage stunts and stresses plant; excreted honeydew promotes sooty mold.

What to Do. Remove by hand on small plants; wash plants with soap and water; wipe with alcohol-soaked swabs; remove heavily infested leaves; encourage or introduce natural predators such as mealybug destroyer beetle (note: larvae resemble very large mealybugs) and parasitic wasps; spray with insecticidal soap (see p. 73) or horticultural oil.

Mildew

Two types, both fungal, but with slightly different symptoms. *Downy mildew:* yellow spots on upper sides of leaves; yellow, white or gray downy fuzz on undersides. *Powdery mildew:* white or gray powdery coating on leaf surfaces; doesn't brush off.

What to Do. Choose resistant cultivars; space plants well; thin out stems to encourage air circulation; tidy any debris in fall. Remove and destroy infected leaves or other parts. For downy mildew, spray foliage with mixture of 5 tbsp. horticultural oil, 2 tsp. baking soda and 1 gal. water; apply once a week for three weeks. For powdery mildew, spray foliage with compost tea (see p. 73) or very dilute fish emulsion (1 tsp. per qt. of water).

Powdery mildew

Mites

Almost too small to see; red, yellow or green, eight-legged relatives of spiders. Do not eat insects but may leave fine webbing on leaves and stems; usually found on undersides of plant leaves. Suck juice out of leaves, which become discolored and speckled, then turn brown and shrivel up. Examples: bud mites, spider mites, spruce mites.

What to Do. Wash off with strong spray of water daily until all signs of infestation are gone. Introduce predatory mites (from garden center). Spray plants with insecticidal soap (see p. 73), or spray horticultural oil at a rate of 5 tbsp. to 1 gal. of water; if necessary, spray again in a month or so.

Mosaic
see Viruses

Needle Cast

Fungal disease causing premature needle drop. Spotty yellow areas turn brown; infected needles drop up to a year later.

What to Do. Ensure good air circulation. Clean up and destroy fallen needles; prune off damaged growth.

To prevent recurrence, treat plants with bordeaux mix (fungicide from garden center) twice, two weeks apart, as candles elongate the next spring.

Nematodes

Tiny, translucent worms of various kinds; can be beneficial (e.g., predatory and decomposer nematodes) or damage plants. *Foliar* and *stem:* yellow spots on leaves turn brown; leaves shrivel and wither; lesions on stems; problem starts low on plant and works upward. *Root-knot:* plant is stunted and may wilt; yellow spots on leaves; roots have tiny bumps or knots.

What to Do. Mulch soil, mix in organic matter, clear garden debris in fall; avoid wetting leaves; don't touch wet foliage of infested plants. Can add parasitic nematodes to soil. In extreme cases, remove infested plants.

Psyllids

Plant lice; treat as for aphids.

Rot

Various, sometimes fatal, fungi and bacteria that cause decay of various plant parts. *Crown rot:* affects base of plant; stems blacken and fall over; leaves yellow and wilt. *Heart rot (wood rot):* decays a tree's heartwood; damage often evident only after high winds bring down branches or whole tree. *Root rot:* yellow leaves; plant wilts; when dug up, plant shows roots rotted away.

What to Do. Keep soil well drained; avoid damaging plant while working around it; keep mulches away from plant base. Destroy completely infected plants; replant area with different, rot-resistant species or cultivars.

Rust

Fungi. Pale spots on upper leaf surfaces; fuzzy or dusty orange spots on leaf undersides. Examples: blister rust, cedar-apple rust, cone rust.

What to Do. Choose rust-resistant varieties and cultivars; avoid handling wet leaves; provide plant with good air circulation; clear up garden debris in fall. Remove and destroy infected plant parts; late-winter lime-sulfur application can delay reinfection.

Sawflies

see Caterpillars

Scab

see Leaf Spot

Scale Insects (Scale)

Tiny, shelled insects that suck sap, weakening and possibly killing plant or making it vulnerable to other problems. Juvenile scale insects (crawlers) are mobile, but once a female scale insect pierces a plant with her mouthparts, she stays there for life.

What to Do. Spray water to dislodge crawlers; wipe adults off using alcohol-soaked swabs. Prune off heavily infested branches. Encourage natural predators and parasites. Spray dormant oil in spring before budbreak.

Skeletonizers

see Beetles

Slugs & Snails

Gray, green, black, beige, yellow or spotted mollusks with slimy, smooth skin; snails have conspicuous,

Large slug on leaf

spiral shells and slugs do not; quite small to 8" long. Can leave large, ragged holes in foliage and silvery slime trails on and around plants.

What to Do. Attaching strips of copper to wood around raised beds or to smaller boards placed around susceptible plants will shock them. Pick off by hand in evening and squish with boot or drop in soapy water. Spread wood ash or diatomaceous earth (from garden center— *not* the kind meant for swimming pool filters) around plants; it will pierce their soft bodies and cause dehydration. Lay damp cardboard on ground in evening, then dispose of it and resting slugs in morning. Shallow dish of beer may be effective. Used according to directions, slug baits containing iron phosphate control slugs without harming humans or animals. If slugs damaged garden late in season, begin controls as soon as green spring shoots appear.

Sooty Mold
Fungus. Thin, black film on leaf surfaces reduces light available to plant.

What to Do. Wipe mold off leaf surfaces; control aphids, mealybugs and whiteflies (their honeydew excretions encourage sooty mold).

Tar Spot
see Leaf Spot

Thrips
Hard-to-see, slender, yellow, black or brown insects with narrow, fringed wings; best seen if disturbed by blowing gently on infested flower. Sucking of plant juices, particularly in flowers and buds, results in mottled petals and leaves, dying buds and distorted and stunted growth.

What to Do. Remove and destroy infested plant parts; encourage native predatory insects with nectar plants such as yarrow; spray severe infestations with insecticidal soap (see p. 73) or neem oil according to directions. Use blue sticky cards to prevent recurrence. Horticultural oil controls adult thrips.

Viruses
May stunt plants and distort, streak or discolor leaves and flowers. Examples: ash yellows,

mosaic virus, ringspot virus.

What to Do. Control disease-spreading insects such as aphids, leafhoppers and whiteflies. Can't be treated; destroy infected plants.

Mosaic virus

Weevils
see Beetles

Whiteflies
Tiny, moth-like, white flying insects; live on leaf undersides; flutter up into air when disturbed. Suck juice out of leaves, causing yellowed foliage and weakened plants; sticky honeydew excretions encourage sooty mold.

What to Do. Destroy weeds inhabited by whiteflies. Attract native predatory beetles and parasitic wasps with nectar plants such as yarrow and sweet alyssum. Make a sticky, flypaper-like trap by mounting a tin can on a stake, wrapping with yellow paper and covering with clear plastic bag smeared with petroleum jelly—discard and replace bag when covered in flies. Spray severe cases with insecticidal soap (see p. 73); apply horticultural oil.

Wilt

If watering doesn't help a wilted plant, one of two wilt fungi may be at fault. *Fusarium wilt:* plant wilts, leaves turn yellow and die; symptoms generally spread from one part of plant. *Verticillium wilt:* plant wilts; leaves curl up at edges, turn yellow and may drop off; plant may die. See also Grubs, Nematodes, Rot.

What to Do. Wilt fungi are difficult to control. Choose resistant varieties; clean up debris in fall. Destroy infected plants; solarize (sterilize) soil before replanting (may help if you've lost an entire bed of plants—contact garden center for assistance); replant with resistant plants.

Witches'-Broom

Twigs become densely clustered together, broom-like, with many dying back in winter. Caused by various microorganisms or insects on many types of plants. Fungal brooms afflict cherry *(Prunus)* and blackberry *(Rubus)*. A virus causes witches'-broom on black locust. Aphids cause honeysuckle witches'-broom. The phytoplasma organisms that cause elm or ash yellows can also cause witches'-broom.

What to Do. Cut out affected portions. Determine cause; improve plant's growing conditions.

Woolly Adelgids
see Aphids

Worms
see Caterpillars, Nematodes

Pest & Disease Control Recipes

Compost Tea
Mix 1–2 lb. compost in 5 gal. of water. Let sit four to seven days, then strain out solids and return them to compost bin. Store liquid out of direct sunlight. For use, dilute until it resembles weak tea. Use during normal watering or apply as a foliar spray to prevent or treat fungal diseases.

Insecticidal Soap
Mix 1 tsp. mild dish detergent or pure soap (biodegradable options are available) with 1 qt. water in a clean spray bottle. Spray surfaces of insect-infested plants. Rinse well within an hour of spraying to avoid foliage discoloration.

Horticultural Oil
Mix 5 tbsp. horticultural oil per 1 gal. water and apply as a spray for a variety of insect and fungal problems. If purchased, follow package directions.

About This Guide

The trees and shrubs in this book are organized alphabetically by common name. Alternative common names and scientific names are given beneath the main headings and in the index. The illustrated Trees & Shrubs at a Glance (pp. 5-9) allows you to become familiar with the different plants quickly, and it will help you find a tree or shrub if you aren't sure what it's called.

Clearly displayed at the beginning of each entry are the plant's special features, height and spread ranges normally expected in our landscapes, preferred planting forms (balled-and-burlapped, container or bare-root), optimal planting seasons and plant hardiness zones (see map, p. 15). Plants differing from these zones are noted within each genus account.

Our favorite species, hybrids and cultivars are listed in each entry's Recommended section. Many more types are often available, so check with your local garden center. Some cultivated varieties are known only by the cultivar name proper, shown in single quotation marks (e.g., 'Little Gem'); others are known instead or also by a trade name registered by a particular company. Trade names are shown in small capitals (e.g., AUTUMN PURPLE). For all plants, we present the most commonly used name first, with any alternative names following in parentheses.

Where height, spread and hardiness zones are not indicated in the Recommended section, use the information under the main heading. The ranges at the beginning of each entry always encompass the measurements for all plants listed in the Recommended section.

Common pests and problems, if any, are also noted for each entry. Consult the Problems & Pests section of the introduction (pp. 62–73) for information on how to address these problems.

The Quick Reference Chart at the back of the book (pp. 342–47) is a handy guide to planning a diversity of features, forms, foliage types and blooming times in your garden.

We refer to seasons only in a general sense. Keep in mind the timing and duration of seasons in your particular area when planning your garden. Hardiness zones, too, can vary locally; consult your local extension agent, horticulturist or garden center.

The Trees
& Shrubs

American Bittersweet

Celastrus

Features: fast growth, fruit, fall color **Habit:** deciduous twining vine or sprawling groundcover **Height:** 20–30' **Spread:** 3–6' **Planting:** B & B, container; spring, fall **Zones:** 2–8

BITTERSWEET IS A ROUGH-AND-TUMBLE, LOW-MAINTENANCE, vining shrub with a wilder appearance than other plants in the Wisconsin and Minnesota landscape. The plant's chief attribute is its highly decorative fruit, which bursts forth in clusters in fall. Lengths of vine with fruit attached are commonly used in dried flower arrangements. The shrub is unsurpassed for naturalizing stone walls and fences. *C. scandens* 'Indian Brave/Maid' (male and female sold together) is the best and most common commercial cultivar; it grows up to 20' tall and has proven hardy to Zone 2.

Growing

American bittersweet grows well in **full sun** and tolerates partial shade. Poor, **well-drained** soil is preferred, because rich soil can create a monster. American bittersweet needs little to no pruning.

Male and female flowers usually bloom on separate plants. For assured fruit production, in addition to regular watering, you need to plant males and females close together. They are often sold together in one pot.

C. scandens (above & below)

Tips

American bittersweet is a great choice for the edge of a woodland garden or in naturalized areas. It quickly covers old trees, fences, arbors, trellises, posts and walls. As a groundcover, it can mask piles of rubble and old tree stumps. It is also very effective as erosion control on hard-to-maintain slopes.

Be careful—the vines can girdle the stems of young trees or shrubs, sometimes damaging or killing them.

Recommended

C. scandens (American bittersweet, staff vine) is a vigorous, twining vine with glossy, dark green foliage that turns bright yellow in fall. With solid support, it can climb to 30'. Small, undistinguished, yellow-green to whitish flowers bloom in late spring. The showy fruit has bright red arils surrounding the orange seeds. The male and female pair of '**Indian Brave**' and '**Indian Maid**' ('Indian Maiden') grow to 20' tall and are hardier than the species.

Problems & Pests

Aphids, leafhoppers, scale insects, canker, fungal leaf spot and powdery mildew can be occasional problems for bittersweet.

Oriental bittersweet (C. orbiculatus) *is far more aggressive than American bittersweet and should not be planted. American bittersweet has pointed leaves; the leaves of oriental bittersweet have rounded tips.*

Aralia
Aralia

Features: foliage, flowers, fruit, stems **Habit:** deciduous small tree or large shrub
Height: 10–30' **Spread:** 10–20' **Planting:** container, bare-root; early spring to
early winter **Zones:** 4–8

ARALIA IS THE BOTANICAL GIRL-WITH-A-CURL; WHEN CONDITIONS
are good, it looks very, very good, but when placement is bad, it is horrid.
Likely because of the invasive nature of *A. spinosa*, finding a nursery near
you that offers aralias may take a few phone calls or time on the Internet.
However, after several years, *A. elata* becomes a season-long showstopper—
few trees or shrubs available to northern gardeners grace the landscape with
such alluring, tropical-like flowers, fruit and foliage. Seek out *A. elata* 'Variegata' and 'Aureo-variegata' for superb adornment of naturalized shady
corners of your landscape.

*Aralias make an excellent burglar
deterrent along the foundation of a house,
but they can easily grow tall enough to
block windows.*

Growing

Aralias prefer **full sun** or **light shade.** They grow best in **fertile, moist, well-drained** soil but tolerate dry, clay or rocky soil. Provide **shelter** from strong winds, which can dry out the foliage.

Pruning is rarely required, but be prepared to spend some time pulling off most or all of the suckers, though barriers such as buildings and driveways can help prevent spread. Young suckers are easier to remove and have softer prickles.

Tough gloves are an absolute requirement when handling aralias. Thick rubber allows a good grip and stretches rather than punctures when prickles are encountered.

Tips

These shrubs are best suited to an informal garden. Try them in a border at the edge of a wooded area. Plant them where their spread can be controlled and where you won't inadvertently brush against the thorny stems.

Do not eat the berries—they are believed poisonous. They rarely last long anyway, because they are quickly eaten by birds.

Recommended

A. elata (Japanese angelica tree) usually grows 20' tall (potentially 30'); it suckers less vigorously than *A. spinosa* and is not quite as spiny. Clusters of creamy late-summer flowers are followed by dark purple berries. The foliage turns purple, orange or yellow in fall. The cultivars below are less vigorous and

A. elata

smaller at maturity. **'Aureo-variegata'** ('Aureovariegata'; golden variegated Japanese angelica tree) has broad, irregularly yellow-margined foliage. **'Variegata'** (variegated Japanese angelica tree) bears irregularly white-edged foliage.

A. spinosa (Hercules' club, devil's walking stick) usually grows 10–15' tall and spreads vigorously through suckering. Be prepared to wade in with thick gloves at least yearly to pull up suckers. Large clusters of white, late-summer flowers are followed by black berries.

Problems & Pests

Fungal leaf spot, aphids or mealybugs may cause occasional trouble.

A. elata 'Variegata'

Arborvitae
Cedar
Thuja

Features: foliage, bark, form **Habit:** small to large evergreen shrub or tree
Height: 1–30' **Spread:** 1–15' **Planting:** B & B, container; spring or fall
Zones: 2–9

ALTHOUGH I'VE RAILED AT TIMES AGAINST THEIR OVERUSE AT
the hands of landscape designers, I must admit that 'arbs' are in many ways
indispensable. Few evergreen genera offer such wide variety in height,
growth, habit and coloration as *Thuja,* and, once established, these plants
suffer little winterburn, all of which makes this genus ideal for our region.
Be advised that the nursery trade seems bent on informing us that most
varieties grow in partial shade. In truth, although arbs don't *die* in partial
shade, they most certainly become loose and somewhat wispy over time,
unless they receive a solid five hours of direct sunlight daily.

Growing

Arborvitae prefer **full sun.** The soil should be of **average fertility, moist** and **well drained.** These plants enjoy humidity and are often found growing near marshy areas. Arborvitae perform best in locations with some **shelter** from the wind, especially in winter, when the foliage can easily dry out, giving entire plants a rather drab, brown appearance.

These plants take very well to pruning and are often grown as hedges. Although they may be kept formally shaped, they are also attractive if just clipped to maintain a loose but compact shape and size.

Tips

Large varieties of arborvitae make excellent specimen trees, and smaller cultivars can be used in foundation plantings, shrub borders and formal or informal hedges.

Deer enjoy eating the foliage of *T. occidentalis.* If deer are a problem in your area, you may wish to avoid using this plant.

Recommended

T. occidentalis (eastern arborvitae, American arborvitae) is native to much of the Midwest and northeastern U.S. In the wild this tree can often grow to about 60' tall (rarely exceeding 100') and 10–15' wide. In cultivation it grows about half this size or less. The following cultivars may be slightly less cold hardy than the species. **'Aurea'** has bright yellow foliage and grows about 36" tall, with an equal spread. **'Emerald'**

'Sunkist'

('Smaragd') can grow 10–15' tall, spreading about 4'. This cultivar is small and very cold hardy; the foliage does not lose color in winter. **'Gold Cargo'** grows 15–25' tall and 6' wide. It has strongly gold-tinged foliage and is resistant to winterburn. **'Hetz Midget'** is a dwarf, rounded cultivar. It grows to 2–4' tall and wide, but it can be kept smaller with pruning. **'Holmstrup'** is small and upright, with whorls of tightly compact foliage. It grows 6–10' tall and 24–36" wide. **'Little Gem'** is a globe-shaped dwarf with dark green foliage. It grows 36" tall and 4–6' wide. **'Little Giant'** is a rounded, bright green cultivar.

'Little Gem' (both photos)

It grows 24–36" tall, with an equal spread. **'Pyramidalis'** is a narrow, upright pyramidal tree with bright green foliage. It grows 20–30' tall and 3–6' wide, but it is susceptible to winterburn. **'Rheingold'** has bright golden yellow foliage that turns coppery gold in winter. It grows to about 6' tall and 5' wide and is popular for hedges. **'Rushmore'** is a narrow, upright selection that grows 15–25' tall and 3–6' wide. It has dark green foliage that holds its color through winter, resisting winterburn and wind desiccation. **'Sunkist'** is a low, slow-growing, pyramidal cultivar with bright yellow foliage. It grows 5–10' tall and 5–8' wide. **'Techny'** is a very hardy cultivar with a broad, pyramidal form. It grows 10–20' tall and 5–8' wide and keeps its bluish green color all winter. **'Teddy'** has feathery, blue-green foliage that turns purple to bronze

in winter. It grows 12–18" tall and 12–24" wide. **'Wintergreen'** has dark green foliage that holds its color through winter. It is a columnar plant, 20–30' tall and 5–10' wide. **'Woodwardii'** is a globe form that grows 3–5' tall and wide. **'Yellow Ribbon'** has golden yellow to yellow-orange foliage that holds its color all year. It is a columnar selection, growing 6–10' tall and 36" wide.

Problems & Pests

Bagworm, leaf miners, red spider mites, scale insects, blight, canker and heart rot are possible, albeit infrequent, problems. Leaf miner damage may resemble winter browning—hold branch tips up to the light and look for tiny caterpillars feeding inside. Trim and destroy infested foliage before June.

'Yellow Ribbon'

Crush some arborvitae foliage between your fingers to enjoy the wonderful aroma. Be cautious, though, if you have sensitive skin— the pungent oils may irritate.

T. occidentalis cultivar

Ash

Fraxinus

Features: fall color, adaptable, fast growing **Habit:** upright or spreading deciduous tree **Height:** 15–80' **Spread:** 15–80' **Planting:** B & B, container, bare-root; spring or fall **Zones:** 2–9

NATIVE TO BOTH MINNESOTA AND WISCONSIN (AND MUCH OF North America), the ashes are handsome, versatile, overall splendid, large shade trees. The credit for several outstanding newer varieties belongs to our Canadian university and nursery friends for decades of experimental propagation. In a large yard, planted a safe 40' or more from the back or side of the house, few large deciduous trees will surpass an ash for century-long beauty. Be aware that, in spite of its common name, a mountain ash is not an ash; the mountain ash is genus *Sorbus* (p. 248), whereas true ash trees are *Fraxinus*—a valuable tidbit of trivia to use when cocktail party chatter turns botanical.

Growing

Ashes grow best in **full sun.** Young plants tolerate partial shade. The soil should be **fertile** and **moist,** with lots of room for root growth. Tolerating drought, poor soil, salt and pollution, these trees adapt to a wide range of conditions, but they are least susceptible to problems when grown in ideal conditions. *F. americana* is more ornamental but less adaptable than *F. pennsylvanica*.

Little pruning is required. Remove dead, damaged, diseased and wayward branches as needed.

Tips

Ashes are popular, quick-growing shade trees. They grow well in the moist soil alongside streams and ponds. *F. americana* is quite large and is best used in spacious areas such as parks.

Although these trees are susceptible to many problems, healthy trees grown in good conditions are very resistant to insect infestation and fungal diseases.

Recommended

F. americana (white ash) is a large, wide-spreading tree that grows 50–80' tall, with an equal spread. The fall color ranges from yellow to purple. **'Autumn Blaze'** is a large tree with an oval crown. It was developed for the prairies in Morden, Manitoba, Canada. It grows 50–60' tall and 25–30' wide. It bears green foliage that turns purple in fall and has very few seeds. (Zones 3–9)

F. nigra (black ash) is an upright tree with a narrow, open crown.

F. pennsylvanica (both photos)

In gardens it grows 40–50' tall and 25–30' wide, but it can grow up to around three times larger in the wild. It occurs in naturally wet areas and bogs and performs best in these types of conditions. **'Fallgold'** is a seedless selection, growing 40' tall and 25' wide. The very disease-resistant leaves turn golden yellow in fall and persist longer than on most other ashes. (Zones 2–7)

F. **'Northern Treasure'** is a cross between *F. nigra* and a hardy Asian species, *F. mandshurica*. It was also developed at Canada's Morden Research Station for application on the cold prairies. It grows 50' tall and 20–30' wide. The green foliage turns yellow to orange in fall. This selection yields minimal seeds. (Zones 3–9)

F. ***pennsylvanica*** (green ash, red ash) is an irregular, spreading tree. It grows 50–70' tall, with an equal

F. americana 'Autumn Blaze' (above)

spread. The foliage turns yellow, sometimes with orange or red, in fall. **'Johnson'** (LEPRECHAUN) is a dwarf of the species, growing only 15–20' tall and wide. It has a dense, oval to rounded crown and is a low water user. **'Marshall's Seedless'** is vigorous, somewhat insect-resistant plant that is supposedly seedless, but it has been known to produce seeds. It grows 40–50' tall and 40' wide and has shiny, dark green foliage. **'Patmore'** is a superior, disease-resistant, seedless selection with a large, oval crown. It has bright green foliage and grows 45' tall and 35' wide. **'Rugby'** (PRAIRIE SPIRE) is a very hardy, seedless selection. It grows 50–60' tall and 25–30' wide and forms a narrowly pyramidal to oval outline. The foliage is glossy dark green, and the young bark is lightly orange tinged. **'Summit'** is a neat, upright tree. It grows up to 50' tall and spreads about 25'. It becomes bright yellow in fall. (Zones 3–9)

Problems & Pests

Among the many possible problems are rust, leaf spot, canker, dieback, borers, leaf miners, sawflies, webworm, flower gall, scale insects, ash yellows and powdery mildew. The emerald ash borer is a new and devastating insect to us. If this imported pest becomes established in our states, it could mean serious problems for all of our ash trees. Consult your county extension agent to determine if ash should be planted in your area.

F. pennsylvanica (both photos)

Barberry

Berberis

Features: foliage, flowers, fruit, spines **Habit:** deciduous shrub **Height:** 1–6'
Spread: 18"–6' **Planting:** container; spring or fall **Zones:** 4–8

THE GREAT JOY OF LANDSCAPING WITH SHRUBS LIES IN THE
exploration of the seemingly endless variations in foliage form, texture and
color. Few shrub families reward this examination as generously as barberries.
Whether they are carrying interest throughout a home's foundation planting
or adding season-long color, height and structure to the perennial garden,
barberries are, in my mind, an essential addition to northern landscapes. The
sturdy, often shiny leaves range from dark green to yellow to red to purple.
When planted in a curving line and sheared, barberries make a good, low
deciduous hedge. About the only objection raised by some homeowners is
that most varieties possess sharp barbs that will indeed prick the skin. Well,
then, be careful!

Extracts from the rhizomes of Berberis
*have been used to treat rheumatic fever
and other inflammatory disorders, as
well as the common cold.*

Growing

Barberries develop the best fall color when grown in **full sun,** but they tolerate partial shade. Any **well-drained** soil is suitable. These plants tolerate drought and urban conditions but suffer in poorly drained, wet soil.

Barberries take heavy pruning well. They make excellent hedges and should be trimmed after they bloom. A plant in an informal border can be left alone or can be lightly pruned. Remove old wood and unwanted suckers in mid- to late winter. Remove dead wood in summer.

Tips

Large barberry plants make excellent hedges with formidable prickles. Barberries can also be included in shrub or mixed borders. Small cultivars can be grown in rock gardens, in raised beds or along rock walls.

B. thunbergii 'Crimson Pygmy'

Recommended

B. **'Bailsel'** (GOLDEN CAROUSEL) is an upright shrub with arching branches. It grows 4–5' tall and 3–4' wide. The new foliage emerges golden yellow but fades with age—the color tends to persist in light shade—becoming orange to red in fall. The fruit is bright red.

B. thunbergii 'Rose Glow'

B. thunbergii cultivar

B. thunbergii 'Helmond Pillar'

B. x 'Tara' (EMERALD CAROUSEL) is a rounded shrub with arching branches. It grows 4–5' tall and wide and has dark green foliage. The foliage turns reddish purple in fall, sooner than on many other barberries. The showy fruit is bright red.

B. thunbergii (Japanese barberry) is a dense shrub with a broad, rounded habit. It grows 3–5' tall and spreads 4–6'. The bright green foliage turns variable shades of orange, red or purple in fall. Yellow spring flowers are followed by glossy red fruit later in summer. **'Aurea'** (golden barberry) grows up to 5' tall, with an equal spread. It has bright yellow new growth. **'Bagatelle'** is a compact, rounded shrub 12–18" tall and wide, with burgundy purple foliage. **'Bailtwo'** (BURGUNDY CAROUSEL) grows 36" tall and spreads 4–5' wide. Its burgundy purple leaves are larger than the leaves of other Japanese barberries. **'Concorde'** is a dwarf cultivar with purple foliage. It grows about 18" tall. **'Crimson Pygmy'** ('Atropurpurea Nana') is a dwarf cultivar with reddish purple foliage. It grows 18–24" tall and spreads up to 36". **'Gentry Cultivar'** (ROYAL BURGUNDY) grows 18–24" tall and 24–30" wide. It has rich, velvety, burgundy foliage that turns deeper burgundy to black in fall. **'Helmond Pillar'** has a narrow, upright form and reddish purple leaves that turn bright red in fall. It grows up to 5' tall and spreads about 24". **'Kobold'** is a mound-forming plant 18–24" tall and 24–30" wide. Kelly green when new, the foliage darkens in summer, becoming yellow with red tinges in fall. GOLDEN NUGGET ('Monlers') is a dense, compact plant 12" tall and 18" wide. Its bright golden yellow foliage develops a good orange fall color. **'Rose Glow'** has purple foliage variegated with white and pink splotches. It grows 5–6' tall.

Problems & Pests

Healthy barberries rarely suffer from problems, but stressed plants can be affected by leaf spot, spider mites, aphids, weevils, root rot, wilt, mosaic or scale insects.

Because some barberry species harbor the overwintering phase of the devastating wheat rust fungus, some regions had banned all Berberis. *Many of these regions are now lifting the ban on certain species, including* B. thunbergii, *which have never been proven to harbor the fungus.*

B. thunbergii 'Concorde'

'Rose Glow' with *Chamaecyparis*

Beech

Fagus

Features: foliage, bark, habit, fall color **Habit:** large, oval, deciduous shade tree
Height: 30–80' **Spread:** 10–60' **Planting:** B & B, container; spring **Zones:** 4–9

IF THE LAND SURROUNDING YOUR CHILDHOOD HOME CONTAINED a mature beech tree, chances are good that the distinctive rumpled, gray bark remains a strong memory, as do the times you climbed the tree darn near to the top. Beeches are magnificent trees, particularly when the homeowner respects these plants' desire to grow their densely foliated branches nearly to the ground. *F. grandifolia* is rarely found at nurseries, but look for the varieties found within *F. sylvatica*, which has superior aesthetics, soil tolerances and use. In very large yards, planting *F. s.* 'Pendula' and watching it mature over your lifetime will astonish you, in addition to bestowing a gift on other people and the planet—one for which you should long be remembered.

Growing

Beeches grow equally well in **full sun** or **partial shade.** The soil should be of **average fertility, loamy** and **well drained,** though almost all well-drained soils are tolerated. *F. grandifolia* suffers in alkaline and poorly drained soils.

F. grandifolia doesn't like having its roots disturbed and should be transplanted only when very young. *F. sylvatica* transplants easily and tolerates varied soil conditions better than *F. grandifolia*.

Very little pruning is required. Remove dead or damaged branches in spring or at any time after the damage occurs. *F. sylvatica* is a popular hedging species and responds well to severe pruning.

Tips

Beeches make excellent specimens. They are also used as shade trees and in woodland gardens. These trees need a lot of space, but *F. sylvatica*'s adaptability to pruning makes it a reasonable choice in a small garden.

The nuts are edible when roasted.

F. sylvatica

Beeches retain their very smooth and elastic bark long into maturity. The leaves and bark of American beech have been used to make an ointment for soothing burns and sores.

F. grandiflora

Recommended

F. grandifolia (American beech) is a broad-canopied tree that can grow 50–80' tall and often almost as wide. This species is native to Wisconsin and most of the eastern U.S.

F. sylvatica (European beech) is a spectacular tree that can grow 60' tall and wide or even larger. Too massive for most settings if unchecked, the species is best kept pruned and used as a hedge in smaller gardens. Several cultivars are small enough to use in the home garden. **'Asplenifolia'** (cutleaf beech, fernleaf beech) has lacier foliage than the species, and it grows in a pyramidal form to 60' tall and 50–60' wide. **'Fastigiata'** ('Dawyck') is a narrow, upright tree that can grow to 80' tall but spreads only about 10'. Yellow- or purple-leaved forms are available. **'Pendula'** (weeping beech) is a dramatic tree whose pendulous branches reach down to the ground. It varies in form; some specimens spread widely, resulting in a cascade effect, whereas other specimens may be rather upright with branches drooping from the central trunk. This cultivar can grow as tall as the species, but a specimen with the branches drooping from the central trunk may be narrow enough for a home garden. **'Purpurea'** (copper beech) is a purple-leaved form with the same habit as the species. Purple-leaved weeping forms are also available. **'Purpurea Tricolor'** has striking dark green foliage with pink

F. sylvatica 'Pendula'

F. grandiflora

and white variegation that develops best in partial shade. This rare, slow-growing tree matures to about 30' tall and wide. It can be grown as a smaller tree if constrained to a large planter. The young foliage of **'Riversii'** is blackish purple when young and holds a purple-bronze color through summer. **'Rotundifolia'** has an upright habit when young, eventually widening with age. The leaves are shiny, deep green and rounded.

Problems & Pests

Aphids, borers, scale insects, bark disease, canker, leaf spot or powdery mildew can afflict beech trees, but without serious problems.

F. sylvatica 'Tricolor'

Beech nuts provide food for a wide variety of animals, including squirrels and birds. They were once a favorite food of the now-extinct passenger pigeon.

Birch

Betula

Features: foliage, fall color, habit, bark, winter and early-spring catkins **Habit:** open, deciduous tree **Height:** 10–90' Spread: 10–60' **Planting:** B & B, container; spring or fall **Zones:** 2–10

I'LL ADMIT FLAT OUT THAT I'M A sucker for *Betula* and that I always will be. For four-season interest (*never* forget that we have long winters up here), I don't believe there is a more important small to mid-sized deciduous tree to plant, grow and enjoy. In winter, the sculptural form and attractive bark of *B. nigra*, *B. lenta* and *B. papyrifera* are tremendous landscape assets. I often include *B.* ROYAL FROST in my designs for small yards; with proper pruning after the first four years of growth, the tree can be planted as close as 10 feet from a house or detached garage.

Some people make birch syrup from the sap of sweet birch. The heavy flow of sap in spring is tapped, and the sap is boiled down, the same way maple syrup is made.

Growing

Birches grow well in **full sun, partial shade** or **light shade.** The soil should be of **average to rich fertility, moist** and fairly **well drained.** Some birch species naturally grow in wet areas, such as along streams, but don't like to grow in places that remain wet for prolonged periods. Provide supplemental water to all birches during periods of extended drought.

Minimal pruning is required. Remove any dead, damaged, diseased or awkward branches as needed. Any pruning of live wood should be done in late summer or fall to prevent excessive bleeding of sap.

Tips

Birch trees are generally grown for their attractive, often white and peeling bark. The bark contrasts nicely with the dark green leaves in summer and with the glossy red or chestnut-colored younger branches and twigs in winter. Yellowish catkins dangle from the branches in early spring.

These trees are often used as specimens. With their small leaves and open canopy, birches provide light shade that allows perennials, annuals or lawns to flourish beneath. Birch trees are also attractive when grown in groups near natural or artificial water features. Most varieties need quite a bit of room to grow, although upright varieties such as B. ROYAL FROST and 'Little King' serve small spaces very well.

The common and popular B. pendula and its weeping cultivars are poor choices for gardens because of their

B. nigra
B. papyrifera

B. papyrifera

B. papyrifera 'Whitespire'

susceptibility to pests and diseases, particularly the fatal bronze birch borer. If you plan to grow or already have one of these trees, consult a tree specialist to begin a preventive program.

Recommended

B. **'Crimson Frost'** is an upright tree with a broad crown that does well in heavy clay soil. It grows 25–35' tall and 10–20' wide and has exfoliating white bark with cinnamon hues. The deep reddish purple foliage varies from crimson to orange-yellow in fall. It is interesting but prone to borers. (Zones 4–7)

B. lenta (sweet birch, cherry birch) has glossy, serrated leaves, brown-black bark, and delicate gold fall color. Excellent for naturalizing, this birch grows 25–50' tall and 20–45' wide. (Zones 3–7)

B. nigra (river birch, black birch) grows quickly to 60–90' tall and 40–60' wide. It has shaggy, cinnamon brown bark that flakes off in sheets when it is young but thickens and becomes ridged as it matures. River birch is very disease resistant and also resists bronze birch borer. **'Little King'** (FOX VALLEY) is a dwarf cultivar with a broad, pyramidal habit. In 10 years it will grow to 10–12' tall, with an equal spread. (Zones 3–9)

B. papyrifera (paper birch, canoe birch) has creamy white bark that peels off in layers, exposing cinnamon-colored bark beneath. It grows about 70' tall and 30' wide and dislikes hot summer weather. **'Renci'**

(RENAISSANCE REFLECTIONS) is a fast-growing, heat-tolerant, pyramidal, single- or multi-stemmed tree that grows 50–60' tall and 25' wide. It is resistant to bronze birch borer. (Zones 2–7)

B. pendula (European white birch) is an upright, pyramidal to rounded tree with graceful, arching branches. It usually grows to a height of 30–40', but it can reach a height of 80' in ideal conditions. The tree spreads about half the height. **'Laciniata'** ('Dalecarlica') has more pendulous branches than the species, and the foliage is deeply cut.

B. populifolia 'Whitespire' (B. platyphylla var. japonica 'Whitespire') has a spire-like habit, chalky white bark and yellow fall color. It is resistant to bronze birch borer, and is moderately susceptible to leaf miners. It grows 40–50' tall and 15–20' wide. Ensure that your plant is a cutting or was produced by tissue culture from the original tree. (Zones 4–8)

B. ROYAL FROST ('Penci-2') is more upright than 'Crimson Frost,' with similar foliage and exfoliating, cinnamon-hued, white bark. It grows 30–40' tall and 15–20' wide. Borer susceptibility is unknown at this time. (Zones 4–7)

The bark of B. papyrifera *(paper birch) has been used to make canoes, shelters, utensils and—as both the botanical and common names imply—paper.*

B. lenta
B. nigra

Problems & Pests

The bronze birch borer is a destructive insect that can quickly kill weakened trees. It is drawn to white-barked forms. Dieback in the top branches indicates that the insects have done their damage. Tree-care companies may be able to stave off the tree's demise but not if wilting is already observed.

Aphids love birch trees. Other potential problems include birch skeletonizer, leaf miners and tent caterpillars.

Blueberry
Vaccinium

Features: mid-spring to early-summer flowers, fruit, foliage **Habit:** bushy, deciduous shrub **Height:** 6"–8' **Spread:** 1–8' **Planting:** container; spring, fall **Zones:** 2–7

WHAT COULD POSSIBLY BE MORE FUN TO GROW THAN SHRUBS offering abundant white spring flowers; appealing, glossy green summer foliage; fiery orange, red or purple fall foliage; and the added bonus of edible fruits for cereal, pancakes and pies? Blueberry bushes delight the eyes and taste buds and can be grown anywhere you find (or create) acidic soil that receives full-day sun. Credit the University of Minnesota for the recent development of many varieties (see below) that are now widely available at nurseries across both states.

Growing

Blueberries grow best in **full sun** but tolerate partial shade. The soil should be **peaty, acidic, moist** and **well drained.** Blueberries are frost hardy.

Very little pruning is required. Deadhead the shrubs after flowering unless fruits are desired.

Tips

Blueberries can be used in a woodland garden or in a shrub or mixed border. Some people grow them just for the fruit and include them in the vegetable garden or with other fruit-bearing plants. Planting two different kinds (such as 'Bluecrop' and 'Blueray') together provides better cross-pollination and fruit production.

Recommended

V. angustifolium (lowbush blueberry) is a densely branched shrub that grows 6–24" tall and 24" wide and spreads by rhizomes. It has glossy, dark green foliage that turns bronze to bright red in fall. In mid- to late spring it produces bell-shaped, white (sometimes pink- to red-tinged) flowers followed by sweet, edible, white-coated, blue-black fruit. (Zones 2–6)

V. corymbosum (highbush blueberry, swamp blueberry) is an upright, dense, well-branched shrub that grows 5–8' tall and wide. It has medium to dark green summer foliage and outstanding orange to red, and sometimes yellow, fall color. It produces hanging clusters of white, sometimes pink-tinged, flowers in late spring to early

V. corymbosum 'Northland'

summer. The fruit is spherical, blue-black and not as sweet as from *V. angustifolium*. **'Bluecrop'** is a drought-resistant plant that ripens tasty fruit in mid-season. It grows 4–5' tall and wide. **'Blueray'** is a vigorous, upright shrub that grows 4–5' tall and wide. It bears light blue fruit and has red stems that stand out in winter. **'Northland'** bears small,

V. corymbosum 'Northland'

V. corymbosum

dark blue, wild-tasting fruit on plants 3–5' tall and wide. It has bright green foliage that turns orange in fall. **'Patriot'** is a disease-resistant plant that has very large, sweet, dark blue fruit. Its dark green foliage turns bright scarlet, yellow and orange in fall. 'Patriot' may have *V. angustifolium* in its parentage. (Zones 3–7)

V. Half-High hybrids are hybrids of *V. angustifolium* and *V. corymbosum* that were developed at the University of Minnesota to handle our cold winters. **'Chippewa'** has sweet, light blue fruit. It grows 3–4' tall and wide, bearing dark green foliage that turns bright red in fall. This cultivar needs a cross-pollinator for good fruit set. **'Northblue'** is a compact shrub with abundant large, dark blue fruit. It grows 20–30" tall and 30–40" wide. It has glossy, dark green foliage and is a vivid deep red

in fall. **'Northcountry'** grows 18–24" tall and 30–40" wide. The dark green foliage turns bright red and orange in fall. The sky blue fruit is mild and sweet. **'Northsky'** is a small, compact plant that grows 12–18" tall and 24–36" wide. It has glossy, dark green foliage that turns dark red in fall. Its sweet fruit is sky blue. **'Polaris'** is an upright shrub, 3–4' tall and wide, with bright orange-red fall color. The firm, fragrant, light blue fruit ripens earlier than the other blueberries listed here. 'Polaris' needs another variety planted nearby for cross-pollination. **'St. Cloud'** is a heavy producer of superior firm, sweet fruit with a great taste. It grows 24–36" tall and 36" wide. The glossy, dark green foliage turns deep red in fall. (Zones 3–7)

V. x **'Top Hat'** is a *V. angustifolium* x *V. corymbosum* hybrid released by the University of Michigan. It is a disease-resistant, dense, compact plant, 12–18" tall and wide. The glossy, dark green foliage turns bright red in fall. This shrub has abundant sweet, light blue fruit and does not need cross-pollination to bear fruit. It is a great plant for containers and bonsai. (Zones 3–7)

Problems & Pests

Occasional problems with caterpillars, scale insects, gray mold, leaf gall, bud gall, crown rot, root rot, powdery mildew or rust are possible but not frequent.

V. angustifolium (above)

The edible, deliciously tart berries of Vaccinium *species can be used to make pies, syrups and wines.*

V. corymbosum 'Bluecrop'

Bog Rosemary
Marsh Rosemary
Andromeda polifolia

Features: foliage, flowers **Habit:** low-growing, evergreen shrub **Height:** 12–24"
Spread: 24–36" **Planting:** container; spring, fall **Zones:** 2–6

BOG ROSEMARY IS A TRAGICALLY UNDERUSED SMALL SHRUB THAT
is slowly gaining popularity across Minnesota and Wisconsin. Its chief asset is
wonderful, powder blue foliage that retains its color all season. The plant's
low stature and naturally mounded form make it ideal for use as a front-of-
the-border accent plant in foundation plantings. I've also seen it planted to
great effect in rock gardens. Bog rosemary is perfectly hardy across the coldest
areas of our region and possesses extremely attractive, light pink, urn-shaped
flowers that persist over several months in early summer. I'll be surprised if
we don't see an expanded lineup of vari-
eties in the years ahead. Start growing
bog rosemary now, and you're
ahead of the curve.

*In Greek mythology,
Andromeda was the
daughter of Cassiopeia.
She angered Poseidon
and was chained to a
rock in the ocean—an
isolation reminiscent of
wild bog rosemary, which
grows on moss hummocks
in a boggy 'sea.'*

Growing

Bog rosemary can grow well in **full sun** or **light shade.** The soil should have **lots of organic matter** worked in and be **acidic, moist** and **well drained.**

It is not the cold of winter but the heat and humidity of summer that are most likely to adversely affect this shrub; give it light shade in a cooler area to protect it from summer heat if your garden tends to get hot and humid. Bog rosemary is one plant that will definitely grow better for us northern gardeners than for our southern neighbors.

A. polifolia (above & bottom)

Tips

Include this pink- or white-flowered plant in a rock garden or woodland garden, by a water feature or as a groundcover underneath other acid-loving shrubs.

Do not make a tea with, or otherwise ingest, bog rosemary—it contains andromedotoxin, which can lower blood pressure, disrupt breathing and cause cramps and vomiting.

Recommended

A. polifolia is an attractive plant that bears light pink flowers in late spring and early summer. It grows 12–24" tall and spreads up to 36". The thick, leathery foliage is dark green. **'Blue Ice'** has icy, slate blue foliage and light pink flowers. Growing 12–16" tall, it reaches 36" across. **'Compacta'** is a dwarf cultivar with pink flowers that grows about 12" tall and spreads about 24".

'Blue Ice' (center)

Boxwood
Box
Buxus

Features: foliage, habit **Habit:** dense, rounded, evergreen shrub **Height:** 2–20'
Spread: equal to height or slightly more **Planting:** B & B, container; spring
Zones: 4–8

AS THE NATURE OF AMERICAN LANDSCAPE DESIGN HAS SLOWLY
loosed itself from the stifling precedent of the English gardening tradition,
boxwoods are being recognized (and planted) with new appreciation. For
generations they have stood on top of the list of good deciduous shrubs for
clipping and coercing into low, dense, formal hedges, and they remain there,
but the rules are changing. Try experimenting with singular placement in
both foundation and perennial beds. Renegade gardeners may even be so
bold as to spare the shears and allow these typically small, rounded, densely
foliated shrubs the chance to grow jagged and wild.

Growing

Boxwoods prefer **partial shade** but adapt to full shade or to full sun if kept well watered. The soil should be **fertile** and **well drained.** Once established, boxwoods are drought tolerant. *B. sempervirens* has a low tolerance of extremes of heat and cold and should be grown in a sheltered spot.

Because boxwoods have roots very close to the surface, a good mulch is beneficial. For the same reason, do not disturb the earth around a boxwood once it is established.

Boxwoods can sprout new growth from old wood. A plant that has been neglected or is growing in a lopsided manner can be cut back hard in spring. By the end of summer, the exposed areas will have filled in with new green growth.

Tips

Many formal gardens include boxwoods because they can be pruned to form neat hedges, geometric shapes or fanciful creatures. A slow rate of growth and small, densely packed leaves that form an even

B. microphylla var. *koreana* (above & below)

surface place boxwoods among the most popular plants for creating topiary. When left unpruned, a boxwood shrub forms an attractive, rounded mound.

These shrubs make excellent background plants in a mixed border. Brightly colored flowers show up well against the even, green surface. Dwarf cultivars can be trimmed into small hedges for edging garden beds or walkways. An interesting topiary piece can create a formal or whimsical focal point in any garden. Large species and cultivars are often used to form dense evergreen hedges.

Boxwood foliage contains toxic compounds that, when eaten, can cause severe digestive upset.

B. sempervirens

The wood of Buxus, *particularly the wood of the root, is very dense and fine grained, making it valuable for carving. Its common name arises from its use for ornate boxes.*

B. m. 'Green Mountain'

Recommended

B. microphylla* var. *koreana (Korean littleleaf boxwood) grows to 4' in height and spread. It is cold hardy and quite pest resistant. The foliage tends to lose its green in winter, turning shades of bronze, yellow or brown.

***B. m.* var. *koreana* x *B. sempervirens* cultivars** have been developed, and some have inherited the best attributes of each parent—hardiness and pest resistance on the one hand and attractive foliage year-round on the other. CHICAGOLAND GREEN ('Glencoe') has a neat, rounded habit and grows quickly to a mature height of 24–36". **'Green Gem'** forms a rounded 24" mound. The deep green foliage stays green all winter. **'Green Mountain'** forms a large, upright shrub, 5' tall, with dark green foliage. **'Green Velvet'** is a hardy cultivar developed in Canada. It has glossy foliage and a rounded habit, growing up to 36" in height and spread.

B. sempervirens (common box-wood) is a much larger species. If left unpruned it can grow to 20' in height and width. It has a low toler-ance to extremes of heat and cold and should be grown in a sheltered spot. The foliage stays green in win-ter. Many cultivars are available with interesting features, such as compact or dwarf growth, varie-gated foliage and pendulous branches. (Zones 5–8)

B. sinica **var.** *insularis* **'Winter-green'** (*B. microphylla* var. *koreana* 'Winter Green') is a dense, mound-ing shrub that grows 2–4' tall and 3–5' wide. The foliage keeps its light green color through winter.

B. **'Wilson'** (NORTHERN CHARM) is a cold-hardy, compact, oval shrub that can grow to 42" tall and 4' wide. This selection has delicate, semi-glossy, emerald green foliage with a bluish cast. The foliage color holds through winter.

B. sempervirens

Problems & Pests

Leaf miners, mites, psyllids, scale insects, leaf spot, powdery mildew and root rot are all problems that can affect boxwoods.

Boxwoods are steeped in legend and lore. The foliage was a main ingredient in an old mad-dog bite remedy, and boxwood hedges were traditionally planted around graves to keep the spirits from wandering.

B. m. 'Green Gem'

Bush Honeysuckle
Diervilla

Features: habit, flowers, foliage, adaptability **Habit:** low, thicket-forming, deciduous shrub **Height:** 2–6' **Spread:** 3–6' **Planting:** container; spring through fall **Zones:** 3–8

INFORMAL, SHADY LANDSCAPES AND PARTS OF LARGE YARDS where a transition from lawn to woods is desired offer great opportunities to use bush honeysuckle, for this tough native likes to roam. It is an excellent choice for naturalizing the spaces under a mature tree canopy, and its shallow, fibrous root system works well anywhere soil erosion is a problem. The small, trumpet-shaped, yellow flowers that appear in mid-summer won't knock your socks off, but the attractive bronze-green foliage (often turning red in fall) and fast growing pace make bush honeysuckles a good choice for massing across large areas.

The bush honeysuckles used to be grouped with Weigela *but have recently been assigned to their own genus.*

Growing

Bush honeysuckles grow best in **full sun** or **partial shade** but tolerate full shade. Any **well-drained** soil will do. These shrubs tolerate dry, rocky soil.

Pruning is rarely required, but the plants can be cut back to within 6–12" of the ground in early spring as the buds begin to swell.

Tips

Bush honeysuckles are hard to beat for difficult and low-maintenance locations. Often used to stabilize banks or to fill in hot, dry flowerbeds close to the house, they can also be added to mixed or shrub borders or to woodland gardens.

Recommended

D. lonicera (bush honeysuckle, northern bush honeysuckle) is a low, suckering shrub. It grows 3–4' tall and spreads 3–5' or more. Small yellow flowers are borne in mid-summer. **'Copper'** has a copper or bronze color to its new foliage.

D. rivularis (Georgia bush honey-suckle) is a rounded shrub growing 6' tall and wide. Clusters of lemon yellow flowers appear in summer.

D. lonicera

'Morton' (SUMMER STARS) is a dwarf about 24–36" tall and 3–4' wide. It sometimes develops a yellow-red fall color. (Zones 4–8)

D. sessifolia (southern bush honey-suckle) spreads by suckers to form a dense thicket. It grows 3–5' tall, with an equal or greater spread. The yellow flowers are produced over a long period, from May through July. **'Butterfly'** is a cultivar with neater, more compact growth that flowers over the same long period. (Zones 4–8)

Problems & Pests

Although these easy-care shrubs rarely suffer any problems, poor air circulation can encourage powdery mildew.

D. sessifolia 'Butterfly'

Butterfly Bush
Summer Lilac
Buddleia (Buddleja)

Features: flowers, habit, foliage **Habit:** large, deciduous shrub with arching branches **Height:** 4–20' **Spread:** 4–20' **Planting:** container; spring to summer **Zones:** 4–9

FEW SHRUBS AVAILABLE TO NORTHERN GARDENERS OFFER AS explosive a display of colorful flowers as does *Buddleia*, but the unfortunate trade-off is that they are only marginally hardy to Zone 4. Many tree and shrub books published as recently as the late 1990s list even the toughest varieties as hardy only to Zone 5, but remember that plants don't read books. This plant is an old-fashioned favorite (and butterfly magnet) well worth attempting in Zone 4, where I have witnessed countless examples of success.

Butterfly bushes are among the best shrubs for attracting butterflies and bees to your garden. Don't spray these plants against pests lest you harm the beautiful and beneficial insects that make their homes in them.

Growing

Butterfly bushes prefer to grow in **full sun.** The soil should be **average to fertile** and **well drained.** These shrubs are quite drought tolerant once established. Plant in sunny locations sheltered from winter wind and unabated cold.

B. davidii blooms on the current year's growth. Early each spring, cut it back within 6 to 12 inches of the ground to encourage new growth and plenty of flowers.

B. alternifolia blooms on the previous year's growth. Prune after flowering is complete in mid-summer. This species may require a sheltered location to prevent winter dieback.

Deadhead to encourage new shoots, extend the blooming period and prevent self-seeding.

Tips

Butterfly bush makes an excellent specimen and is beautiful in shrub and mixed borders. The forms under 5' tall are suitable for small gardens.

Recommended

B. alternifolia (alternate-leaved butterfly bush) grows 10–20' tall, with an equal or slightly narrower spread. In late spring to early summer, clusters of light purple flowers form at the branch ends. If the branches have room to arch down around the trunk, it can be trained to form a tree. **'Argentea'** has silvery gray leaves.

B. davidii (orange-eye butterfly bush, summer lilac) grows 4–10' tall, with an equal spread. Flowers in

B. davidii

Butterfly bushes have a habit of self-seeding, and you might find tiny bushes popping up in unlikely places. The seedlings are easily pulled up from places they aren't wanted.

bright and pastel shades of purple, white, pink or blue bloom over a long period from mid-summer to fall. **Var. *nanhonensis* 'Nanho Blue'** grows 4–8' tall and wide. It has lilac blue flowers and a more refined look with narrower foliage and slimmer branches. **Var. *nanhonensis* 'Nanho Purple'** is similar to 'Nanho Blue.' It grows 4–6' tall and wide, bearing very fragrant, deep burgundy purple flowers. **'Pink Delight'** bears pink flowers. **'Windy Hill'** has large clusters of purple flowers on plants 5' tall and wide and is rated to Zone 4. (Zones 5–9)

Problems & Pests

Spider mites present occasional trouble, but good air circulation helps keep them and any fungal problems at bay.

Cherry
Plum, Almond
Prunus

Features: spring to early-summer flowers, fruit, bark, fall foliage **Habit:** upright, rounded, spreading or weeping, deciduous tree or shrub **Height**: 3–75'
Spread: 3–50' **Planting:** B & B, container, bare-root; spring **Zones:** 2–9

THIS VERY LARGE GENUS OF TREES INCLUDES A VARIETY OF EDIBLE 'stone' fruits—apricots, peaches and nectarines, plus those drawing our attention here: cherry, plum and almond. Most are native to the Northern Hemisphere, and dozens of varieties thrive in even the coldest portions of both Minnesota and Wisconsin. Although not all bear edible fruit (birds likely have a different viewpoint), the plants mentioned below have numerous terrific uses. Compact sizes, wonderful forms, breathtaking spring blooms and vivid fall colors make these trees and shrubs worth much consideration.

Growing

These plants prefer **full sun** and **moist, well-drained soil** of **average fertility.** Plant on mounds when possible to encourage drainage. Shallow roots will come up from the ground if the tree isn't getting enough water.

Most plants listed here need little or no pruning when grown individually. Simply remove damaged growth and wayward branches. Specific pruning requirements are noted below. All pruning should take place after flowering is complete.

Tips

These trees and shrubs make beautiful specimens. Many are small enough to include in almost any garden. Use small species and cultivars in borders, or group to form informal hedges or barriers. 'Atropurpurea' and *P.* x *cistena* can be trained as formal hedges.

Cherries can be short-lived. If you plant a pest-susceptible species, such as *P. serrulata,* enjoy it while it thrives, but be prepared to replace it once problems surface.

P. pensylvanica

Recommended

P. americana (American plum) is a large, spreading shrub with spiny branches that can be trained as a single-stemmed tree. It grows 15–25' tall and 10–15' wide, bearing small clusters of white flowers in spring, and spherical, red to yellow fruit. It spreads by suckers and thrives on neglect. Prune one-third of the old wood to the ground each year and remove all wayward suckers. (Zones 3–8)

P. besseyi (western sand cherry) is an erect to prostrate shrub that grows 3–5' tall and wide, bearing small clusters of white flowers in early to mid-spring, and spherical to slightly oblong, black to red-yellow

fruit. Fall foliage is reddish orange. This shrub tolerates hot, dry conditions and is an effective plum pollinator. Prune one-third of the old wood to the ground each year and remove wayward suckers. (Zones 3–8)

P. cerasifera (cherry plum, myrobalan) is an erect, bushy tree with a rounded, spreading crown that grows 15–30' tall and 15–25' wide and tolerates dry conditions. It bears small, very fragrant white flowers in abundance in spring. The small, edible fruit is red to yellow. When the tree is young, remove vertical shoots that compete with the main stem. If training as a hedge, start with very young plants, 36" apart, and prune back immediately after flowering. **'Atropurpurea'** (Pissard plum) is a shrubby, often multi-stemmed tree that grows 20–30' tall and wide. Light pink flowers, which fade to white, emerge before the deep purple

P. glandulosa 'Rosea Plena'

P. serrulata 'Kwanzan'

foliage. The purple fruit is edible. MOUNT SAINT HELENS ('Frank threes') is a vigorous, upright selection with a rounded crown. It has light pink flowers, and the purple foliage holds its color. **'Newport'** grows 15–20' tall and wide. More cold hardy than the species, it blooms earlier, with light pink to white flowers. New foliage is light bronze-purple, aging to deep purple. The fruit is dull purple. **'Thundercloud'** is a rounded, bushy tree, 15–20' tall and wide, that bears fragrant, light pink flowers and glossy purple foliage. (Zones 4–8)

P.* x *cistena (purple-leaf sand cherry, purple-leaf dwarf plum) is an upright shrub that grows 5–10' high, with an equal or lesser spread. It has deep purple leaves, fragrant white or slightly pink flowers in mid- to late spring, and purple-black fruit. (Zones 3–8)

P. glandulosa (dwarf flowering almond) grows 3–4' tall and wide. Pink or white single or double flowers completely cover the stems in early spring. Although it's attractive when flowering, plant it with other trees and shrubs so it can fade into the background as the season wears on. It may spread by suckers. Prune one-third of the old wood to the ground each year. **'Rosea Plena'** features pink double flowers. (Zones 4–8)

P. maackii (Amur chokecherry) grows 30–45' tall and spreads 25–45'. Fragrant, white, mid-spring flowers are followed by red fruit that ripens to black. The peeling, glossy, reddish to golden brown bark provides year-round interest. (Zones 2–6)

P. x *cistena*

P. mandshurica (*P. armeniaca* var. *mandshurica;* Manchurian apricot) is a small, frost-resistant tree with a rounded, spreading crown. It grows 15–20' tall and wide, bearing pale pink flowers in spring and spherical, red-yellow fruit. **'Moongold'** grows 10–15' tall and wide, bearing white flowers and high yields of mild-flavored, sweet, orange fruit. **'Sungold'** is an upright tree that

P. pensylvanica

P. sargentii
P. tomentosa

grows 10–15' tall and wide and bears mild-flavored, sweet, golden orange fruit. 'Sungold' and 'Moongold' are an excellent pair for cross-pollination. (Zones (3)4–8)

P. nigra (Canada plum) is an upright tree with a narrow, oval-shaped crown. It grows 15–25' tall and 10–15' wide, producing small clusters of white, sometimes pink-tinged, flowers. The gray, plate-like bark flakes off like scales. The fruit is yellow-red to red. **'Princess Kay'** grows 10–15' tall and 8–12' wide and has fragrant white double flowers. It produces little or no fruit but blooms freely at a young age. The bark is very dark red-brown to almost black, with contrasting white lenticels. Fall foliage is orange to red. (Zones 2–6)

P. pensylvanica (pin cherry) is a fast-growing tree with a rounded, spreading crown and yellow to red fall color. It grows 18–30' tall and 12–25' wide and has attractive, peeling, reddish orange bark. Small clusters of white flowers in mid- to late spring yield small, light red fruit that birds enjoy. This species likes very moist soil, performing well by streams and in light boggy conditions. (Zones 2–6)

P. sargentii (Sargent cherry) is a rounded or spreading tree that grows 20–40' tall and 20–30' wide with glossy, red-brown bark and orange fall color. Fragrant light pink or white flowers appear in mid- to late spring, followed by deep red fruit. **'Columnaris'** is a narrow, upright cultivar, suitable for tight spots. (Zones 4–9)

P. serrulata (Japanese flowering cherry) grows up to 75' tall and up to 50' wide. It bears white or pink flowers in mid- to late spring. **'Kwanzan'** (Kwanzan cherry) has drooping clusters of pink double flowers. It is sometimes grafted onto a single trunk, creating a small, vase-shaped tree. Grown on its own roots, it becomes a large, spreading tree, 30–40' tall and wide. (Zones 5–8)

P. tomentosa (Nanking cherry, Manchu cherry) grows 6–10' tall and spreads up to 15'. It has pink buds that yield fragrant white flowers in mid-spring and tart, edible, bright red fruit in mid-summer. The exfoliating, shiny, reddish bark is attractive in winter. Prune out some of the lower branches for better viewing. (Zones 2–7)

P. virginiana (chokecherry) is a small, suckering tree with an oval, rounded or pyramidal crown and dark green foliage. It grows 20–30' tall and 15–25' wide. Small, dense clusters of white flowers bloom in late spring, followed by small red fruits that mature to purple. **'Canada Red Select'** has a rounded crown and dense foliage that begins green but turns bright reddish purple in summer. **'Schubert'** is a more pyramidal selection. Its dark green leaves turn dark red-purple in summer. (Zones 2–8)

Problems & Pests

Potential problems include aphids, borers, caterpillars, leafhoppers, mites, nematodes, scale insects, canker, crown gall, fire blight, powdery mildew and viruses. Root rot can occur in poorly drained soils.

P. tomentosa

Introduced into cultivation in 1880, Pissard plum was one of the first purple-leaved Prunus *cultivars.*

P. virginiana 'Schubert'

Chokeberry
Aronia
Aronia

Features: flowers, fruit, fall foliage **Habit:** suckering, deciduous shrub
Height: 3–6' **Spread:** 3–8' **Planting:** container, bare-root; spring or fall
Zones: 3–8

SEVERAL YEARS AGO I ENTERED INTO THAT SUBLIME STAGE OF
gardening when one realizes the importance of planting residential landscapes with ample numbers of shrubs. Soon afterward, I happened upon a
chokeberry in blazing red fall splendor. Checking back the next spring, I was
treated to fragrant, lovely white flowers. Later that summer, I witnessed the
plant's handsome, upright form clad in shiny, dark green foliage and saw it
bearing glossy, bright red berries. No doubt the variety was *A. arbutifolia*
'Brilliantissima.' Chokeberries are tough, easy-to-grow shrubs, and I have
been designating them for single and massed placement in landscape designs
ever since.

*High in vitamins, especially vitamin C,
chokeberry fruit is used as a local
alternative to citrus in parts of Russia.*

Growing

Chokeberries grow well in **full sun** or **partial shade,** with the best flowering and fruiting and strongest branches in full sun. In partial shade the weight of the fruit may cause the branches to splay downward. The soil should be of **average fertility** and **well drained,** but these plants adapt to most soils and generally tolerate poor, wet or dry soil. *A. arbutifolia* 'Brilliantissima' prefers moist to wet soil.

Up to one-third of a mature chokeberry's oldest stems can be pruned out annually.

Tips

Chokeberries are useful in a shrub or mixed border. They also make interesting, low-maintenance specimens. Left to their own devices, they can colonize a fairly large area.

Recommended

A. arbutifolia (*Photinia floribunda;* aronia, red chokeberry) is an upright shrub, 3–6' tall, with white flowers in late spring and persistent, waxy, bright red fruit. Shades of orange and red color the fall leaves. **'Brilliantissima'** has brilliant red fall foliage.

A. melanocarpa (black chokeberry) is an upright, suckering shrub that grows 3–6' tall and 6–8' wide, bearing white flowers in late spring and early summer. Ripening in fall, the dark fruit persists through winter. The foliage turns red to purplish red in fall. **'Autumn Magic'** has bright red to purple fall foliage. **Var.** *elata* has larger flowers, foliage and fruit than the species. IROQUOIS BEAUTY

A. melanocarpa

('Morton') is a compact cultivar just 36" tall and slightly wider than tall. **'Viking'** grows 3–5' tall and 6–8' wide. It has glossy, dark green foliage that turns dark red in fall. The persistent, large, dark fruit is edible but bitter.

Problems & Pests

Major problems are rare, but fungal leaf spot is possible.

Too bitter even for birds unless fermented, chokeberry fruit usually persists all winter. Copious amounts of sugar are needed when making jam or juice.

A. melanocarpa 'Autumn Magic'

Cotoneaster

Cotoneaster

Features: foliage, early-summer flowers, persistent fruit, variety of forms **Habit:** deciduous groundcover or shrub **Height:** 1–10' **Spread:** 4–10' **Planting:** container; spring, fall **Zones:** 2–8

TALL VARIETIES OF COTONEASTERS HAVE BEEN POPULAR HEDGE plants in Minnesota and Wisconsin yards for generations, but when it comes to relatively low-growing, horizontal deciduous shrubs, there are few alternatives better than the short, spreading varieties. *C. adpressus* features wonderful, bluish green groundcover foliage that turns a rich red in fall. For tall hedges, the classic *C. lucidus* takes to shearing well, and it can be planted only 18 inches apart. The absence of suckering adds to the value of cotoneasters when used for hedges; the width is up to you, not the plant. Attractive red to black fruit is a prime feature of all cotoneasters.

C. horizontalis

Growing

Cotoneasters grow well in **full sun** or **partial shade.** The soil should be of **average fertility** and **well drained.**

Although pruning is rarely required, these plants tolerate even hard pruning. Prune cotoneaster hedges in mid- to late summer to see how much you can trim off while still leaving some of the ornamental fruit in place. Hard pruning encourages new growth and can rejuvenate plants that are looking worn out.

Tips

Cotoneasters can be included in shrub or mixed borders. The low spreaders work well as groundcovers, and shrubby species can be used to form hedges. Some low growers are grafted onto standards and grown as small, weeping trees.

Although cotoneaster berries are not poisonous, they can cause stomach upset if eaten in large quantities. The foliage may be toxic.

Recommended

C. acutifolius (Peking cotoneaster) is a rounded to erect shrub with arching branches that grows 6–10' tall and wide. It has dull, gray-green to dark green foliage, and it produces pink-tinged white flowers in summer. The small red fruit is egg-shaped. Fall turns the leaves orange-yellow. (Zones 4–8)

C. adpressus (creeping cotoneaster) is a low-growing, deciduous species that is used as a groundcover. It grows only 12" high and spreads up to 7' wide. Red-tinged white flowers are produced in summer. In fall the foliage turns reddish purple and the fruit ripens to red. (Zones 4–6)

C. apiculatus (cranberry cotoneaster) is a deciduous species that forms a mound of arching, tangled branches. It grows about 36" high and spreads up to 7'; sometimes it is available in a grafted, tree form. Small pink flowers bloom in late spring. The bright red fruit persists until winter. (Zones 4–7)

C. divaricatus (spreading cotoneaster) grows 5–6' tall and 5–8' wide. A rounded to spreading, deciduous shrub, it has dense, somewhat arching branches and glossy, dark green foliage. Small, reddish pink to white flowers appear in late spring but are often concealed by the foliage. The ovoid fruit is red to dark red. The long-lasting fall leaf color is maroon to bright red. This species takes clipping very well, so it can be used in a hedge border. (Zones 4–7)

C. horizontalis
C. apiculatus

C. horizontalis (rockspray cotoneaster) is a low-growing, deciduous species with a distinctive, attractive, herringbone branching pattern. It grows 24–36" tall and spreads 5–8'. Light pink flowers in early-summer are followed by red fruit in fall. The leaves turn bright red in fall. (Zones 5–7)

C. integerrimus (European cotoneaster) forms a dense, tangled mound of stems, 3–5' tall and 4–6' wide. It has dull, dark green foliage and produces rose-tinged white flowers in spring. It bears persistent, small, red to red-purple fruit. (Zones 2–7)

C. lucidus (hedge cotoneaster) is an erect to rounded shrub with glossy, dark green foliage and superb yellow to red fall color. Often slightly taller than wide, it grows 5–7' tall and wide. The small, pink-tinged white flowers of mid- to late spring are followed by small, persistent, shiny black fruit. This species is an excellent hedge plant and also looks great when left in its natural form. (Zones 2–7)

C. acutifolius
C. lucidus

Problems & Pests

These plants are generally problem free, but occasional attacks of lace bugs, scale insects, slugs, snails, spider mites, canker, fire blight, powdery mildew or rust are possible.

'Cotoneaster' is pronounced cuh-TONE-ee-aster rather than cotton-easter.

Crabapple
Malus

Features: spring flowers, late-season and winter fruit, fall foliage, habit, bark
Habit: small to medium, rounded, mounded or spreading, deciduous tree **Height:**
6–35' **Spread:** 5–30' **Planting:** B & B, container; spring, fall **Zones:** 2–8

OF ALL THE ORNAMENTAL TREES, CRABAPPLES ARE THE MOST
popular with northern gardeners. The available varieties range from small
and compact to quite large, and their mid-May show of big, blousy blooms is
a joy to behold. Many crabapples fall into the small tree category, making
them ideal for small yards and for multiple plantings throughout large properties. Many varieties introduced over the past 20 years have combined good
winter hardiness with much-improved disease resistance.

Growing

Crabapples prefer **full sun** but tolerate partial shade. The soil should be of **average to rich fertility, moist** and **well drained.** These trees tolerate damp soil.

Crabapples require very little pruning but adapt to aggressive pruning. Remove damaged or wayward branches and suckers when necessary. Vertical branches should be removed because they won't flower as much as horizontal branches. The next year's flower buds form in early summer, so any pruning done to form the shape of the tree should be done by late spring, or as soon as the current year's flowering is finished.

Tips

Crabapples make excellent specimen plants. Many varieties are quite small, so there is one to suit almost any size of garden. Some forms are small enough to grow in large containers. The flexibility of the young branches makes crabapples good choices for creating espalier specimens along walls or fences.

If planted in full sun, crabapples will mature into magnificent, fully rounded focal points of the landscape.

Many pests overwinter in the fruit, leaves or soil at the base of the tree, so one of the best ways to prevent the spread of crabapple pests and diseases is to clean up all the leaves and fruit that fall off the tree. Clearing away their winter shelter helps keep their populations under control.

Recommended

The following are a few suggestions from among the hundreds of crabapples available. When choosing a species, variety or cultivar, look for disease resistance. Ask for information about new resistant cultivars at your local nursery or garden center.

All of the following crabapples flower in mid- to late spring, unless otherwise noted.

M. **'Adams'** has good disease resistance. This upright, rounded tree grows about 20–25' tall and 20' wide. Carmine pink buds open to dull pink flowers. The fruit is a glossy dark red. The foliage is tinged red when young and tinged purple when mature. (Zones 5–8)

M. **'Amaszam'** (AMERICAN MASTERPIECE) is a disease-tolerant, upright tree with an oval to rounded crown and dark maroon foliage. It grows 20–25' tall and 18–20' wide. The red buds produce bright red flowers, and the fruit is pumpkin orange. (Zones 4–8)

M. **'Cinzam'** (CINDERELLA) is an upright tree, 8' tall and 5' wide. Although disease resistant, it has a slight susceptibility to scab. It develops an oval to rounded crown and dark green, deeply lobed foliage. Red buds open to white flowers, followed by small gold fruit. (Zones 4–8)

Some gardeners use crabapple fruit to make preserves, cider or even wine.

M. **'Coralcole'** (CORALBURST) is disease resistant. This crabapple has a rounded habit and can be grown as a small tree or large shrub, 8–15' tall, with an equal spread. Red buds open to coral pink semi-double flowers. This cultivar produces some, but not a lot of, orange fruit. (Zones 4–8)

M. **'David'** grows 12–15' tall and wide and offers good disease resistance. It bears abundant pink buds and white flowers, mid- to dark green foliage that turns yellow in fall, and persistent, scarlet fruit. (Zones 4–8)

M. **'Dolgo'** is a vigorous, hardy tree that grows 25–35' tall and 20–30' wide. The fragrant white flowers appear from light pink buds, and the tree may flower heavily only in alternate years. It has yellow fall foliage and bright purple-red fruits. It has fair to good disease resistance. (Zones 2–7)

M. **'Donald Wyman'** is resistant to all diseases except apple scab and powdery mildew, which can be prevented by pruning out enough growth to allow good air circulation. This open, rounded tree grows up to 20' tall and 25' wide. Dark pink buds open to white flowers in mid-spring. Flowering tends to be heavier in alternating years. The persistent fruit is bright red. (Zones 4–8)

M. **'Doubloons'** has bright red buds and double white flowers, followed by small, persistent, yellow to gold fruit. It is an upright, dense tree with a rounded crown that grows to 10–12' tall and 8–10' wide. It may

reach a height of 18' and a width of 16' in ideal conditions. It has good disease resistance. (Zones 4–8)

M. GOLDEN RAINDROPS (*M. transitoria* 'Schmidtcutleaf') is a fast-growing, vase-shaped tree, 15–20' tall and 10–15' wide, with a susceptibility to fire blight. It has deeply cut foliage, white flowers and tiny, golden yellow fruit. (Zones 4–8)

M. **'Hargozam'** (HARVEST GOLD) is a highly disease-resistant tree growing 20–25' tall and 15–25' wide, with an upright, spreading to rounded habit. The pink buds open to white flowers, followed by persistent yellow fruit. (Zones 3–8)

M. **'Lanzam'** (LANCELOT) is a compact, disease-resistant tree that grows 10–15' tall and 8–15' wide. It has red buds that open to white flowers, small, persistent, gold fruit and golden yellow fall foliage. This cultivar requires no pruning to maintain its form. (Zones 4–8)

M. **'Lollizam'** (LOLLIPOP) grows 10' tall and wide and has a tight, rounded crown; no pruning is needed to maintain its form. This disease-resistant tree bears abundant white flowers from white buds, and golden yellow fruit. The leaves turn yellow in fall. (Zones 4–8)

M. **'Mazam'** (MADONNA) is fairly resistant to disease. This upright tree grows about 20' tall and 10' wide. The pink buds open to long-lasting white double flowers. The yellow fruit is flushed with red. (Zones 4–8)

M. **'Pink Spires'** is a narrow, upright tree. Growing 20–25' tall and 10–12' wide, it has dark lavender buds and lavender flowers, which fade with age. The bright purple-red fruit is persistent. Tinged red in spring, the green foliage becomes bronzy in fall. (Zones 2–8)

M. sargentii (Sargent crabapple) is a small, mounding tree, 6–10' tall and 8–15' wide, that is fairly resistant to disease. White flowers open from red buds in late spring. The long-lasting fruit is dark red. **'Candymint Sargent'** ('Candymint') has a horizontal spreading to somewhat weeping form with attractive reddish brown bark. It grows 8–10' tall and 10–15' wide, producing abundant deep pink or red buds that open to red-edged pink flowers. The fruit is purple. The purple-tinged foliage turns bronze-purple in fall. FIREBIRD ('Select A') is a slow-growing, rounded form that has good disease resistance and very persistent fruit. (Zones 4–8)

Problems & Pests

Aphids, Japanese beetles, leaf rollers, leaf skeletonizers, scale insects and tent caterpillars are insect pests to watch for, but the damage is largely cosmetic. Leaf drop caused by apple scab is the most common problem with susceptible cultivars. Cedar-apple rust, fire blight, leaf spot or powdery mildew can also be problematic, depending on the weather.

To help your crabapples become the much-admired mature specimens that they are capable of being, be sure to properly prune them while they are young.

Currant

Ribes

Features: spring flowers, foliage, fruit **Habit:** upright, deciduous shrub
Height: 3–8' **Spread:** 3–8' **Planting:** container; spring, fall **Zones:** 2–7

CURRANTS ARE EUROPEAN NATIVE SHRUBS OFFERING MUCH OF
value to northern gardeners. If you desire a dense, clipped, formal, deciduous
hedge, look no farther than *R. alpinum.* For single placement at the back of
the garden or in the foundation planting, *R. aureum* will quickly develop into
a large shrub featuring reddish brown
bark and fragrant yellow
flowers. *R. odoratum* is
perhaps the best for fall
color, with both fruit and
foliage developing a rich, purplish tinge.

The edible red currants
(R. rubrum) *produce mouth-
watering fruit that can be
eaten right off the bush or
used for jellies, jams and pies.*

Growing

Currants grow well in **full sun** to **partial shade** in **moist, well-drained soil** of **average fertility, rich in organic matter.** Currants do tolerate drought. Avoid overhead watering.

Unless fruit is desired, each flowering shoot can be cut back to a strong bud or branch after flowering; up to one-third of the growth can be removed annually. Hedges can be trimmed back after flowering.

Tips

Currants can be used in shrub or mixed borders, or at the edge of a woodland garden. Alpine currant makes an excellent hedge, remaining branched to the ground.

The female flowers and showier male flowers of *R. alpinum* are borne on separate plants; both are needed if fruit is desired.

Recommended

R. alpinum (alpine currant) is a dense, bushy, rounded shrub, 3–6' tall and wide, bearing early, bright green foliage, clusters of chartreuse flowers and persistent scarlet fruit. It tolerates shade and urban conditions. GREEN JEANS ('Spreg') has clean, deep green foliage that persists throughout summer, especially in adverse climatic conditions. **'Green Mound'** is a 3–4' tall and wide male selection that has disease-resistant, dark green foliage.

R. aureum (golden currant) is an upright, open, 5' tall and wide shrub with slightly arching stems and mid- to blue-green foliage that turns red in

R. alpinum

fall. The spicy yellow flowers may be tinged red. The fruit is purple-black.

R. odoratum (clove currant, buffalo currant) is an erect, drought-resistant, suckering shrub, 6–8' tall and wide, with slightly arching stems, bluish green foliage and clove-scented, yellow flowers. It often gets leggy with age. (Zones 3–6)

R. rubrum **'Red Lake'** is a vigorous, well-branched, mounding shrub, 3–4' tall and wide. It bears large, bright, translucent red fruit. A late frost may damage the flowers.

Problems & Pests

Anthracnose, aphids, caterpillars, dieback, downy mildew, leaf spot, powdery mildew, rust and scale insects can be problems. Some currants, including *R. aureum* and *R. odoratum,* are alternate hosts for white pine blister rust, a devastating pine fungus, and are banned in many communities.

Daphne
Daphne

Features: foliage, fragrant spring flowers **Habit:** upright, rounded or low-growing, evergreen, semi-evergreen or deciduous shrub **Height:** 6"–5'
Spread: 2–5' **Planting:** container; early spring or early fall **Zones:** 4–7

ALTHOUGH DESERVING OF THEIR REPUTATION FOR BEING something of a challenge to grow, daphnes are well worth the extra effort, if just for their long, oval, variegated foliage and soft, dainty flowers. Daphnes highly deserve being placed within the perennial garden or as focal points near the front of shrub borders. The key to success in growing these shrubs is to prepare neutral to slightly alkaline soil that drains freely. Daphnes most often die because of overwatering, so it's best to water them once a week the first month after planting, then cut back to once every two weeks during periods of no rain. Once established, these plants prefer life on the dry side.

Growing

Daphnes grow best in **full sun** but tolerate partial shade. The soil should be of **average fertility** and **well drained.** Loose, sandy soils serve well. Avoid overfertilizing or overwatering. A layer of mulch keeps the roots cool, and daphnes overwinter best when covered with a thick layer of snow or mulch.

The neat, dense growth needs very little pruning. Remove damaged or diseased branches right away. Spent inflorescences can be removed, if desired, once flowering is finished. To preserve the natural growth habit of the shrub, cut the flowering stems back to where they join main branches.

Tips

Daphnes can be included in shrub or mixed borders. *D. cneorum* makes an attractive groundcover in a rock garden or woodland garden. Plant daphnes near paths, doors, windows or other places where the wonderful scent can be enjoyed.

Although generally considered hardy only to Zone 4, daphnes often thrive as smaller plants in even colder climates. Daphnes do, however, have a strange habit of dying suddenly, and experts have various theories to explain why. The best advice is to plant them in well-drained soil and then leave them alone. Avoid any disturbance that could stress the plants, and don't move them after they have been planted.

All parts of daphnes are toxic if eaten, and the sap may cause skin

D. cneorum 'Variegata'

irritations. Avoid planting these species where children may be tempted to sample the berries.

Recommended

D. x burkwoodii (Burkwood daphne) is a semi-evergreen, upright shrub that grows 3–5' in height and spread. It bears fragrant white or light pink flowers in late spring and sometimes again in fall. **'Briggs Moonlight'** has yellow foliage with green margins and bears clusters of fragrant pink flowers. **'Carol Mackie'** is a common cultivar; its dark green leaves have creamy margins. **'Somerset'** has darker pink flowers than *D. x burkwoodii.*

D. x burkwoodii 'Somerset'

D. cneorum (rose daphne, garland flower) is a low-growing, evergreen shrub. It grows 6–12" tall and can spread up to 4'. The fragrant, pale to deep pink or white flowers are borne in late spring. **'Alba'** has white flowers. **'Eximia'** is a vigorous selection that grows only 8" tall. It has larger flowers and foliage than the species. The flower buds are crimson red, opening to deep pink. **'Ruby Glow'** (sometimes attributed to *D. mezereum*) has reddish pink flowers. **'Variegata'** is a vigorous plant with cream-edged foliage.

D. mezereum (February daphne) is an upright, rounded to spreading shrub, 24–36" tall and wide, that tends to get leggy with age. One of the earliest flowering shrubs we can grow, it produces small, closely spaced clusters of very fragrant flowers in shades of pink-purple that appear in late winter to early spring,

D. cneorum 'Variegata'

D. x burkwoodii 'Briggs Moonlight'

before the foliage emerges. A medium to dull blue-green, the foliage is borne in whorls on the stems. The fruit is scarlet red. This species does not tolerate lime soils or heavy soils.

Problems & Pests

Aphids, scale insects, crown rot, root rot, leaf spot, twig blight and viruses can affect daphnes, and plants grown in poor conditions can be more susceptible to these problems. Diseased daphnes may wilt and die suddenly.

In late winter, cut a few daphne stems and arrange them in a vase indoors—they should come into bloom in a warm, bright room. Enjoy both the sweet scent and the delicately beautiful flowers.

D. x *burkwoodii* 'Somerset'

D. x *burkwoodii* 'Carol Mackie'

Deutzia
Deutzia

Features: early-summer flowers **Habit:** bushy, deciduous shrub **Height:** 1–7'
Spread: 3–7' **Planting:** container; spring to fall **Zones:** 4–9

DEUTZIAS ARE A GREAT EXAMPLE OF HOW THE POPULARITY OF
certain shrubs rises and falls over decades. There was a time when tall, flop-
ping deutzias, laboring under heavy bloom in May and June, grew in yard
after yard across the Midwest—arresting, if not always lovely. Gardeners
eventually recognized that the shrub offered little more than mediocre form
and foliage the rest of the year. Enter *D. gracilis*, a lower, mounding form of
the plant that features masses of white, star-shaped flowers in summer and
pleasant, pale green foliage that turns burgundy in fall. Voilà—a much
improved, finely textured, smaller deutzia that is useful in both the perennial
border and as undercarriage for larger shrub and tree plantings.

*D. gracilis is lovely as a small, easily managed,
informal hedge or in a mid-border planting.
The fine texture creates a beautiful contrast
with many larger, coarser shrubs.*

Growing

Deutzias grow best in **full sun;** in light shade they produce fewer flowers. The soil should be of **average to high fertility, moist** and **well drained.**

These shrubs bloom on the previous year's growth. After the bloom, cut flowering stems back to strong buds, main stems or basal growth as required to shape the plant. To encourage new growth on established plants, remove one-third of the old growth at ground level.

D. gracilis (above & below)

Tips

Include deutzias in shrub or mixed borders or in rock gardens—or use them as specimen plants.

Deutzias are quite frost hardy. If you live in a colder area than is generally recommended for these plants, try growing them in a sheltered spot.

Recommended

D. gracilis (slender deutzia) is a low-growing, mounding species 2–4' high and 3–7' wide. In late spring it is completely covered with white flowers. The species is hardy only to Zone 5. **'Nikko'** has white double flowers and purple fall foliage. It grows 12–24" tall and spreads about 5'. (Zones 4–8)

D. x *lemoinei* is a dense, rounded, upright hybrid 5–7' tall, with an equal spread. The early-summer blooms are white. **'Avalanche'** has arching branches and abundant white flowers in dense clusters. **'Compacta'** ('Boule de Neige') has denser, more compact growth than the species. It bears large clusters of white flowers. (Zones 5–9)

Problems & Pests

Problems are rare, but aphids, leaf miners or fungal leaf spot may cause some trouble.

The name Deutzia honors Johan van der Deutz, an 18th-century Dutch patron of botany who supported expeditions of the famous botanist Carl Peter Thunberg.

Dogwood
Cornus

Features: late-spring to early-summer flowers, fall foliage, fruit, habit
Habit: deciduous large shrub or small tree **Height:** 2–30' **Spread:** 2–30'
Planting: B & B, container; spring to summer **Zones:** 2–9

LANDSCAPING WITH AN EYE TOWARD THE WINTER MONTHS IS AN
important skill to acquire. Wisconsin and Minnesota homeowners who
ignore the relatively large number of days falling between November 1 and
April 30 tend to create something less than beautiful landscapes. Don't aban-
don ship in winter—grow dogwoods. Red- and yellow-twigged varieties are
a must in the north, giving much-needed color to our white winter world.
They happen to look good in summer as well. *C. alternifolia* is one of my top
choices for adding a focal point to a lightly shaded area. Although its bark is
gray, the magnificent forms of both the tree and shrub varieties add graceful
elegance year-round.

*Ornamental dogwoods fall into
two main categories: the tree or
flowering dogwoods (including
C. florida and C. kousa), with
large, showy blooms; and the
shrubby dogwoods (including
C. alba and C. sericea), which
often have colorful stems.*

Growing

Tree dogwoods grow well in **light** or **partial shade.** Shrub dogwoods prefer **full sun** or **partial shade,** with the best stem colors developing in full sun. For all dogwoods, the soil should be of **average to high fertility, rich in organic matter, neutral to slightly acidic** and **well drained.** Shrub dogwoods adapt to most soils but prefer **moist** soil. *C. sericea* tolerates wet soil.

Tree dogwoods and *C. alternifolia* require very little pruning. Simply remove damaged, dead or awkward branches in early spring.

C. alba and *C. sericea*, which are grown for the colorful stems that are so striking in winter, need ongoing rejuvenation pruning to maintain a steady supply of colorful young growth. *C. racemosa* and *C. sanguinea* 'Winter Flame' also respond well to rejuvenation pruning. A drastic, but effective, method to encourage new growth is to cut back all stems to within a few buds of the ground in early spring. To make up for the loss of the top growth, feed the plant once it starts growing. A less drastic approach is to cut back only the oldest branches, the ones that have lost the most color—up to about one-third of the stems—to within a few buds of the ground early each spring.

Tips

The tree species make wonderful specimen plants and are small enough to include in most gardens. Use them along the edge of a woodland garden, in a shrub or mixed

C. sericea

border, alongside a house or near a pond, water feature or patio. Shrub dogwoods can be included in a shrub or mixed border. They look best in groups rather than as single specimens.

Recommended

C. alba (red-twig dogwood, Tartarian dogwood) is a shrub grown for the bright red stems that provide winter interest. Green all summer, they turn red as winter approaches. This species can grow 5–10' tall, with an equal spread. It prefers cool climates and can develop leaf scorch and canker problems if the weather gets very hot. **'Argenteo-marginata'** ('Elegantissima') has gray-green leaves with creamy margins. **'Bud's Yellow'** has bright yellow stems and is disease resistant. IVORY HALO ('Bailhalo') is a compact, rounded

C. *alba* cultivar

C. *alba*

shrub with creamy white edges to its green foliage. It grows 5–6' tall and wide. **'Sibirica'** (Siberian dogwood) has pinkish red to bright red winter stems. (Zones 2–7)

C. alternifolia (pagoda dogwood) is a native dogwood that can be grown as a large, multi-stemmed shrub or a small, single-stemmed tree. It grows 15–25' tall and spreads 10–25'. The branches have an attractive layered appearance. Clusters of small white flowers appear in early summer. This species prefers light shade. (Zones 3–8)

C. baileyi (red-twig dogwood) is a rounded, open shrub that grows 6–8' tall and wide. It produces medium to dark green foliage that turns reddish purple in fall. Bright red when young, the stems turn dull brown-red to gray with age. Early summer brings clusters of white flowers on old wood. The white fruit

turns bluish with age and is enjoyed by birds and other wildlife. This species has been listed as a cultivar of *C. sericea* in many references. The main difference is that *C. baileyi* does not have stolons. (Zones 2–7)

C. kousa (Kousa dogwood) is grown for its flowers, fruit, fall color and interesting bark. This tree grows 20–30' tall and spreads 15–30'. The white-bracted, early-summer flowers are followed by 1" round, bright red fruit that is often quite palatable. The foliage turns red and purple in fall. **'Milky Way'** produces a plethora of white flowers and bronze-purple fall foliage. (Zones 5–9)

C. mas (Cornelian cherry dogwood) can be grown as a small tree or large shrub. It grows to 15–25' in height and spreads 15–20'. Clusters of small yellow flowers appear in

C. kousa

late winter, and the tart, edible, bright red fruits ripen in late summer. The foliage turns shades of red and purple in fall. **'Golden Glory'** has larger foliage and larger, more abundant flowers than the species. (Zones 4–9)

C. pumila (dwarf dogwood) is a slow-growing, rounded shrub that reaches only 2–4' tall and wide. The dark green leaves, which have

C. alba IVORY HALO

carmine red tips and a red tinge when young, turn orange in fall. Spring clusters of small white flowers result in black fruit that birds enjoy eating. (Zones 4–7)

C. racemosa (gray dogwood) is an erect, multi-stemmed shrub that grows 8–10' tall and wide and spreads by rhizomes to form colonies. It has dark green foliage and attractive gray bark on mature stems. In late spring it bears abundant clusters of white flowers at the stem tips. The white fruit is enjoyed by many bird species. The following cultivars are North Dakota State University releases. **'Emerald'** (SNOW LACE) is a dense, rounded shrub growing 7–9' tall and wide. It has emerald green, semi-glossy foliage and abundant flowers. The rosy pink individual fruit stems contrast well with the silver gray branches and main stems. **'Jade'** (SNOW MANTLE) is a small, multi-stemmed tree with a layered, umbrella-shaped crown. It grows 12–15' tall and wide and also bears flowers in abundance, followed by persistent, pink-stemmed fruit. The wonderful folks at NDSU suggest this tree is best with three to five main stems. (Zones 3–8)

C. sanguinea (bloodtwig dogwood) is a large, rounded to upright, multi-stemmed shrub with dull, mid- to dark green foliage that turns blood red in fall. Purple to dark red and often flushed with green when new, the stems turn gray-green with age. Growing 6–10' tall and 6–8' wide, it spreads by suckers to form colonies. It produces floriferous clusters of white flowers in late spring; their

C. sericea 'Isanti'
C. racemosa

odor is attractive to insects but not to humans. **'Winter Flame'** ('Midwinter Fire,' 'Winter Beauty') is a great selection for winter interest. The stems are yellow at the base, turning to orange and red at the tips. In fall the foliage turns bright yellow and orange. This cultivar grows 5–8' tall and wide. 'Winter Flame' is sometimes attributed to *C. alba* or to *C. sericea*. You may also see 'Winter Flame' and 'Midwinter Fire' listed as separate cultivars. (Zones 4–7)

C. sericea (*C. stolonifera;* red-osier dogwood, red-twig dogwood) is a widespread, vigorous shrub that has bright red stems and spreads by stolons. This Minnesota and Wisconsin native grows about 6' tall, spreads up to 12' and bears clusters of small white flowers in early summer. The fall color is red or orange. **'Cardinal'** has pinkish red stems that become bright red in winter. **'Isanti'** is a compact plant, 3–4' tall and wide, with thin, bright red stems and abundant white flowers. **'Silver and Gold'** has excellent variegated (white and green) leaves and yellow-green stems. (Zones 2–8)

Problems & Pests

The many possible problems include aphids, borers, leafhoppers, nematodes, scale insects, thrips, weevils, anthracnose, blight, canker, leaf spot, powdery mildew and root rot.

C. alba 'Sibirica'

The showy parts of tree dogwood blooms are actually bracts, not petals; the small true flowers are clustered in the center of the four bracts.

C. alba cultivar

Douglas-Fir

Pseudotsuga

Features: foliage, cones, habit **Habit:** conical to columnar (with age), evergreen
tree **Height:** 6–80' **Spread:** 6–30' **Planting:** container; year-round **Zones:** 4–9

IT'S A PITY THAT SPRUCE TREES HAVE ENJOYED SUCH WIDESPREAD
popularity in the north, whereas the equally (some would say more) handsome
Douglas-fir remains somewhat obscure. When choosing large, dense evergreens
for your yard, give Douglas-fir serious consideration, for at all stages of growth
you will find it to be a majestic, beautiful tree. Douglas-fir possesses a more
rugged, less uniform appearance than do spruces, particularly as it approaches
maturity. A single specimen set a proper distance from the house is stunning,
and its dense, billowy form plays well with spruce and pines when combined in
large evergreen stands.

*According to legend, the
unique three-pronged
bracts of Douglas-fir cones
are the hind feet and tails
of tiny mice trying to hide
inside them.*

Growing

Douglas-fir prefers **full sun.** The soil should be of **average fertility, acidic, moist** and **well drained,** but Douglas-fir adapts to most soils with good drainage. Pruning is generally not required.

Tips

The species can be grown as a single large specimen tree or in groups of several trees. The smaller cultivars can be grown in smaller gardens as specimens or as part of shrub or mixed borders. When purchasing, select plants grown from local seed sources for the best performance.

Recommended

P. menziesii is native to the Pacific Northwest and as far south as Mexico. In its native habitat on the West Coast, Douglas-fir has been known to exceed 300' in height. In our region, it typically grows 70–80' tall and 20–30' wide. For gardeners with small gardens, several cultivars of Douglas-fir are not quite as imposing. **'Fletcheri'** is a dwarf cultivar that grows about 6' tall and can spread 6–8'. **'Fretsii'** is a slow-growing cultivar that matures to a height of about 20'. Some new seedling varieties on the market are a striking blue, much like Colorado blue spruces.

Problems & Pests

Canker, leaf cast (needle version of leaf spot), borers, weevils, spruce budworm and other caterpillars, scale insects, adelgids or aphids can cause occasional problems.

D. menziesii (above & below)

Elderberry
Elder
Sambucus

Features: early-summer flowers, fruit, foliage **Habit:** large, bushy, deciduous shrub
Height: 5–20' **Spread:** 5–20' **Planting:** bare-root, container; spring or fall
Zones: 3–9

DISMISS THE NOTION THAT ELDERBERRIES ARE WEEDY, COMMON natives besmirching the roadsides and abandoned clearings of America. Elderberries are fantastic ornamental shrubs that are now gaining deserved recognition. Newer varieties are proving very popular with homeowners across America, and some of the best have proven hardy in Zones 3–5. *S. nigra* 'Gerda' is a knockout that features purplish black (yes, black) foliage and huge, lemon-scented, pink flowers in June. Even varieties derived from the native *S. canadensis* have improved on both foliage color and texture, in addition to their production of highly desirable, edible fruit.

Growing

Elderberries grow well in **full sun** or **partial shade.** Cultivars grown for burgundy or black leaf color develop the best color in full sun, but cultivars with yellow leaf color show their finest color in light or partial shade. The soil should be of **average fertility, moist** and **well drained.** Established plants tolerate dry soil.

S. canadensis 'Aurea'

Although elderberries do not require pruning, they can become scraggly and untidy if ignored. They tolerate even severe pruning. Plants can be cut back to within a few buds of the ground in early spring. This treatment controls the spread of these vigorous growers and encourages the best foliage color on specimens grown for this purpose.

If you desire flowers and fruit as well as good foliage color, remove only one-third to one-half of the growth in early spring because flowers are not produced on new growth. Fertilize or apply a layer of compost after pruning to encourage strong new growth.

Tips

Elderberries can be used in shrub or mixed borders, in natural woodland gardens or next to ponds or other water features. Plants with interesting or colorful foliage can be used as specimen plants or to create focal points.

Both the flowers and the fruit of *S. canadensis* and *S. nigra* can be used to make wine. The berries are also popular for pies and jelly—or try them in place of blueberries in scones or muffins. Cooking elderberry fruits before eating them is recommended. Raw, they are not really edible and can cause nausea, vomiting, diarrhea and gastrointestinal pain, particularly in children. Although less tasty, the fruit of *S. racemosa* can be used for similar purposes, but the berries of most other *Sambucus* species are considered inedible.

All parts of elderberries other than the berries are toxic.

Recommended

S. canadensis (*S. nigra* subsp. *canadensis;* American elderberry) is a shrub about 8–12' tall, with an equal spread. The white flowers of midsummer are followed by dark purple berries. A widespread native across the eastern and central U.S., this

S. racemosa

S. racemosa
S. nigra 'Gerda'

species is generally found growing in damp ditches and alongside rivers and streams. **'Adams'** has bright green foliage. It was selected for its large clusters of abundant fruit, which is excellent in pies and jams. **'Aurea'** has yellow foliage and red fruit. **'Laciniata'** ('Acutiloba') has deeply dissected leaflets that give the shrub a feathery appearance. **'York'** is another producer of abundant fruit that is larger and of higher quality than the berries of any other known elderberry; it is especially productive when planted alongside 'Adams.' It grows 12' tall and wide. (Zones 4–9)

S. nigra (*S. nigra* subsp. *nigra;* European elderberry, black elderberry) is a large shrub that can grow 15' tall and wide. The yellowish white to creamy white flowers of early summer are followed by purple-black fruit. **'Gerda'** (BLACK BEAUTY) has

dark foliage that gets blacker as the season progresses. It bears pink flowers and grows 8–12' tall, with an equal spread. **'Guincho Purple'** grows 8–15' tall and wide and has purple-red stems. The purple-green foliage fades to dark green in summer and turns red in fall. The flowers are tinged pink. **'Madonna'** grows 6–10' tall and wide and has dark green foliage with wide, irregular, golden yellow margins. **'Pulverulenta'** has mottled, unusually dark green and white foliage. It grows slower than other cultivars but can reach 10' in height and spread. (Zones 4–8)

S. pubens (American red elderberry, scarlet elderberry) is a deciduous, multi-stemmed, vase-like, large shrub or small tree that grows 12–20' tall and wide, with a dense, rounded crown of shiny, dark green foliage. This native plant bears flattened clusters of creamy white flowers in late spring. The scarlet red fruit is much used and enjoyed by birds. (Zones 3–6)

S. racemosa (red elderberry, European red elderberry) grows 8–12' tall, with an equal spread. This shrub bears pyramidal clusters of white flowers in spring, followed by bright red fruit. **'Sutherland Gold'** has deeply cut, yellow-green foliage. It grows 5–10' tall and wide. (Zones 3–7)

Problems & Pests

Borers, canker, dieback, leaf spot or powdery mildew may occasionally affect elderberries.

S. canadensis (above & below)

The versatile elderberries can be cut back hard each year or trained into small tree form.

The genus name Sambucus *is derived from the Greek word for a musical instrument made with elderberry wood.*

Elm

Ulmus

Features: habit, fall color, bark **Habit:** variable, rounded to vase-shaped, deciduous tree **Height:** 40–80' **Spread:** 30–60' **Planting:** container, B & B, bare-root; spring or fall **Zones:** 2–9

SOME OF YOU MAY BE THINKING, *HEY, WAIT A MINUTE, I THOUGHT this was a new book—how can they be recommending elms?* Let's make an important fact clear: reports of the American elm's death have been greatly exaggerated. Yes, Dutch elm disease wiped out millions of elms across America beginning in the 1960s. But it didn't take them all, and from those very trees that shrugged off the attack, new, disease-resistant elms have been developed, meaning that today you can plant elms with confidence. That's fabulous news, because there is a good reason why elms were once chosen to grace yards, streets and boulevards across the Midwest: they are gorgeous, magnificent trees.

Growing

Elms grow well in **full sun** or **partial shade**. They adapt to most soil types and conditions but prefer a **fertile, moist** soil. Elms tolerate urban conditions, including salt from roadways.

Pruning, which is rarely needed, can be done in fall. Remove damaged, diseased or dead growth as needed. The elm bark beetle, which spreads Dutch elm disease, is attracted to wounds and freshly cut elm wood. Avoid pruning between early April and late July, when the beetle is active. Do not transport or store elm firewood. Immediately burn, bury or chip all wood from tree removal or pruning.

Tips

Many elms are large trees that are attractive when given plenty of room to grow on large properties and in parks. Smaller species and cultivars make attractive specimen and shade trees.

Recommended

U. americana (American elm) is a long-lived, large, vase-shaped native tree with pendulous branches and a large, rounded to oval crown. It usually grows 60–80' tall and spreads 30–60'; in the wild it can reach heights well over 100'. The shiny, dark green foliage turns an attractive golden yellow in fall. With age, the thick, gray bark becomes deeply furrowed. This species is susceptible to Dutch elm disease, but disease-resistant cultivars are becoming available. **'New Harmony'** has a broad, vase-shaped habit. **'Princeton'** is a

U. 'Morton Glossy'

quick-growing, narrow, vase-shaped selection with attractive foliage. Likely the best of the three cultivars listed here, it is becoming more common in commerce. **'Valley Forge'** is an upright tree with arching branches and high resistance to Dutch elm disease.

U. **'Cathedral'** is a vigorous, spreading hybrid of Japanese and Siberian elm. It was developed at the University of Wisconsin. It grows 40–50' tall and 40–60' wide. Highly tolerant of Dutch elm disease and *Verticillium* wilt, it is also resistant to elm leaf miner. The medium green foliage turns yellow in fall. (Zones 4–7)

U. americana 'New Harmony'

U. americana

U. **'Homestead'** (*U. carpinifolia* 'Homestead') is an upright, vase-shaped tree, 40–50' tall and 40–60' wide, with a roughly pyramidal to oval crown, arching branches and blemish-free, disease-resistant foliage. This hybrid is also resistant to Dutch elm disease. (Zones 5–8)

U. **'Morton'** (ACCOLADE) is a vigorous, upright tree with an oval to vase-shaped crown and arching branches. It grows 60–70' tall, spreads 45–60' and has shiny, dark green foliage that turns bright yellow in fall. Along with having excellent disease resistance and foliage resistant to the elm leaf beetle, it is very drought tolerant. (Zones 4–7)

U. **'Morton Glossy'** (TRIUMPH) is an upright tree, 50–60' tall and 40–50' wide, with an oval to vase-shaped crown. It has glossy, dark green foliage and excellent disease and pest resistance. The dark gray bark

eventually becomes deeply fissured. (Zones 4–7)

U. **'Morton Red Tip'** (DANADA CHARM) is a very graceful, vase-shaped tree up to 70' tall and 60' wide. It is resistant to Dutch elm disease. The new foliage is tinged with red. (Zones 4–9)

U. **'Morton Stalwart'** (COMMENDA-TION) is a vigorous tree that forms an upright, oval crown. It grows up to 60' tall, spreads 40–50' and has excellent drought tolerance and good disease resistance. The green foliage turns yellow in fall. (Zones 4–9)

U. **'Regal'** is a European elm hybrid introduced by the University of Wisconsin. It has a pyramidal to oval shape, grows up to 60' tall by 35' wide, tolerates stress and has good disease resistance. (Zones 4–7)

Problems & Pests

In addition to the fatal Dutch elm disease fungus, elms can suffer attack from aphids, bark and leaf beetles, borers, caterpillars, Japanese beetles, leafhoppers, leaf miners, canker, dieback, leaf spot, powdery mildew, rot or *Verticillium* wilt.

Dutch elm disease was first identified by seven female Dutch scientists in 1917.

A single elm tree on the south side of your house provides summer cooling that rivals many models of home air-conditioning units.

U. 'Morton' (above & below)

Elms attract wildlife. The seeds are food for many small birds, and the trees provide shelter and nest sites. The flower buds, flowers and fruit are eaten by mice, squirrels, ruffed grouse and northern bobwhite.

Euonymus

Euonymus

Features: foliage, corky stems, habit **Habit:** deciduous or evergreen shrub, small tree, groundcover or climber **Height:** 2–20' **Spread:** 2–20' **Planting:** B & B, container; spring, fall **Zones:** 3–8

OF THE TREES AND SHRUBS THAT CAN BE GROWN BY NORTHERN gardeners, only a handful match the breathtaking fall color of *E. alatus*. I grow 'Compacta' up close to my dark green house, flanked tightly by a 'Skyrocket' juniper on one side and a variegated dogwood more loosely on the other, with various low evergreens in front. When the 'Compacta' erupts into blistering, red-orange splendor in October, you'd think the house was on fire. It's arresting in summer as well, with arching, textured branches that host delicate, soft green foliage.

Growing

Euonymus prefer **full sun** but tolerate light or partial shade. They also tolerate heavy shade but with diminished fall color. Soil of **average to rich fertility** is preferable, but any **moist, well-drained** soil will do.

Use only hand pruners (or loppers for larger wood) to prune any euonymus species. *E. alatus,* *E. bungeanus* and *E. atropurpureus* require very little pruning except to remove dead, damaged or awkward growth as needed. To thin congested shrubs, remove older stems to the base. *E. alatus* tolerates severe pruning and can be used as a hedge. *E. fortunei* is a vigorous, spreading plant that can be trimmed as required to keep it within the desired growing area. It tolerates severe pruning.

Tips

E. alatus adds season-long color in a shrub or mixed border, as a specimen,

E. alatus

in a naturalistic garden or as a hedge. Dwarf cultivars can be used to create informal hedges. *E. fortunei* can be grown as a shrub in a border or as a hedge. It is an excellent substitute for boxwood. Its trailing habit also makes it suitable as a groundcover or container plant.

Recommended

E. alatus (burning bush, winged euonymus) is an open, mounding, deciduous shrub. It grows 15–20' tall and wide or slightly wider. The foliage turns vivid red in fall, but

E. fortunei 'Canadale Gold'

E. alatus (above)
E. fortunei 'Emerald 'n' Gold' (below)

only with five or more hours of sunlight per day. The small red fall berries are somewhat obscured by the bright foliage. The corky ridges or 'wings' that grow on the stems and branches provide winter interest. This wide-spreading plant can be invasive. CHICAGO FIRE ('Timber Creek') grows 8–10' tall and 6–8' wide. It has early, bright red fall foliage and conspicuous orange fruit. It is hardier than the species, with better branching. **'Compacta'** ('Compactus') has denser, more compact growth, reaching up to 10' tall and wide, and has less prominently corky ridges on the branches. During unusually cold winters it may suffer winter damage. FIRE BALL ('Select') is a hardier selection of 'Compacta' that suffers no winter damage. It grows up to 7' tall and wide and provides brilliant red fall color. **'Nordine'** ('Nordine Strain') has larger, denser foliage and larger corky 'wings' than the species. It grows 5–10' tall and wide, with horizontal branching almost to the ground. It produces more flowers and fruit than the species, and it has orange fall color.

E. atropurpureus (eastern wahoo, burning bush) is a narrow, deciduous, upright shrub that broadens with maturity. It grows 10–15' tall and 8–12' wide and has slightly corky ridge-like lines on the stems. Its dark green foliage turns yellow to red-brown in fall. The very showy fruit is crimson red with scarlet red arils. (Zones 4–8)

E. bungeanus (winterberry euonymus) is a refined, deciduous shrub or small tree with pendulous stems and branches. It grows 15–20' tall and wide and has light to medium green foliage with yellow fall color (sometimes with pink tinges). It bears pink-tinged yellow fruit with orange arils and white seeds. (Zones 4–8)

E. fortunei (wintercreeper euonymus) is the progenitor of a wide and attractive variety of evergreen cultivars that can be prostrate, climbing or mounding and often have attractive variegated foliage. **'Canadale Gold'** is a robust, compact shrub with large, bright green foliage variously edged with golden yellow. It grows 3–4' tall and wide. **'Emerald Gaiety'** is a vigorous shrub that grows about 5' tall, with an equal or greater spread. It sends out long shoots that will attempt to scale any nearby wall. This rambling habit can be encouraged, or the long shoots can be trimmed back to maintain the plant as a shrub. The foliage is bright green with irregular, creamy margins that turn pink in winter. **'Emerald 'n' Gold'** is a bushy selection, 24" tall and 36" wide. It has green leaves with wide gold margins. The foliage turns pinky red during winter and spring. **'Moonshadow'** is a compact, dense shrub that grows 24–36" tall and wide. It has bright, light yellow foliage with narrow, dark green margins. This cultivar is extremely useful in shady areas where a very low, variegated, spreading shrub is desired. (Zones 4–8)

Problems & Pests

The two worst problems are crown gall and scale insects, both of which can prove fatal to the affected plant. Other possible problems include aphids, leaf miners, tent caterpillars, leaf spot and powdery mildew.

The name Euonymus *translates as 'of good name' — ironic considering that all parts of this plant are poisonous and can cause stomach upset.*

E. alatus

False Cypress
Chamaecyparis

Features: foliage, habit, cones **Habit:** narrow, pyramidal, evergreen tree or shrub
Height: 10"–100' **Spread:** 1–55' **Planting:** B & B, container; spring or fall
Zones: 3–8

CHAMAECYPARIS IS A SPLENDID GENUS OF EYE-CATCHING TREES
and shrubs that are starting to catch on with homeowners across Minnesota
and Wisconsin. A susceptibility to winterburn in the north often results in the
tallest tree species, *C. nootkatensis*, being hard to find at local nurseries. *C.
obtusa* is making inroads in availability, whereas *C. pisifera* is now both common at local nurseries and, in my mind, indispensable. 'Heather Bun' is a
rounded, plum-colored variety with feathery foliage and hardiness to Zone 3.
'King's Gold' is all over my property—I may actually have planted
too many, but I can't seem to get enough of its golden yellow,
rag-tag-floppy foliage. Combine either (or both) with blue-
tinged junipers and spruces, and everyone will think you're
a genius.

In the wild, rare C. nootkatensis
*specimens have been known to
reach a height of 200' and
exceed 1800 years in age.*

Growing

False cypresses prefer **full sun;** growth in shaded areas may be sparse or thin. The soil should be **fertile, neutral to acidic, moist** and **well drained;** alkaline soils are tolerated.

No pruning is required on specimen trees. Plants grown as hedges can be trimmed anytime during the growing season. Avoid severe pruning because new growth will not sprout from old wood. To tidy shrubs, pull dry, brown leaves from the base by hand.

Tips

Tree varieties are used as specimen plants and for hedging. The dwarf and slow-growing cultivars are used in shrub or mixed borders, in rock gardens, as foundation plants and as bonsai.

As with the related arborvitae and junipers, the foliage of false cypresses may be irritating to sensitive skin. Wear gloves and long sleeves when planting or pruning.

C. pisifera cultivar

C. nootkatensis

Recommended

C. nootkatensis (yellow-cedar, Nootka false cypress) is native to the Pacific Northwest. In our area, it grows 30–100' tall, with a spread of about 25'. The species is rarely grown. **'Pendula'** is much preferred. It has even more pendulous foliage and a very open habit. It grows to 50' in height and 20–25' in spread.

C. obtusa (Hinoki false cypress), a native of Japan, has foliage arranged in fan-like sprays. It grows about 70' tall, with a spread of 20'. **'Minima'** is

C. *nootkatensis* 'Pendula'

C. *obtusa* 'Nana Gracilis'

a very dwarf, mounding cultivar. It grows about 10" tall and spreads 16". **'Nana Aurea'** grows 3–6' in height and spread. The foliage, which is gold-tipped in full sun but greener in shade, becomes bronzy in winter. **'Nana Gracilis'** (dwarf Hinoki false cypress) is a slow-growing cultivar that reaches a height of 24–36", with a slightly greater spread. (Zones 4–7)

C. pisifera (Japanese false cypress, Sawara cypress) is another Japanese native. It grows 70–100' tall and spreads 15–25'. The cultivars are more commonly grown than the species. **'Boulevard'** ('Squarrosa Cyano-viridis') is a dense, pyramidal cultivar that needs a moist site. It grows 10–12' tall and 5–6' wide. The soft, blue-green needles fade to gray-blue in winter, and old, brown needles persist on the branches. **'Filifera'** (threadleaf false cypress) is a slow-growing cultivar with dark green, thread-like foliage borne on slender, pendent, sparsely branched shoots. It usually grows 6–8' tall and wide but can reach a height of 40–50' and a width of 10–20'. **'King's Gold'** is a dwarf threadleaf variety that grows slowly to about 24" tall and wide. The burn-resistant foliage is very gold in color. **'Nana'** (dwarf false cypress) is a dwarf cultivar with feathery foliage similar to that of the species. It grows into a mound about 12" in height and width. **'Plumosa'** (plume false cypress) has very feathery foliage. It grows 30–50' tall, with a 10–20' spread. **'Squarrosa'** (moss false cypress) has less pendulous foliage than the other cultivars. Young plants grow very densely, looking like fuzzy stuffed animals. The growth becomes more relaxed and open with maturity. This cultivar grows about 65' tall, with a spread of about 55'.

C. thyoides (Atlantic white cedar, white cedar, white false cypress, swamp cedar) is a narrow, conical tree, 40–50' tall and 10–20' wide. Its natural habitat is swamps and wet lowlands. The sharply pointed, gray-green foliage turns brown in its second year and persists on the tree. With age, this tree loses one-half to two-thirds of its lower branches. **'Heather Bun'** ('Heatherbun') is a compact, mounded to round shrub that grows 6–10' tall and 4–5' wide. The soft, blue-green foliage turns purplish in winter. (Zones 3–8)

Problems & Pests

False cypresses are not prone to problems, but they can occasionally be affected by spruce mites, blight, gall or root rot.

C. pisifera

Chamaecyparis, *which comes from the Greek, means 'low cypress,' even though many species are very tall trees.*

C. pisifera threadleaf cultivar

False Spirea
Ural False Spirea
Sorbaria

Features: summer flowers, foliage **Habit:** large, suckering, deciduous shrub
Height: 5–10' **Spread:** 10' or more **Planting:** container; any time **Zones:** 2–8

PERHAPS BECAUSE OF ITS PROLIFIC SUCKERING HABIT (READ 'borderline invasive'), false spirea remains on the dusty list of little-used shrubs, but this northern Asian native is not without merit. The one you'll find at nurseries, *S. sorbifolia,* has blemish-free, feathery, tropical-like foliage; each leaf has up to two dozen narrow, rough-textured, 2–4" long leaflets, with spring growth tinged a rich red. The mid-summer show of long clusters of white flowers resembles gargantuan astilbes in bloom, and it is impressive. That it's hardy to Zone 2 is noteworthy. For naturalizing large areas, and for controlling soil erosion on slopes, false spirea can be an excellent choice.

Growing

False spirea grows equally well in **full sun, partial shade** or **light shade.** The soil should be of **average fertility, high in organic matter, moist** and **well drained,** but this plant tolerates hot, dry periods.

S. sorbifolia (all photos)

Pruning false spirea is both easy and important. Each year after it flowers, remove about one-third of the oldest growth. When needed, rejuvenation pruning can be done in spring as the buds begin to swell—cut the entire plant back to within a few buds of the ground. To help prevent excessive spread, use a barrier in the soil and remove any suckers whenever they appear in undesirable places.

Remove the faded brown seedheads if you find them unattractive.

Tips

Use false spirea in large shrub borders, as a barrier plant, in naturalized gardens or in lightly shaded woodland gardens. This plant can be aggressive, but its spread is most troublesome in small gardens.

Recommended

S. sorbifolia is a large, many-stemmed, suckering shrub that is native to Asia. Long clusters of many tiny, fluffy, white or cream flowers are produced in mid-summer. This plant is very cold hardy.

Problems & Pests

False spirea has no serious problems but can fall victim to fire blight in stressful conditions.

Fir

Abies

Features: foliage, cones, form **Habit:** narrow, pyramidal or columnar, evergreen tree or shrub **Height:** 1–80' Spread: 2–30' **Planting:** B & B, container; spring **Zones:** 3–7

WELCOME TO THE WONDERFUL WORLD OF *ABIES*, IN WHICH YOU will find many varieties of attractive and unusual evergreen trees sure to add arresting splendor to any northern landscape. *A. balsamea* is an excellent choice where a tall but relatively narrow evergreen is desired, and it can be planted as close as 16 feet from a house. It is the dwarf varieties, however, that give gardeners the greatest opportunities for creative use. *A. balsamea* 'Nana,' *A. concolor* 'Compacta,' *A. koreana* 'Horstmann's Silberlocke' and *A. lasiocarpa* var. *arizonica* 'Compacta' should all be thoroughly investigated. These dwarf evergreens have wide-ranging forms and needle colorations that assure year-round interest and add distinction to mixed shrub borders, foundation plantings and perennial gardens.

The genus name Abies *is derived from the Latin word* abire, *'to rise up,' referring to the great heights some fir trees reach.*

Growing

Firs prefer **full sun** but tolerate partial shade. The soil should be **rich, neutral to acidic, cool, moist** and **well drained.** *A. balsamea* tolerates wet soil. *A. concolor* prefers a **loose, sandy** soil and does not tolerate heavy clay.

These trees generally don't tolerate extreme heat or polluted, urban conditions, but *A. concolor* accepts such situations far better than do other *Abies*.

No pruning is required. Remove dead or damaged growth as needed.

Tips

Firs make impressive specimen trees for large areas. The natural species tend to be too large for the average home garden, but several compact or dwarf cultivars can be included in shrub borders or used as specimens.

Recommended

A. balsamea (balsam fir) is quite pyramidal when young but narrows as it ages. A slow-growing tree native

A. balsamea 'Nana' (above & below)

to the northeastern U.S., it can reach a height of 45–75' (100' in the wild), with a spread of 15–25'. **'Nana'** is a slow-growing, dense, rounded shrub with dark green needles that have silvery white undersides. It grows to 12–24" tall and 24–36" wide. This coneless dwarf cultivar is more suitable to a small garden than the much larger parent species. It benefits from some afternoon shade from the hot sun. (Zones 3–6)

A. concolor (white fir, silver fir) is an impressive specimen that grows 30–50' tall and spreads 20–30' in garden conditions but can exceed 200'

in height in the wild. A whitish coating on the needles gives the tree a hazy blue appearance. **'Candicans'** is a narrow, upright tree with silvery blue needles. **'Compacta'** is a dwarf cultivar that makes an attractive specimen tree to 4–6' in height and spread. It has whiter needles than the species.

A. koreana (Korean fir) is slow growing and small, by evergreen standards, with a height of 15–30' and a spread of 10–20'. Even young trees produce the unusual, attractive purple-blue cones. **'Horstmann's Silberlocke'** ('Silberlocke') has unusual, twisted needles that show off the silvery stripes on their undersides. **'Prostrata'** ('Prostrate Beauty') is a low-growing cultivar with bright green needles. It reaches about 24" in height and spreads 3–6'. **'Starker's Dwarf'** takes on a flat-topped nest form when young, becoming mounded with age. It grows 24–36" tall and its dark green needles are

A. balsamea

A. koreana 'Horstmann's Silberlocke'

wide and round-tipped. This cultivar prefers light shade. (Zones 4–7)

A. lasiocarpa (alpine fir, subalpine fir) is a slow-growing columnar to narrowly cone-shaped tree. In gardens it grows 50–80' tall and 10–20' wide; in the wild it can exceed 160' in height. It has smooth gray bark and gray-green to blue-green foliage with silver stripes. The purple cones, with orangy hairs on the scales, mature to brown. Recent research has determined that *A. lasiocarpa* plants from the Rocky Mountains are different from the ones found closer to the West Coast. The former, including the following two cultivars, will likely be reassigned to *A. biflora*. **Var. *arizonica* 'Compacta'** is a dense, cone-shaped plant, 8–10' tall and 4–6' wide, with silver-blue foliage. **'Green Globe'** is a dwarf, globe-shaped, densely branched shrub that grows 36" tall and wide. (Zones 4–6)

A. concolor 'Candicans'

Problems & Pests

Firs are susceptible to problems with aphids, bagworm, bark beetles, spruce budworm, needle blight, root rot or rust.

A. koreana

Forsythia
Forsythia

Features: early to mid-spring flowers **Habit:** spreading, deciduous shrub with upright or arching branches **Height:** 5–10' **Spread:** 4–15' **Planting:** B & B or container in spring or fall; bare-root in spring **Zones:** 4–9

FORSYTHIAS SEEM TO SHARE A SENTIMENT WITH NEARLY ALL gardeners across Wisconsin and Minnesota—they can barely wait for spring. With the first blush of April's warmth, before most other shrubs have leafed out, forsythias explode into riveting, golden yellow bloom. If planted where they are visible from inside the house, their profuse, vibrant flowers will cheer the soul when much of the rest of the landscape remains in drab disarray. The summer foliage cannot be considered out-standing, but these plants quickly develop a wild, irregu-lar growth habit that fits well into a naturalized setting.

The genus name Forsythia *honors Scotsman William Forsyth (1737–1804), who served as superintendent of the Royal Gardens at Kensington Palace, London, England.*

Growing

Most forsythias grow best in **full sun** but tolerate light shade. The soil should be of **average fertility, moist** and **well drained.**

Correct pruning is essential to keep forsythias attractive, but prune young plants only minimally. Flowers are usually produced on growth that is at least two years old. Mature plants should be thinned annually, removing old wood back to vigorous shoots and removing one or two of the oldest stems to the ground. Pruning should take place after flowering is finished.

Trimming these shrubs into formal hedges often results in uneven flowering. An informal hedge allows the plants to grow more naturally. Restrict the size of a hedge by cutting the shoots back to strong junctions.

Tips

Forsythias are gorgeous early-season bloomers. Include them in shrub or mixed borders among other plants that can take over once the forsythias are finished.

Forsythias quite happily survive in Zone 3. The flower buds, however, which form in summer, are vulnerable to winter cold. The hardiness zones listed here apply to bud and flower hardiness.

For an early touch of spring indoors, cut some dormant forsythia branches for forcing. Smash the stem ends with a hammer and place them in warm water. Change the water daily, and you should have blooms in about a week.

Forsythia heralds spring in this community garden.

F. x *intermedia*

F. ovata 'Northern Gold'

In the coldest areas, a tall shrub may flower only on the lower half—which was buried in protecting snow. Don't despair, therefore, if your garden is outside the recommended zonal region. With dependable snowfall and a hardy cultivar, simply pile some salt-free snow over the plant in winter to enjoy flowers each spring.

Recommended

F. x *intermedia* is a large shrub with upright stems that arch as they mature. It grows 5–10' tall and spreads 5–12'. Yellow flowers emerge in early to mid-spring, before the leaves. Many cultivars have been developed from this hybrid. **'Beatrix Farrand'** grows 8–10' tall and 6–8' wide, producing large, bright, golden yellow flowers up to 2" in diameter. **'Lynwood'** ('Lynwood Gold') grows to 10' in both height and width. The light yellow flowers open widely and are distributed evenly along the branches. **'Spring Glory'** is a bushy shrub with arching branches and shiny green foliage that changes to purple-tinged yellow in fall. It grows 6–8' tall and 5–6' wide and bears abundant clear yellow flowers. (Zones 6–9)

F. mandshurica **'Vermont Sun'** is an upright shrub with erect stems that grows 6–8' tall and 4–6' wide. The dark lemon yellow flowers emerge from the dark yellow to blackish buds about a week before *F. ovata* blooms. Orange to purple tinges mark the yellow fall foliage. (Zones 4–7)

F. ovata (early forsythia) is an upright, spreading shrub that grows up to 6' tall. This species has the hardiest buds, and its flowers open in early spring. It has been crossed with other species to create more attractive, floriferous, hardy hybrids such as the ones below. **'Meadowlark'** is considered to have the hardiest flower buds and can withstand temperatures of -35° F. This open shrub, 8–10' tall and 6–10' wide, has a fountain-like habit and arching branches. It bears bright yellow flowers in abundance. The dark green foliage turns a good yellow color in fall. **'New Hampshire Gold'** is an attractive compact cultivar with very hardy buds. This reliable bloomer grows up to 6' tall. The red-purple fall foliage is an added attraction. **'Northern Gold'** was developed in Canada to produce cold-hardy, bright yellow flowers— even after -28° F temperatures. This upright shrub grows 5–8' tall and spreads up to 10', becoming more arching as it matures. **'Northern Sun'** is hardy to -30° F and bears clear yellow flowers. It has a spreading habit and can reach a height of 8–10' and a width of 8–15'. (Zones 4–7)

F. x intermedia (above & below)

Problems & Pests

Most problems are not serious; they may include root-knot nematodes, leaf spot and stem gall.

Allow a clematis to twine through your forsythia for an ongoing display of flowers and color.

Forsythias can be used as hedging plants, but they look most attractive when grown informally.

Fringe Tree

Chionanthus

Features: early-summer flowers, fall and winter fruit, bark, habit **Habit:** rounded or spreading, deciduous large shrub or small tree **Height:** 10–25' **Spread:** 10–25'
Planting: B & B, container; spring **Zones:** 4–9

ALTHOUGH IT MAY TAKE A BIT OF EXTRA EFFORT TO LOCATE A nursery that stocks fringe trees, you will not regret purchasing and planting them. The smooth, slender leaves are attractive all summer, turn yellow in fall, then drop to reveal an irregular form that adds winter interest to the landscape. The brief, early-summer blooming period (two weeks in ideal conditions) graces the landscape with a tropical elegance unequalled by other shrubs. As with most shrubs that prefer full sun, the flowering is noticeably diminished for fringe trees grown in partial shade.

By your choice of pruning technique you can shape a fringe tree into either a large, full shrub or a lovely small, multi-stemmed specimen tree.

Growing

Fringe trees prefer **full sun** but do grow in partial shade. They do best in soil that is **fertile, moist** and **well drained** but adapt to most soil conditions, including salt. Fringe trees appreciate regular watering and fertilizing, particularly while young, and benefit greatly from winter mulching. In the wild they are often found growing alongside streams and in rock crevices near water.

Mature fringe trees require little pruning. To encourage an attractive habit, thin out the stems of young plants. Prune young plants that aren't yet flowering in spring, and older plants after flowering.

Tips

Fringe trees work well as specimen plants, in borders or beside water features. They begin flowering at a very early age.

The fruit attracts birds. Male flowers, which are sometimes on the same tree as the female flowers, must be present to produce fruit.

Recommended

C. retusus (Chinese fringe tree) is a rounded, spreading shrub or small tree. It grows 15–25' tall, with an equal spread. In early summer it bears erect, fragrant white flowers. Late summer brings dark blue fruit. (Zones 5–9)

C. virginicus (white fringe tree) is a spreading small tree or large shrub that is native to the eastern U.S. It is available in both single-trunk and clump forms. It grows 10–20' tall, with an equal or greater spread.

C. virginicus (above & below)

In early summer it bears fragrant, drooping, white flowers. Only occasionally does the dark blue fruit follow.

Problems & Pests

Borers, canker, leaf spot or powdery mildew can affect fringe trees, but any problems are rarely serious.

Small and tolerant of pollution, fringe trees are good choices for city gardens.

Ginkgo
Maidenhair Tree
Ginkgo

Features: summer and fall foliage, habit, bark **Habit:** deciduous tree; conical in youth, variable with age **Height:** 40–60' **Spread:** 15–30' or more
Planting: B & B, bare-root, container; spring or fall **Zones:** 3–9

BOTANISTS HAVE CONCLUDED THAT GINKGO IS ONE OF THE VERY oldest and least-changed trees, appearing the same today as 150 million years ago, which may explain why its leaves are so distinctive (and a bit prehistoric-looking). Ginkgo matures into a tall, handsome tree with a somewhat loose, cascading canopy. The clam-shaped leaves typically turn buttery yellow in fall. A ginkgo is a tremendous asset to the landscape from the first year the tree is grown. A plant can be either male or female. Be certain the tree you bring home is a male; the rarely sold female ginkgo produces a fruit that drops, rots, makes a mess and stinks to high heaven.

Ginkgo appears to have been saved from extinction by its long-time use in Asian temple gardens. Today this 'living fossil' grows almost entirely in horticultural settings.

Growing

Ginkgo prefers **full sun.** The soil should be **fertile** and **well drained;** this tree adapts to most soil types. It also tolerates urban conditions and cold weather. Little or no pruning is necessary.

Tips

Although its growth is slow until it becomes established, ginkgo eventually becomes a large tree that is best suited as a specimen in parks and large gardens. It can also be used as a street tree. If you buy an unnamed plant, make sure that it has been propagated by grafting because seed-grown trees may prove to be female.

Recommended

G. biloba varies in habit; it grows 50–60' tall and 30' wide or possibly wider. A few cool fall nights usually turn the leaves an attractive yellow. Several cultivars are available. **'Autumn Gold,'** a broadly conical male cultivar, grows 50' tall and spreads 30'. Its fall color is bright

G. biloba (all photos)

golden yellow. **'Magyar'** has stiff, upright branches and survives in difficult situations, making it a good choice for urban streets. This male selection grows up to 50' tall and 20–30' wide. PRINCETON SENTRY ('PNI 2720') is a narrow, upright, male cultivar, 40–60' tall and 15–25' wide.

Problems & Pests

This tree seems to have outlived most of the pests that might have afflicted it. A leaf spot may affect ginkgo, but it doesn't cause any real trouble.

Hawthorn
Crataegus

Features: late-spring or early-summer flowers, fruit, foliage, thorny branches
Habit: rounded, deciduous tree, often with a zigzagged, layered branch pattern
Height: 15–40' **Spread:** 15–40' **Planting:** B & B, container; early spring
Zones: 3–7

INTERESTED IN UNUSUAL CHOICES FOR SMALL, FLOWERING TREES
for prime placement? Take a long look at the hawthorns before committing
automatically to crabapples. They are spectacular ornamental trees for hot,
sunny spots. *C. ambigua*, with its golden bark, showy white flowers and finely
textured, dark green foliage outsparkles the smaller crabapples any day. For
pure form and focal point, *C. crus-galli* var. *inermis* is unmatched. The dense,
wide, horizontal branching is stunning in summer or when covered in snow
or frost, but, in an unfortunate trade-off, some people find the blooms malodorous. Rampant across Europe and hardy here, *C. laevigata* (English
hawthorn) is not widely sold because of susceptibility to blight; varieties of
C. x mordenensis are much wiser choices.

*The thorniness of most
hawthorns can be an asset
for blocking access with an
impenetrable hedge or repelling
burglars from windows.*

Growing

Hawthorns grow well in **full sun.** They adapt to any **well-drained** soil, are moderate to low water users and tolerate urban conditions.

Hawthorns should be pruned much like crabapples. Cut out crossing interior limbs and dead inner wood of dormant plants in late winter to early spring. Also prune to keep branches away from pedestrian walkways. Hawthorn hedges can be pruned after flowering, in fall or in late winter to spring. Remove any diseased growth immediately. It is prudent to wear leather gloves and safety goggles when pruning hawthorns.

Tips

Hawthorns can be grown as specimen plants or hedges in urban sites and exposed locations.

Hawthorns trees are small enough to include in most gardens, but the long, sharp thorns may make them inadvisable for yards with children.

Recommended

C. ambigua (Russian hawthorn) is a slow-growing tree, 15–20' tall and 20–25' wide, with a rounded crown and sparse thorns. It is resistant to cedar-apple rust. The bright green, finely textured, deeply cut foliage develops a yellow fall color. Flattened clusters of pink-tinged white flowers in late spring yield abundant spherical, red fruit. (Zones 3–6)

C. crus-galli (cockspur hawthorn) grows 20–30' tall and 20–35' wide. It features stout, curved thorns, horizontal branching and a large, spreading crown that flattens with age. It is resistant to cedar-apple rust on the foliage and moderately resistant to cedar-quince rust on the fruit. Floriferous clusters of foul-smelling white flowers appear in late spring to early summer. The rounded, dark red fruit persists past fall. The spoon-shaped, shiny, dark green leaves turn bright red in fall. **'Inermis'** (var. *inermis*) is a thornless selection with good disease resistance. (Zones 4–7)

C. crus-galli

C. crus-galli (in behind *Cladrastis kentuckea*)

C. x mordenensis is a dense, upright tree, 15–20' tall and wide, with a rounded to oval crown, white flowers and red fruit. It closely resembles *C. laevigata*, but with larger leaves and flowers. The following cultivars are highly resistant to cedar-apple rust. **'Snowbird'** is hardier than the original hybrid species. It bears double flowers and sparse, pinkish red fruit. **'Toba'** grows up to 15' tall and wide and is resistant to leaf spot. It has a twisted trunk, large, sturdy branches and fragrant white double flowers that age to pink. The fall foliage is yellow-orange.

C. x nitida (glossy hawthorn) is an often thornless cross of *C. viridis* and *C. crus-galli*. It grows 25–30' tall and wide, with a dense, rounded crown. Clusters of small white flowers in mid- to late spring are followed by persistent, dull red fruit. The shiny, dark green foliage turns orange to red in fall. (Zones 4–6)

C. punctata (dotted hawthorn) grows 20–30' tall and wide or slightly wider. The rounded to spreading crown flattens with age. This native of Minnesota and Wisconsin is highly prone to cedar-apple rust on the foliage. It has softly hairy, dark green leaves and short, stout thorns. Pink stamens mark the abundant clusters of malodorous, white, late-spring flowers. The rounded to slightly pear-shaped fruit is dark red with pale speckles. (Zones 4–7)

Hawthorn fruits are edible but dry and seedy. Some people make jelly from them. A liqueur can be made using fermented berries and brandy.

C. viridis (green hawthorn) is a rounded, thorny tree with a dense habit. It grows 20–40' tall, with an equal or slightly lesser spread. The glossy green leaves, which are slightly susceptible to cedar-hawthorn rust, can turn red to purple in fall. Late spring brings white flowers; the fall fruit is bright red. **'Winter King'** has an attractive, rounded to vase-shaped habit. The red fruit is larger and persists longer than that of the species. (Zones 4–7)

C. x mordenensis

Problems & Pests

Borers, caterpillars, leaf miners, scale insects, skeletonizers, canker, fire blight, fungal leaf blight, fungal leaf spot, powdery mildew, rust and scab are all possible problems. Stress-free hawthorns are less susceptible.

The genus name Crataegus *comes from the Greek kratos, 'strength,' a reference to the hard, fine-grained wood.*

Hazelnut
Filbert
Corylus

Features: early-spring catkins, nuts, foliage, habit **Habit:** large, dense, deciduous shrub or small tree **Height:** 8–50' **Spread:** 6–25' **Planting:** B & B, container; spring, fall **Zones:** 3–9

HAZELNUTS NOT ONLY LOOK GOOD, BUT MANY KINDS ALSO YIELD tasty nuts—if you can beat the squirrels to them, that is. *C. americana* grows into an attractive, low-maintenance shrub that is highly recommended for use in large, mixed shrub borders or for planting in multiples to create informal hedges. The large leaves are a nice background foil for shrubs with finer foliage. *C. avellana* 'Contorta' is a lovely accent plant with twisted stems that add winter interest. All varieties develop a wide, wild, irregular shape that can be moderated with pruning as the shrubs gain maturity.

Forked hazelnut branches have been used as divining rods to find underground water or precious metals.

Growing

Hazelnuts grow equally well in **full sun** or **partial shade.** The soil should be **fertile** and **well drained.**

These plants require very little pruning but tolerate it well. Entire plants can be cut back to within six inches of the ground to encourage new growth in spring. On grafted specimens of *C. avellana* 'Contorta,' straight-growing suckers that come up from the roots can be easily spotted and cut out.

C. americana expands at a moderate clip, with new shoots emerging from the base each spring, so plant these shrubs 10 feet apart or a good 6 to 8 feet from other shrubs.

Tips

Use hazelnuts as specimens or in shrub or mixed borders. *C. americana* is a good choice for naturalized areas and woodland gardens.

Male and female flowers are produced on the same plant, but planting at least three plants assures better nut production. The male flowers are the long, showy, dangling catkins; the nuts arise from the rather inconspicuous female flowers.

C. avellana 'Contorta'

The alternative name for corkscrew hazelnut, Harry Lauder's walking stick, comes from the gnarled, twisted cane the famous vaudeville comedian used.

C. americana

Recommended

C. americana (American hazelnut, American filbert) is a rounded, multi-stemmed, suckering shrub that gets leggy with age. This native grows up to 10' tall and 6' wide, and it features showy catkins in early spring and dark green foliage that turns orange-yellow in fall. The edible nuts are enclosed in attractive, hairy, papery, frilled bracts that turn from green to brown when ripe. (Zones 4–9)

C. avellana (European hazelnut, European filbert) grows as a large shrub or small tree that reaches a height of 12–20' and spreads up to 15'. It bears long, dangling, male catkins in late winter and early spring. Various cultivars are more commonly grown than the species. **'Aurea'** has bright yellow foliage that fades to yellow-green in summer.

C. avellana 'Contorta'
C. maxima var. *purpurea*

'**Contorta**' (corkscrew hazelnut,
Harry Lauder's walking stick), perhaps the best-known cultivar, grows
8–10' tall and wide. The twisted and
contorted stems and leaves are a particularly interesting feature in winter, when the bare stems are most
visible. '**Pendula**' is a weeping form
that reaches a height of 8' and a
width of 16'. This cultivar is often
found grafted as a standard. '**Red
Majestic**' is a purple-leaved form of
corkscrew hazelnut, a selection to
keep your eyes open for. The leaves
emerge deep red in spring and
mature to a purple color that lasts
through early summer. (Zones 3–8)

C. colurna (Turkish hazelnut, Turkish filbert) grows 40–50' tall, with a
20–25' spread. It tolerates a range of
soil types and adverse conditions.
This species has good yellow fall
color. (Zones 4–7)

C. maxima (giant filbert) is a large
shrub or small tree that is rarely seen
in cultivation. **Var. *purpurea*** (purple giant filbert), which is more
common, adapts to many soils and
makes a fine addition to the spring
garden. Growing 10–12' tall, with an
equal spread, this variety adds deep
purple leaf color. The rich color
develops best in full sun, but it usually fades to dark green with the heat
of summer.

Problems & Pests

Bud mites, Japanese beetles, tent
caterpillars, webworm, blight, canker,
fungal leaf spot, powdery mildew or
rust may cause occasional problems.

C. avellana 'Contorta'

C. americana

Heather
Scots Heather, Scotch Heather, Ling
Calluna

Features: flowers, foliage **Habit:** mat-forming, evergreen groundcover
Height: 4–30" **Spread:** 24–30" **Planting:** container; spring, fall **Zones:** 3–7

YES, FRIENDS, WE CAN GROW HEATHER IN THE NORTH—RELIABLY
in Zones 4 and 5, and, with a bit of gardening skill, in Zone 3. The only difficulty northern gardeners may encounter is finding the stuff—you'll need to
seek out the better specialty nurseries or do some searching on-line, but it's
worth it. The fine, grayish green foliage contrasts splendidly with the foliage
of countless other shrubs and perennials, and the late-summer bloom comes
at a time when fresh bloom is needed most. Heather is beautiful when massed
or grown as singles in key spots at the front of the foundation planting or
perennial garden.

The genus name Calluna *comes from
the Greek work* kallunein, *which
means 'to beautify,' referring to the
use of* Calluna *as the business end of
old-time brooms.*

Growing

Heather prefers **full sun** and **poor to moderately fertile, acidic, moist** and **well-drained** soil. Too rich a soil causes rank, unruly growth. Amend the soil with peat moss or compost before planting. Ample snow cover may help heather survive in Zone 3. When cultivating near heather, be careful not to damage the shallow roots.

In early spring, before new growth begins, stems that have flowered can be cut back to just above last season's new growth. Heather does not rejuvenate well from older wood. Scraggly old plants should be replaced; propagate new plants by mound layering or by tip cuttings.

Tips

Heather is excellent as a dense, weed-smothering groundcover and for binding sandy soils. Try it as bed and border edging or in a rock garden.

Recommended

C. vulgaris is a mat-forming, evergreen shrub with densely branched, erect stems. The scale-like gray-green foliage, which is held tightly to the branch, becomes purple tinged in winter. Mid-summer to early fall brings dense, spike-like flower clusters. The actual petals are usually concealed in the showy pink to purple-pink sepals. Over 1000 cultivars are listed in the reference literature. Additional flower colors available include red, rosy pink, purple and white. The alternative foliage options encompass dark green, yellow, orange-yellow, bronze

C. vulgaris cultivar (above & below)

and variegated green-white, with winter colors ranging from bronze to red to red-orange to purple. **'Silver Knight'** is a vigorous, very erect plant with woolly, gray foliage that turns purple-gray in winter. It grows up to 12–16" tall and bears lavender pink flowers.

Problems & Pests

Heather may have infrequent problems with Japanese beetles, scale insects or spider mites. Alkaline soil causes chlorosis (leaf yellowing).

Hemlock
Eastern Hemlock
Tsuga

Features: foliage, habit, cones **Habit:** evergreen, pyramidal or columnar to rounded tree, or low-growing to prostrate shrub **Height:** 1–80' **Spread:** 2–35' **Planting:** B & B, container; spring, fall **Zones:** 3–8

COME UPON A MATURE *T. CANADENSIS* IN EITHER A PLANNED landscape or the wild, and you will be smitten. The hemlocks are an extremely attractive genus of graceful, beguiling trees and shrubs that gain new popularity each year. They are among the few evergreens that prefer partial shade. If you like plants that develop a broad, weeping form, no evergreen would be a better choice than 'Pendula.' And as a vertical accent plant in foundation plantings or perennial gardens, or where a dense evergreen hedge is needed in less than full sun, 'Monler' is superb—in partial shade it performs much better than any arborvitae.

Unlike the unrelated herb that killed Socrates, hemlocks of the genus Tsuga *are not poisonous.*

The name Tsuga *(pronounced SOO-gah) is derived from a Japanese word meaning 'tree-mother.'*

Growing

Hemlocks generally grow well in any light from **full sun** to **full shade;** 'Monler' is susceptible to winterburn and should remain mostly shaded in winter. The soil should be **humus rich, moist** and **well drained.** These drought-sensitive plants grow best in cool, moist conditions. Avoid roadways because of a sensitivity to air pollution and salt damage.

Hemlock trees need little pruning, but they respond well to it. The cultivars can be pruned to control their growth as required. Trim hemlock hedges in summer.

Tips

With their delicate needles, hemlocks are among the most beautiful evergreens to use as specimen trees—or shape them to form hedges. Small cultivars may be included in a shrub or mixed border. The many dwarf forms are especially useful in small gardens.

Recommended

T. canadensis (eastern hemlock) is a graceful, narrowly pyramidal tree. Native to the eastern U.S., it usually grows 40–80' tall (occasionally double that in the wild) and spreads 25–35'. Many cultivars are available, including groundcovers and dwarf forms. **'Cole's Prostrate'** is a low, spreading plant about 12–24" tall and about 3–5' wide. **'Monler'** (EMERALD FOUNTAIN) is an upright plant, 6–10' tall and 24–36" wide, that prefers partial shade. Great for screening, it has dark green foliage and weeping

T. canadensis

branches. **'Pendula'** is a small, upright, weeping form that grows 5–15' tall, with an equal spread.

Problems & Pests

Stress-free hemlocks have few problems. Aphids, mites, scale insects, weevils, woolly adelgids, gray mold, needle blight, rust or snow blight may cause trouble.

Don't use hemlock boughs as holiday decorations. The needles drop quickly once the branches are cut.

Holly
Inkberry, Winterberry
Ilex

Features: glossy, sometimes spiny, leaves; fruit, habit **Habit:** erect or spreading, evergreen or deciduous shrub or tree **Height:** 3–15' **Spread:** 3–15'
Planting: B & B, container; spring or fall **Zones:** 3–9

NEWCOMERS TO OUR TWO GREAT STATES ARE OFTEN SHOCKED to learn that a fair variety of hollies can be grown in the north, though we can't grow the classic evergreen *I. aquifolium* (English holly) that is so popular in Europe. The closest we come is *I.* x *meserveae,* which can be successfully grown as far north as Zone 4 when planted in a sheltered location on the north or east side of the home. *I. verticillata* is hardy to Zone 3, but, alas, this deciduous species does not carry its glossy, dark green foliage past fall—the dense, red berries look terrific splayed out atop a blanket of snow, however.

Showy scarlet holly berries look tempting, especially to children, but they are not edible.

Growing

Hollies prefer **full sun** but tolerate partial shade. The soil should be of **average to rich fertility, humus rich, acidic** and **moist.** Apply a summer mulch to keep the roots cool and moist. Evergreen hollies are susceptible to winterburn, so plant them where they do not receive much, if any, winter sun or wind.

Hollies require little pruning. Simply remove damaged growth in spring. Hollies grown as hedges can be trimmed in summer.

Tips

Hollies can be used in groups, in woodland gardens and in shrub and mixed borders or shaped into hedges.

I. glabra looks much like boxwood and has similar uses in the land-scape. Use it as a low hedge or in a mass planting. It adapts to regular shearing and forms a fuller, more appealing plant when cut back hard on a regular basis.

All hollies have male and female flowers on separate plants. In order to guarantee berries, one male plant within 10 feet of any compatible female plant should be sufficient.

Recommended

I. glabra (inkberry) is a rounded shrub with evergreen, glossy, deep green foliage and dark purple fruit. It grows 6–10' tall and spreads 8–10'. **'Compacta'** is a female cultivar with a dense branching habit. It grows 3–6' tall. **'Nigra,'** a dwarf female shrub cultivar that grows up to 36" tall, with an equal spread, has glossy, dark leaves that develop a purple

I. verticillata cultivar

winter hue. NORDIC ('Chamzin') is a compact, rounded, male cultivar that grows to about 4' tall, with an equal spread. **'Shamrock'** has bright green foliage and an upright habit. It grows 3–4' tall. (Zones 4–9)

I. x meserveae (blue holly) is an erect or spreading, dense, evergreen shrub. It grows 10–15' tall, with an equal spread. This pruning-tolerant holly

I. x m. 'Blue Prince'

makes a formidable hedge or barrier. The glossy red fruit persists past fall. Many cultivars have been developed. Often available in male and female pairs, they can be mixed or matched. **'Blue Boy'** and **'Blue Girl'** grow about 10' tall, with an equal spread, and both are quite cold hardy. 'Blue Girl' bears abundant red berries. **'Blue Prince'** and **'Blue Princess'** have larger leaves, and 'Blue Princess' bears fruit prolifically. These cultivars grow 10–12' tall, with an equal spread. (Zones 5–8)

I. verticillata (winterberry, winterberry holly) is a deciduous native species grown for its explosion of red fruit, which persists past fall. It naturalizes well in moist sites and grows 6–8' tall, sometimes taller, with an equal spread. **'Afterglow'** is a rounded shrub, 5–8' tall and slightly wider than tall. It has orange to red-orange fruit and is hardy to

I. glabra 'Nigra'

I. verticillata

Zone 4. The fall color of the small, shiny, green leaves is bright orange and yellow on young plants and greenish yellow on mature ones. **'Cacapon'** bears dark red fruit. It grows 3–8' tall, with a lesser to equal spread. **'Jim Dandy'** is a compact male cultivar up to 6' tall. It is very useful for pollinating. **'Shaver'** is a dense, upright shrub that grows 5–6' tall and 3–6' wide. It has large, orange-red fruit and shiny, light green foliage. **'Southern Gentleman'** is a popular male pollinator; not as compact as 'Jim Dandy,' it grows up to 9' tall.

I. verticillata x *I. serrata* **hybrids** are vigorous plants with a faster rate of growth than *I. verticillata* and leaves that emerge purple to red. The following two upright shrubs grow 10–12' tall and wide. **'Apollo'** is a male selection with purple-red new foliage that makes an excellent pollinator for 'Sparkleberry.' **'Sparkleberry'** produces long-lasting, bright red fruit in abundance. With age, it becomes somewhat leggy. (Zones 4–9)

Problems & Pests

Aphids may attack young shoots. Scale insects or leaf miners can present problems, as can root rot in poorly drained soils.

A vase of cut winterberry branches is a perfect way to brighten a room during the long, gray months of winter.

I. x *meserveae*
I. x *m.* cultivar

Honeylocust
Gleditsia

Features: summer and fall foliage, habit **Habit:** rounded, spreading, deciduous tree **Height:** 30–50' **Spread:** 30–35' **Planting:** B & B, container; spring or fall **Zones:** 4–8

IF NOT FOR ITS PROPENSITY TO LITTER ROOF, YARD, STREET AND alley with large, brown, green-bean-like seedpods every fall, honeylocust would certainly be planted more widely, for it is a very handsome tree. Fast growing and salt tolerant, it is commonly grown as a street tree in urban areas. If you don't mind a little extra fall cleanup—the seed pods are an excellent compost additive—SUNBURST is stellar. It grows well in light shade and matures into a graceful, spreading tree with yellow spring foliage that turns bright green as the season progresses. SKYLINE is seedless and therefore worthy of consideration where a tidier, medium-sized shade tree is needed in full sun.

Unlike its popular cultivars, the species form of G. triacanthos *is heavily armored with branched thorns up to 6" long.*

Growing

Honeylocust prefers **full sun** and **fertile, well-drained** soil but adapts to most soils, including alkaline, acidic or salty kinds, and tolerates flooding and drought.

Prune young plants to establish a good branching pattern. Mature trees often require removal of dead interior wood.

Tips

Use honeylocust as a specimen tree. Often used as a street tree, it is a poor choice for narrow streets—the vigorous roots can break up pavement and sidewalks.

Recommended

G. triacanthos var. *inermis* (thornless honeylocust) is a thornless, spreading, rounded tree, usually 30–40' tall and 30–35' wide (can exceed 100' tall and 70' wide in the wild), with a warm golden yellow fall color. The flowers are inconspicuous, but the long pods persist from late summer as late as fall, sometimes after leaf-drop. The cultivars below are generally fruitless. **'Impcole'** (IMPERIAL) is a rounded tree, 30–35' tall and wide. Attached at wide angles, the branches resist storm damage. **'Majestic'** grows 50' tall and 30–35' wide, with ascending branches and dense, dark green foliage. It tolerates partial shade. SKYLINE ('Skycole') is an upright cultivar, 45–50' tall and 30–35' wide, with dense foliage and good resistance to honeylocust plant bug. SUNBURST ('Suncole'), a relatively broad spreader for its height, grows

Young specimen of SUNBURST

35' tall and 30–35' wide. Emerging bright yellow in spring, the foliage matures to light green over summer.

Problems & Pests

Aphids, borers, caterpillars, honeylocust plant bug, mites, webworm, canker, heart rot, leaf spot, powdery mildew or tar spot can cause problems. Abundant honeylocust aphid can cause serious damage.

Honeylocust does not fix nitrogen on its roots the way most other members of the pea family do.

Honeysuckle
Lonicera

Features: flowers, habit, fruit **Habit:** deciduous or semi-evergreen, rounded, upright shrub or twining climber **Height:** 3–20' **Spread:** 3–20' **Planting:** container, bare root; spring **Zones:** 3–9

THE COLORFUL, TROPICAL-LOOKING, OFTEN FRAGRANT SPRING blooms of *Lonicera* are reason enough to grow these popular shrubs and vines. Add the credentials that honeysuckles are long-lived, drought resistant and easy to grow, and it's no wonder they have graced northern gardens for many generations. Although these plants can survive and expand in partial shade, the bloom's the thing, so grow them in full sun or you'll be disappointed. *L.* x 'Honey Rose' exists on the planet courtesy of the University of Minnesota, and it is a superior variety, with rose red flowers and blue-green foliage. All the shrub varieties below make marvelous clipped or informal deciduous hedges and windbreaks.

Growing

Honeysuckles grow well in **full sun** and tolerate partial shade. The soil should be **average to fertile** and **well drained.** Climbing honeysuckles prefer a **humus-rich, moist** soil.

Shrub honeysuckles benefit from annual thinning (renewal pruning) after flowering is complete. Trim hedges twice a year (usually in early summer and again in mid- to late summer) to keep them neat. To control their direction or size, trim back climbing honeysuckles in spring.

Tips

Shrub honeysuckles can be used in mixed borders, in naturalized gardens and as hedges; most are large and take up a lot of space when mature. Climbing honeysuckles can be trained to grow up a trellis, fence, arbor or other structure; to fill the space provided, they can spread as widely as they climb.

L. xylosteum

Recommended

L.* x *brownii (scarlet trumpet honeysuckle, Brown's honeysuckle) is a twining, deciduous climber that bears red or orange flowers in summer. This vine can grow 10–20' tall. **'Dropmore Scarlet'** bears bright red flowers for most of summer. One of the cold-hardiest climbing honeysuckles, this cultivar is hardy to Zone 4. (Zones 5–8)

L. x *xylosteoides* cultivar

L. sempervirens

L. x heckrottii

L. fragrantissima (winter honey-suckle, sweet breath of spring) is a large, bushy, deciduous or semi-evergreen shrub. It grows 6–10' high, with an equal spread. Over a long period in early or mid-spring it bears small, lemon-scented, creamy white flowers. (Zones 4–8)

L. x heckrottii (goldflame honey-suckle) is a twining, deciduous to semi-evergreen vine with attractive blue-green foliage. It grows 10–20' tall and bears fragrant pink-yellow or pink and yellow flowers profusely in spring and then sporadically until sometime in fall. (Zones 4–8)

L. hirsuta (hairy honeysuckle, yellow honeysuckle) is a twining, climbing, hairy vine that reaches a height of 10–20'. The foliage is a dull dark green. The small clusters of yellow to orange flowers in late spring and early summer produce red fruit. (Zones 3–8)

L. HONEY BABY ('Novso') is a stout, bushy shrub with shiny green foliage that grows 4–6' tall and 3–5' wide. From summer to early fall, purple-red buds open into fragrant, creamy yellow flowers that fade to yellow-orange. (Zones 4–8)

L. x 'Honey Rose' is a large, upright to rounded shrub with dark blue-green foliage that grows 8–10' tall and wide. It is both drought tolerant and resistant to honeysuckle witches' broom aphid (Russian aphid). It produces deep rose red flowers and red fruit. (Zones 4–7)

L. sempervirens (trumpet honeysuckle, coral honeysuckle) is a twining, deciduous climber that is native to the eastern U.S. It grows 10–20' tall and bears orange or red flowers in late spring and early summer. Many cultivars are available, with flowers in yellow, red or scarlet. **'Sulphurea'** bears yellow flowers. *L. sempervirens* is also a parent of many hybrids, including *L. x brownii*. (Zones 4–8)

L. tatarica (Tatarian honeysuckle) is a large, bushy, suckering, deciduous shrub. It grows 8–12' tall, with an equal spread. It bears pink, white or red flowers in late spring and early summer. **'Arnold Red'** is a dense shrub with arching branches and blue-green foliage that bears fragrant, very red flowers and bright red fruit. It is resistant to Russian aphid. (Zones 3–8)

L. x xylosteoides is an erect, well-branched shrub that grows 8–10' tall and wide. It has blue-green foliage and bears pink to light red flowers in late spring to early summer. The fruit is yellow to red. **'Claveyi'**

L. tatarica

(Clavey's Dwarf) grows 3–6' tall and wide. (Zones 4–8)

L. xylosteum (European fly honeysuckle) is a rounded to spreading shrub, 8–10' tall and 10–12' wide, with arching branches and gray-green foliage. Its white to yellow-white summer flowers are sometimes tinged with red, and the fruit clusters are dark red. This species is well adapted to growing in urban conditions. (Zones 4–8)

Problems & Pests

Occasional problems with aphids, leaf miners, leaf rollers, scale insects, blight or powdery mildew can occur.

L. x brownii 'Dropmore Scarlet'

Hornbeam

Carpinus

Features: habit, fall color **Habit:** pyramidal, deciduous tree **Height:** 10–50'
Spread: 10–40' **Planting:** B & B, container; spring **Zones:** 3–9

WHY HORNBEAMS ARE NOT PROMOTED AND GROWN MORE IN
northern zones is difficult to fathom. *C. betulus* shrugs off great variance in
soil moisture, fertility and pH, performs splendidly in full sun to shade and
matures into a magnificent, well-proportioned, medium-sized tree. *C. b.*
'Columnaris' is magnificent as a corner specimen in foundation plantings.
C. caroliniana is the smaller cousin, and, although its preference is for more
evenly moist, acidic soil, it brings the same easy care and attractive, smooth,
steely gray bark as its European counterpart. Use *C. caroliniana* in city lots or
anywhere a handsome, smaller tree is needed in partial shade.

*To create a pleasing visual balance, plant
slow-growing hornbeams as an understory
for very large older trees.*

Growing

Hornbeams prefer **full sun** or **partial shade. Average to fertile, well-drained** soil is best. *C. caroliniana* prefers **moist** soil conditions and grows well near ponds and streams.

Although hornbeams are very tolerant of heavy pruning, pruning is rarely required. Remove damaged, diseased and awkward branches as needed. Do any formative pruning in late summer to early winter to reduce bleeding. Trim hedge varieties in late summer.

Tips

These small to medium-sized trees can be used as specimens or shade trees in small gardens. *C. betulus* 'Columnaris' and 'Globosa' and *C. caroliniana* can be used as large hedges, but begin training early. The narrow, upright cultivars are often used to create barriers and windbreaks.

Recommended

C. betulus (European hornbeam) is a pyramidal to rounded tree, 40–50' tall and 30–40' wide, with bright yellow or orange fall foliage. **'Columnaris'** is a narrow, slow-growing cultivar. It grows 30' tall and spreads 20'. **'Fastigiata'** is an upright cultivar that grows 50' tall and spreads 40'. Narrow when young, it broadens as it matures. **'Globosa'** is a densely branched, rounded to globe-shaped tree with no central trunk. It grows 15–20' tall and wide. The foliage is produced in abundance near the branch tips. (Zones 4–8)

C. caroliniana

C. caroliniana (American hornbeam, ironwood, musclewood, bluebeech) is a small, slow-growing tree, 10–30' tall, with an equal spread. It tolerates both shade and city conditions. The fall foliage is yellow to red or purple.

Problems & Pests

Borers are becoming prevalent. Canker, dieback, powdery mildew or rot also occur rarely.

C. betulus

Horsechestnut
Buckeye
Aesculus

Features: late-spring or summer flowers, foliage, spiny fruit **Habit:** rounded or spreading, deciduous tree or shrub **Height:** 8–75' **Spread:** 8–50' **Planting:** B & B, container; spring or fall **Zones:** 3–9

FEW TREES AVAILABLE TO NORTHERN GARDENERS WILL STOP viewers in their tracks as quickly and assuredly as *A.* x *carnea* 'Briotii' in bloom, unless perhaps your taste for spectacular blooming trees is more attuned to the sublime *A. hippocastanum. Aesculus* is a diverse group of extremely attractive trees and shrubs featuring unusual, often rugose foliage, billowing forms and wide options in size, habit, and bloom color. As is always recommended, note the proper botanical name *(Aesculus)* in your research and shopping, because both 'buckeye' and 'horsechestnut' are bandied about as common names in the trade.

Growing

Aesculus species grow well in **full sun** or **partial shade.** The soil should be **fertile, moist** and **well drained.** These plants dislike excessive drought.

Little pruning is required. Remove wayward branches in winter or early spring.

Tips

Large forms of *Aesculus* are best suited as specimen and shade trees for large gardens. Their roots can break up nearby sidewalks and patios. The heavy shade of these trees is excellent for cooling buildings but difficult to grow grass beneath; use a shade-loving groundcover instead.

The smaller, shrubbier types are useful in a space-restricted setting, where they can be used as specimens, in shrub or mixed borders or in mass plantings to fill unused corners or cover hard-to-mow banks.

All parts of *Aesculus* plants, especially the seeds, are toxic. People have been poisoned when they confused the nuts of these trees with edible sweet chestnuts (*Castanea* species).

Recommended

A. x *arnoldiana* 'Autumn Splendor' is a tree 30–40' tall, with an equal spread and an oval to rounded crown. The scorch-resistant foliage remains dark green all summer, turning brilliant purple-red in fall.

A. parviflora

Erect clusters of yellow spring flowers with orange and red markings are followed by round, spiked, yellow-brown fruit. (Zones 4–8)

A. x *carnea* (red horsechestnut) is a dense, rounded to spreading tree that grows 30–40' tall, with a spread of 30–50'. It is smaller than common horsechestnut but needs more regular water in summer. Spikes of dark pink flowers are borne in late spring and early summer. The light brown fruit is slightly prickly. 'Briotii' bears large, lobed leaves and stunning red flowers. It grows 25–40' tall, with an equal spread. This cultivar is hardy in

A. hippocastanum

A. glabra

A. hippocastanum

Zones 5–9. **'O'Neill'** grows slowly to 35' in height and 25' in spread. It bears bright red flowers. (Zones 4–8)

A. flava (*A. octandra;* yellow buckeye) is a large tree, 50–75' tall and 30–50' wide, with an upright oval to spreading crown. The shiny, dark green foliage, which turns orange-yellow in fall, is much more resistant to diseases than that of other *Aesculus* plants. Upright clusters of yellow flowers in late spring are followed by large, smooth, oblong to pear-shaped, light brown fruit. (Zones 3–8)

A. glabra (Ohio buckeye) is a rounded tree with a dense canopy. It grows 20–40' tall, with an equal spread. The flowers are not very showy, and the fruit is less spiny than that of other *Aesculus* species. This native of Minnesota and Wisconsin is susceptible to scorch and looks best when grown in damp, naturalized situations, such as next to a stream or pond. (Zones 3–7)

A. hippocastanum (common horsechestnut) is a large, rounded tree, 50–75' tall and spreading 40–50', that branches right to the ground if grown in an open setting. White flowers with yellow or pink marks, borne in spikes up to 12" long, appear in late spring. Spiky, light brown fruit follows. **'Baumannii'** bears spikes of white double flowers and produces no fruit. (Zones 3–7)

A. parviflora (bottlebrush buckeye) is a spreading, mound-forming, suckering shrub, 8–12' tall and 8–15' wide. In early to mid-July the plant is covered with spikes of white flowers. It produces smooth, oblong to pear-shaped, light brown fruit. This species is not susceptible to the pests and diseases that plague its larger cousins. (Zones 4–9)

A. pavia (red buckeye) is a low-growing to rounded, shrubby tree that grows 15–20' tall, with an equal spread. It needs consistent moisture. The foliage ranks among the most handsome of the genus. Cherry red flowers appear in late spring to early summer, followed by smooth, egg-shaped, light brown fruit. (Zones 4–8)

Problems & Pests

Scale insects, anthracnose, canker, leaf scorch, leaf spot, powdery mildew and rust can all cause problems. Stressed plants are most susceptible to disease.

A. flava

A. glabra

The common name 'buckeye' arises from the resemblance of the smooth-skinned, dark brown seeds to the eyes of a deer.

A. x carnea

Hydrangea

Hydrangea

Features: flowers, habit, fall foliage of some species **Habit:** deciduous mounding shrub, woody climber or spreading shrub or small tree **Height:** 3–30'
Spread: 3–20' **Planting:** container; spring or fall **Zones:** 3–9

HYDRANGEAS NOT ONLY OFFER A BOUNTIFUL MIX OF WORTHY, blooming shrubs to the northern plant pallet, but are also a good example of the importance of knowing the species of the shrubs you buy, not just the genus. In the north we have four hydrangea species to choose from. *H. anomala* and *H. macrophylla* bloom on old wood (last year's bud set), which is why blooming is spotty, or nonexistent, following severe winters. In contrast, *H. arborescens* and *H. paniculata* bloom on new wood (spring bud set), which is why they bloom every year. Could this difference be the reason why 'My hydrangeas didn't bloom, but my neighbor's did'?

Growing

Hydrangeas grow well in **full sun** or **partial shade.** *H. arborescens* tolerates heavy shade. Shade or partial shade reduces leaf and flower scorch in our hottest regions. The soil should be of **average to high fertility, humus rich, moist** and **well drained.** These plants perform best in cool, moist conditions.

H. macrophylla responds to the level of aluminum ions in the soil, which depends on the pH. In acidic soil the flowers tend to be blue, whereas the same plant grown in an alkaline soil tends to have pink flowers. Most cultivars develop their best color in one soil type or the other.

Pruning requirements vary from species to species. See the Recommended section for specific suggestions.

Tips

Hydrangeas come in many forms and have many uses in the landscape. Include them in shrub or

H. macrophylla cultivar (above)

H. macrophylla (below)

Traces of cyanide are found in the leaves and buds of some hydrangeas. Wash your hands well after handling these plants, and avoid burning clippings—the smoke can be toxic.

H. paniculata

H. paniculata 'Grandiflora'
H. arborescans 'Annabelle'

mixed borders, use them as specimens or informal barriers, or plant them in groups or containers. Climbing varieties can be trained up trees, walls, fences, pergolas and arbors. They will also grow over rocks and can be used as groundcovers.

A hydrangea inflorescence (flower cluster) consists of inconspicuous fertile flowers, showy sterile flowers or both. Mophead (or hortensia) inflorescences consist almost entirely of showy sterile flowers clustered together to form a globular, snowball-like shape. Lacecap inflorescences consist of a combination of sterile and fertile flowers. The showy sterile flowers form a loose ring around the smaller fertile ones, giving this flatter inflorescence a delicate, lacy appearance. Both types are well worth growing.

Recommended

H. anomala subsp. *petiolaris* (*H. petiolaris;* climbing hydrangea) is considered by some gardeners to be the most elegant climbing plant available. It grows up to 30' tall, clinging to any rough surface by means of little rootlets that sprout from the stems. For more than a month in summer, the vine is covered with white lacecap flower clusters, and the entire plant appears to be veiled in a lacy mist. Although this plant is shade tolerant, it produces the best flowers when exposed to some direct sun each day. If you must restrict its growth, it can be pruned after flowering. The glossy, dark green leaves sometimes show yellow fall color. (Zones 4–9)

H. arborescens (smooth hydrangea, wild hydrangea) forms a rounded shrub 3–5' tall and wide. It looks most attractive if grown as a perennial and cut right back to the ground in fall; the new growth that forms from the base each year bears the flowers. The flowers of the species are not very flashy, but its cultivars have large, showy blossoms. **'Annabelle'** bears large, ball-like mophead clusters of white flowers from early to mid-summer. A single inflorescence may be up to 12" in diameter. More compact than the species, this cultivar is useful for brightening up a shady wall or corner of the garden. It's common for this plant to collapse under its own weight, especially after a rain. **'Grandiflora'** (hills of snow hydrangea) bears its white flowers in 6" diameter mophead clusters, blooming about 10 to 14 days earlier than 'Annabelle.' The individual sterile flowers are larger than those of 'Annabelle,' but the clusters are smaller.

H. macrophylla (bigleaf hydrangea) is a rounded or mounding shrub that grows 3–5' tall and spreads up to 6'. It flowers from mid- to late summer on the previous season's growth, and a severe winter or late-spring frost can kill this species back to the point where no flowering occurs. Prune flowering shoots back to the first strong buds once flowering is finished or early the following spring. On mature, established plants you can remove one-third of the oldest growth yearly or as needed to encourage vigorous new

H. macrophylla ENDLESS SUMMER

Softwood cuttings of smooth hydrangea are easy to root.

H. paniculata 'Pink Diamond'

H. macrophylla

H. paniculata

Considered the Cadillac of vines, climbing hydrangea is beautiful, especially when grown up a tall, high-limbed tree.

H. anomala subsp. *petiolaris*

growth. The many cultivars can have mophead or lacecap clusters with flowers in shades of pink, red, blue or purple. **'All Summer Beauty'** bears dark blue mophead clusters on the previous and sometimes the current season's growth, making this cultivar useful where other bigleaf hydrangeas are frequently killed back in winter. ENDLESS SUMMER bears deep pink mophead flower clusters over a long season on current and prior-year growth. The only bigleaf hydrangea reliably hardy to Zone 4, it survives cold winters and late-spring frosts well. **'Nikko Blue'** bears many large, blue to deep lavender mophead clusters. **'Variegata'** features leaves with mottled, creamy white margins and bears light purple lacecap flower clusters. (Zones 5–9)

H. paniculata (panicled hydrangea) is a spreading to upright large shrub or small tree. It grows 10–22' tall, spreads to 8' and bears white flowers from late summer to early fall. This species requires little pruning. When young it can be pruned to encourage a tree-like or shrub-like habit, and the entire shrub can be cut to within a foot of the ground each fall to encourage vigorous new growth the following summer. **'Compact'** ('Compacta,' 'Grandiflora Compacta') is a compact version of 'Grandiflora,' the Pee Gee hydrangea. It grows 5–6' tall and wide, and it bears clusters of white flowers that fade to pink with age. **'Grandiflora'** (Pee Gee hydrangea) is a spreading, large shrub or small tree, 15–25' tall and 10–20' in spread. The mostly sterile white flowers are borne in mophead clusters up to 18" long, fading to pink with age. **'Kyushu'** bears lacy white blooms from July to frost. **'Peewee'** grows up to 10' tall. Its flower clusters are very similar to, and somewhat smaller than, those of 'Grandiflora.' **'Pink Diamond'** bears large lacecap clusters of white flowers that turn an attractive deep pink in fall. **'Tardiva'** bears 6" long clusters of sterile and fertile flowers, blooming later than the species and other cultivars. **'Unique'** bears large, upright mophead clusters of white flowers that turn pink in fall. (Zones 3–8)

Problems & Pests

Occasional problems for hydrangeas include gray mold, slugs, powdery mildew, rust, ringspot virus and leaf spot. Hot sun and excessive wind can dry out the petals and turn them brown.

H. arborescens 'Annabelle'

Mophead hydrangea flowers can be used in fresh or dried arrangements. For the longest-lasting fresh flowers, water the plant deeply the evening before cutting to help keep the petals from wilting. For drying, wait until the blooms begin to change color in late summer before cutting.

H. anomala subsp. *petiolaris*

Juniper
Juniperus

Features: foliage, variety of colors, sizes and habits **Habit:** evergreen, conical or columnar tree, rounded or spreading shrub, or prostrate groundcover **Height:** 4"–70' **Spread:** 1–25' **Planting:** B & B, container; spring or fall **Zones:** 2–9

THE CREAM INDEED RISES TO THE TOP, AS EVIDENCED BY THE long-standing and wide use of junipers in all manner of landscapes across the north. Junipers are extremely durable evergreen shrubs. These plants run the gamut from low-growing, spreading groundcovers to wide, arching, mid-sized shrubs to tall, pyramidal trees. When properly grown, they rarely suffer winterburn. There are many, many junipers to choose from, so I encourage you to visit a large nursery carrying at least two dozen varieties (some carry 40 or more).

Growing

Junipers prefer **full sun** but tolerate light shade. Ideally, the soil should be of **average fertility** and **well drained,** but these plants tolerate most conditions.

Although these evergreens rarely need pruning, they tolerate it well. They can be used for topiary; trim them in summer as required to maintain their shape or limit their size.

Tips

There are endless uses for the wide variety of junipers available. They make prickly barriers and hedges, and they can be used in borders, as specimens or in groups. The larger species make good windbreaks, while the low-growing species work well in rock gardens and as ground-covers.

It is a good idea to wear long sleeves and gloves when handling junipers because the prickly foliage gives some gardeners a rash. Juniper 'berries' are poisonous if eaten in large quantities.

Recommended

J. chinensis (Chinese juniper) is a conical tree that grows 50–70' tall and spreads 15–20'. It is rarely grown; its many cultivars, which lend themselves to use in small gardens, are generally preferred. **'Daub's Frosted'** is a spreading shrub with drooping branch tips that grows 3–4' tall and wide. The new, light golden-yellow foliage contrasts well with the older, blue-green foliage in the plant's interior.

J. chinensis (above), *J. virginiana* cultivar (below)

The blue 'berries' (actually fleshy cones) of junipers are used to season meat dishes and to give gin its distinctive flavor. They also make a nice addition to potpourri.

J. squamata

J. horizontalis cultivar

'Hetzii Columnaris' forms an attractive, narrow pyramid about 20' tall and 5–8' wide. **'Maney'** ('Maneyi') is a dense, semi-erect, rounded to spreading shrub with powdery, blue-green foliage. It grows 4–8' tall and 6–12' wide and is salt tolerant. MINT JULEP ('Monlep') is a compact, vase-shaped shrub with arching branches. It grows 4–6' tall and 6–8' wide and has bright, mint green foliage. This cultivar is sometimes considered to be the same plant as 'Sea Green.' **'Old Gold'** is a spreading cultivar with yellow foliage on new spring growth. It grows 24–36" tall and spreads 3–4'. **Var.** *sargentii* **'Viridis'** (green Sargent juniper) is a low-growing, spreading variety that holds its light green color well year-round. It grows only 12–24" tall but can spread 5–10'. **'Sea Green'** has arching branches in a fountain pattern and strong green color through winter. It grows 6' tall and up to 8' wide. (Zones 3–9)

J. communis (common juniper) is a native species that is widespread over the Northern Hemisphere. It grows in two distinct forms: a spreading shrub or a small, columnar tree. The variably sized plants may reach a height of 2–20' and a width of 3–15'. Many cultivars take advantage of, and improve on, one growth form or the other. **Var.** *depressa* **'AmiDak'** (BLUEBERRY DELIGHT) is a dense, low-growing, spreading shrub that grows to 12–18" tall and up to 5' wide. The dark green needles have silver-blue lines on top, and the foliage color is retained well through winter. This cultivar produces a plethora of berry-like blue cones. (Zones 2–6)

J. horizontalis (creeping juniper) is a prostrate, creeping groundcover that is native to Minnesota, Wisconsin and boreal regions across North America. It grows 12–24" tall and spreads up to 8'. The blue-green foliage develops a purple hue in winter. This juniper looks attractive cascading down rock walls, but a susceptibility to diseases often makes it relatively short-lived. '**Blue Chip**' grows 8–10" tall and spreads 6–10' wide. The silvery blue foliage is lightly tinged purple in winter. '**Blue Prince**' grows only 6" tall and spreads 3–5' wide, bearing dense, intensely blue foliage that holds its color in winter. '**Prince of Wales**' bears bright green foliage with a bluish cast that turns light purple in winter. This mat-like shrub is just 4–6" tall but 5–8' wide. The center opens with age. '**Webberi**' grows 6–12" tall and 6–8' wide. Its blue-green foliage takes on bronze tints in winter. '**Wiltonii**' ('Blue Rug') has trailing branches and silvery blue foliage. Very low growing, it is just 4–6" tall but spreads 6–8'. (Zones 3–9)

J. procumbens (Japanese garden juniper) is a wide-spreading, stiff-branched, low shrub, 12–36" tall and 6–15' wide. '**Greenmound**' is a low, dense spreader with light green foliage. It grows 4–6" tall and spreads about 6'. '**Nana**' is a dwarf, compact, mat-forming shrub, 12–24" tall and 6–12' across. (Zones 4–9)

J. sabina cultivar

Junipers come in all shapes and sizes and can suit almost any garden. Grow them in the sun to avoid open, straggly growth.

J. horizontalis cultivar

J. sabina (Savin juniper) is a variable, spreading to erect shrub. It grows 4–15' tall and may spread 5–20'. Many popular cultivars are available. **'Arcadia'** has dense, gently arching branches and bright green foliage. It grows 12–18" tall and 4–6' wide, and it is resistant to twig blight. **'Broadmoor'** is a low spreader with erect branchlets. It grows 24–36" tall and spreads up to 10'. **'Buffalo'** has feathery, bright green foliage that holds its color well in winter. It grows 12" tall and spreads about 8'. CALGARY CARPET ('Monna') is a low, spreading plant about 12" tall and 4–5' in spread. **'Skandia'** is a gray-green sister plant to 'Arcadia' with a similar growth habit. It grows 12–16" tall and 4–8' wide and is also resistant to twig blight. (Zones 3–7)

J. scopulorum (Rocky Mountain juniper) is a rounded or spreading tree or shrub that grows 30–50' tall and spreads 3–20'. The species is highly prone to twig blight; the cultivars are less susceptible. **'Blue Heaven'** is an upright, pyramidal tree that grows 10–20' tall and 3–6' wide. It has beautiful silver-blue foliage year-round and an abundance of cones. **'Medora'** is a dense, upright, columnar shrub that grows slowly to 10–15' tall and 2–4' wide. It has blue-green foliage. **'Moonglow'** has intensely silver-blue foliage. It is a dense, cone-shaped shrub growing 10–20' tall and 5–10' wide. **'Skyrocket'** is a very narrow, columnar tree with gray-green needles. It grows up to 20' tall but spreads only 12–24". **'Tolleson's Weeping'** has arching branches and pendulous, string-like, silvery blue foliage. It grows about 20' tall and spreads 10'. It is sometimes grafted to create a small, weeping standard tree. This cultivar can be used in a large planter. **'Welchii'** is a columnar to cone-shaped shrub growing 8–12' tall and 5–6' wide. The blue-green foliage has a silvery sheen when new. **'Wichita Blue'** ('Wichita') is an upright pyramidal cultivar that grows 15–20' tall and spreads about

J. sabina 'Broadmoor'

4'. It has attractive silvery blue foliage. (Zones 3–7)

J. squamata (singleseed juniper) forms a prostrate or low, spreading shrub or a small, upright tree. It grows up to 30' tall and spreads 3–25'. Rarely grown, it is less popular than its cultivars. **'Blue Star'** is a compact, rounded shrub with silvery blue needles. It grows 12–36" tall and spreads about 3–4'. (Zones 4–7)

J. virginiana (eastern redcedar) is a durable tree of variable form, from upright to wide-spreading. It usually grows 40–50' tall but can grow taller, and it spreads 8–20'. This species is native to Wisconsin, Minnesota and most of eastern and central North America. **'Grey Owl'** has threadlike branchlets of blue foliage that contrast with its yellow twigs. It has a spreading habit and grows to 10' tall and wide. **'Hillspire'** is a uniform, pyramidal tree with upright branches and bright green to yellow-green foliage that holds its color through winter. It grows 15–30' tall and 5–15' wide.

Problems & Pests

Although junipers are tough plants, occasional problems may be caused by aphids, bagworm, bark beetles, leaf miners, mites, scale insects, canker, caterpillars, cedar-apple rust or twig blight.

Juniper was used traditionally to purify homes affected by sickness and death.

J. chinensis MINT JULEP

J. scopulorum 'Wichita Blue'

Kentucky Coffee Tree

Gymnocladus

Features: summer and fall foliage, fruit, bark, habit **Habit:** upright to spreading, deciduous tree **Height:** 50–75' **Spread:** 20–50' **Planting:** B & B; spring or fall **Zones:** 3–8

THIS SPLENDID NATIVE IS FINALLY RECEIVING THE ATTENTION IT deserves, and it should be given serious consideration when choosing a large shade tree for the landscape. Kentucky coffee tree grows across much of the United States, and it has proven highly adaptable to a wide variety of soil conditions. It has striking bluish green foliage that appears to float upward from the dense branches, and its fall color is a rich yellow. This tree matures into an elegant, billowy, feathered cloud of beauty that will be much admired for years to come.

Kentucky coffee tree seeds are poisonous when raw. Early settlers roasted them to use as a coffee substitute, hence the common name.

Growing

Kentucky coffee tree grows best in **full sun**. It prefers **fertile, moist, well-drained** soil but adapts to a range of conditions, tolerating alkaline soil, drought and urban situations.

Pruning is rarely required. Remove dead, diseased or damaged growth as needed. Do any necessary formative pruning in fall or spring.

Tips

Ideal for spacious landscapes, parks and golf courses, Kentucky coffee tree makes an attractive specimen tree.

Recommended

G. dioicus grows 60–75' tall, with a spread of 40–50'. This Wisconsin and Minnesota native has compound leaves up to 36" long, each consisting of many dark green to blue-green leaflets that turn yellow in fall. Large clusters of white flowers appear in late spring or early summer. Female trees produce leathery pods, 5–12" long, that ripen to reddish brown and persist past fall before littering the ground. The ridged bark adds interest to the winter landscape. **'Espresso'** is an upright, vase-like, male tree with arching branches. It grows 50' tall and 25–30' wide. **'J.C. McDaniel'** (PRAIRIE TITAN) is a male clone with an upright, spreading habit, blue-green foliage that turns yellow in fall and a wonderful winter form. It grows 10–15' tall and 6–8' wide in 10 years (50–70' tall and 20–40' wide at maturity). **'Stately Manor'** is another upright, vase-like, male tree. Growing 50–70' tall and 20–40' wide, it was introduced by the Minnesota Landscape Arboretum.

G. dioicus (above & below)

Kerria
Japanese Kerria, Japanese Rose
Kerria

Features: mid- to late-spring flowers, habit **Habit:** mounding or arching, suckering, deciduous shrub **Height:** 3–7' **Spread:** 3–8' **Planting:** B & B, container; spring or fall **Zones:** 4–9

MY FIRST ENCOUNTER WITH JAPANESE KERRIA OCCURRED IN spring some years ago as I strolled around a large woodland park preserve south of the Twin Cities. I spied the shrub, or shrubs, from what seemed like a mile away—a large cloud of buttery yellow blooms resembling *Coreopsis* 'Moonbeam' on steroids. Sightings and use of this unusual shrub are sporadic, so if you are intrigued enough to seek one out, you may find mail order your easiest option. This collector's plant is good for naturalized settings and as background foil in large, informal perennial gardens. Native to China, the shrub is extremely easy to grow and very long-lived.

Kerria flowers can resemble old-fashioned yellow roses, and this plant is indeed a member of the rose family.

Growing

Kerria prefers **partial shade** but adapts to other light levels. The soil should be of **average fertility** and **well drained.** Overly fertile soil results in fewer flowers.

Prune after the bloom. Cut flowering shoots back to young side shoots, strong buds or right to the ground. The entire plant can be cut back to the ground after flowering if it becomes overgrown and needs rejuvenating.

K. japonica 'Picta'

Tips

Kerria is useful in group plantings, woodland gardens and shrub or mixed borders.

Most flowers emerge in spring, but some may appear sporadically in summer.

Recommended

K. japonica grows 3–6' tall and spreads 3–8'. It has yellow single flowers. **'Albiflora'** ('Albescens') bears light yellow to white flowers. **'Aurea-variegata'** has gold-edged foliage. **'Golden Guinea'** bears large single blooms over a long period. **'Picta'** has grayish blue-green foliage with creamy margins. **'Pleniflora'** ('Flora Pleno') has double flowers. It grows 6–7' tall, with an equal spread, and its habit is more upright than that of the species. **'Superba'** has large single flowers and grows 6' tall and wide, sometimes wider.

Problems & Pests

Canker, leaf blight, twig blight, leaf spot or root rot may occur but are not serious.

K. japonica 'Pleniflora'

Kiwi

Actinidia

Features: early-summer flowers, edible fruit, foliage, habit **Habit:** woody, climbing, deciduous vines **Height:** 15–30' **Spread:** indefinite **Planting:** spring, fall **Zones:** 3–8

ALTHOUGH THEY ARE AMONG THE MORE USEFUL, VIGOROUS AND cold-hardy vining shrubs available to northern gardeners, kiwis are unfortunately not common at nurseries, for a couple of ill-founded reasons. First, the small, white, fragrant flowers are mostly covered by the foliage—but so what? Boston ivy doesn't flower at all, yet it's grown all across the northland. Kiwis perform much better than ivies in shade, and the stunning pink-and-green foliage of *A. kolomikta* is unequalled by other vines. Kiwis gallop up fences, trellises, walls (with support) and trees with such vigor that I sense nurseries fear homeowners will complain they're unwieldy. So prune them. No better choice exists for covering fences, trellises and pergolas in partial shade.

These kiwi species offer hairless fruits high in Vitamin C, potassium and fiber. They make good substitutes for the commercially available brown, hairy-skinned fruit of A. chinensis (A. deliciosa).

Growing

Kiwis grow best in **full sun,** but they also grow well in partial shade. The soil should be **fertile** and **well drained.** These plants require **shelter** from strong winds.

Prune in late winter. The plants can be trimmed to fit the area they've been given. If greater fruit production is desired, the side shoots can be cut back to two or three buds from the main stems.

Tips

These vines need a sturdy structure to twine around. Given a trellis against a wall, a tree or some other upright structure, kiwis will twine upwards all summer. They can also be grown in containers.

Both male and female vines are needed to produce fruit. All species listed here have fragrant white flowers that are borne in small clusters in early summer, and small, smooth-skinned, yellowish green fruit.

Recommended

A. arguta (hardy kiwi, bower actinidia) grows 20–30' high, but it can be trained to grow lower through the judicious use of pruning shears. The heart-shaped leaves are dark green.

A. kolomikta (variegated kiwi vine, kolomikta actinidia) grows 15–20' high. The green leaves are strongly variegated with pink and white; some leaves may be entirely white. (Zones 4–8)

A. polygama (silver vine) grows up to 15' high. The dark green foliage has silver-white markings on the leaf tips and sometimes over the

S. arguta (above & below)

entire upper leaf surface. (Zones 4–8)

Problems & Pests

Kiwis are occasionally afflicted with fungal diseases, but they are not a serious concern.

Lilac

Syringa

Features: mid-spring to early-summer flowers, habit **Habit:** rounded or suckering, deciduous shrub or small tree **Height:** 3–30' **Spread:** 3–30' **Planting:** B & B, container; late winter or early spring **Zones:** 2–8

WE LOVE OUR LILACS IN THE NORTH. I DOUBT THAT MANY NATIVE residents of our states are without fond childhood memories tinged with the sweet fragrance of lilacs in spring (I can close my eyes and smell lilacs right now). We are blessed that this large group of long-lived shrubs and small trees love cold climates. Lilacs perform far better here than in warmer climes. The nursery industry has devoted millions of dollars to the development of new varieties, and they seem to come up with spectacular new specimens each year. So take your time while choosing, and take care to plant lilacs where existing trees won't shade them in the decades to come.

Growing

Lilacs grow best in **full sun.** The soil should be **fertile, humus rich** and **well drained.** These plants tolerate open, windy locations, and the improved air circulation helps keep powdery mildew at bay.

Lilacs benefit from renewal pruning. On established plants of *S. x chinensis, S. x hyacinthiflora, S. x josiflexa, S. laciniata, S. x prestoniae* and *S. vulgaris,* remove one-third of the oldest growth each year after the bloom to make way for vigorous new growth and to prevent the plants from becoming leggy and overgrown. *S. meyeri, S. microphylla, S. patula, S. pekinensis* and *S. reticulata* need only minimal pruning each year after the bloom to remove dead, damaged, diseased and wayward growth. Except for *S. reticulata* and *S. pekinensis* plants being grown as single-trunk trees, all lilacs listed here respond well to hard pruning during dormancy. This pruning can be done all at once, but is best spread over two years. On mature plants, remove the thickest stalks at the base after the plants become dormant for the season—borers tend to tunnel into these woody havens, and they can kill the entire bush.

Deadhead lilacs as much as possible to keep the plants neat. Remove the flower clusters as soon as they are spent to give the plant plenty of time to produce next season's flowers.

S. vulgaris cultivar

The wonderfully fragrant flowers of S. vulgaris *have inspired the development of some 800 to 900 cultivars to date.*

S. meyeri 'Palibin'

C. vulgaris 'Charles Joly'
S. x hyacinthiflora cultivar

Tips

Include lilacs in shrub or mixed borders or use them to create informal hedges. *S. reticulata* can be used as a specimen or small shade tree.

Recommended

S. x *chinensis* (Chinese lilac, Rouen lilac) is a graceful shrub, 8–12' tall and wide, with many slender, spreading to slightly arching branches. In mid- to late spring it produces long, nodding clusters of lilac-purple flowers. **'Alba'** bears light pink to white flowers. (Zones 3–7)

S. x *hyacinthiflora* (hyacinth-flowered lilac, early-flowering lilac) is an upright hybrid that spreads as it matures. It grows up to 15' tall and wide. Clusters of fragrant flowers appear in mid- to late spring. The following cultivars are among those resistant to powdery mildew and bacterial blight. **'Blanche Sweet'** grows 8–10' tall and wide. The blue buds yield whitish blue flowers with pink-tinged petals. **'Dr. Chadwick'** is a dwarf cultivar with blue flowers. It grows 4–6' tall, with an equal spread. **'Evangeline'** bears light purple double flowers. It grows 8–10' tall and wide and doesn't sucker. **'Mt. Baker'** bears large clusters of white flowers that completely cover the plant. **'Pocahontas'** grows 10–12' tall and wide, producing very fragrant reddish purple flowers. (Zones 3–7)

S. x *josiflexa* is an upright to rounded shrub, 8–12' tall and wide. This late bloomer bears pendent clusters of flowers in a range of pink, purple, red and white. **'Royalty'** is a vigorous plant that bears deep red-purple flowers. (Zones 4–7)

S. laciniata (cutleaf lilac) is a dense, rounded shrub, 6' tall and 6–10' wide. The blue-green foliage is deeply cut, with each leaf having three to nine lobes. In mid- to late spring the small, open clusters of fragrant, light mauve flowers are borne from deep purple buds where the leaves meet the stem. This species tolerates heat and resists mildew. (Zones 4–8)

S. meyeri (Meyer lilac, dwarf Korean lilac) is a compact, rounded shrub that grows 3–8' tall and spreads 3–12'; it does not sucker profusely. It bears fragrant pink or lavender flowers in late spring and early summer and sometimes again in fall. The **Fairy Tale Series** is a new group of hybrids that grow 5–6' tall and wide. FAIRY DUST ('Baildust') bears fragrant, dusty pink flowers. TINKERBELLE ('Bailbelle') bears fragrant, bright pink flowers that open from dark pink buds. Both hybrids may bloom sporadically over summer. **'Palibin'** bears clusters of fragrant mauve pink flowers. (Zones 3–7)

S. microphylla (littleleaf lilac) is an upright, broad-spreading shrub that grows 6' tall and spreads 9–12'. It offers small, tidy leaves and attractive, airy clusters of fragrant, lilac pink flowers in early summer and sometimes again in fall. **'Superba'** grows 7' tall and up to 12' wide. Its deep red flower buds open to rich pink single blooms. This cultivar is quite resistant to powdery mildew. (Zones 4–7)

S. vulgaris cultivar

Lilacs are frost-loving shrubs that don't flower at all in the warm southern U.S.

S. meyeri TINKERBELLE

S. x prestoniae 'Miss Canada'

S. vulgaris

S. patula (Manchurian lilac) grows 5–10' tall, spreads 3–8' and bears small clusters of fragrant lilac-colored flowers. This species produces very few suckers. **'Miss Kim'** is similar to the species in shape and size but is denser in habit. The dark green leaves turn burgundy in fall. (Zones 3–8)

S. pekinensis (Pekin lilac) forms a small, multi-stemmed tree. It grows 15–20' tall, with an equal spread. It bears nodding clusters of creamy white flowers in early summer. Although similar to *S. reticulata,* it has a more delicate appearance. (Zones 3–7)

S. x prestoniae (Preston hybrid lilacs) is a group of upright hybrids that bear nodding clusters of flowers in early summer, two to three weeks after *S. vulgaris.* They generally grow 8–12' tall and 8–10' wide but can achieve up to 25' in height and width. These typically nonsuckering hybrids can be trained into small trees. **'Agnes Smith'** (*S. x josiflexa* 'Agnes Smith') has spicy-smelling, pure white single flowers. **'Donald Wyman'** bears deep rose-purple flowers. **'Hiawatha'** has reddish purple buds that open to pale pink flowers. **'Miss Canada'** is a vigorous, non-suckering plant with abundant bright pink flowers arising from deep rosy pink to bright red buds. (Zones 2–7)

S. reticulata (Japanese tree lilac) is a rounded large shrub or small tree that grows 20–30' tall and wide. It does not produce many suckers, and it bears fragrant cream-colored flowers in early summer. This species and its cultivars are resistant to powdery mildew, scale insects and borers. **'Summer Snow'** has a rounded crown and grows slightly smaller than the species. (Zones 3–7)

S. vulgaris (French lilac, common lilac) grows 8–15' tall, spreads 6–15' and bears fragrant lilac-colored flowers in late spring and early summer. This suckering, spreading shrub has an irregular habit, but consistent maintenance pruning keeps it neat and in good condition. Many cultivars are available. **'Albert F. Holden'** has deep violet-purple flowers with silver on the petal backsides. **'Arch McKean'** has abundant large clusters of bright red-purple flowers, and it suckers minimally. **'Charles Joly'** has magenta double flowers. **'Katherine Havemeyer'** is a vigorous, mildew-resistant plant with purple flower buds and fragrant, lavender blue double flowers. **'Krasavitsa Moskvy'** ('Beauty of Moscow,' 'Pride of Moscow') bears white flowers that open from pink buds. **'Mme. Lemoine'** has large white double flowers. **'Miss Ellen Willmott'** has very fragrant, creamy white double flowers with large individual florets. It does not sucker. **'Wonderblue'** ('Little Boy Blue') grows 4–5' tall and wide and bears clusters of fragrant, sky blue single flowers. (Zones 3–8)

Problems & Pests

Powdery mildew, leaf spot, bacterial blight, stem blight, borers, caterpillars, scale insects and root-knot nematodes are all possible troublemakers for lilacs.

S. reticulata (above & below)

Linden

Tilia

Features: habit, foliage **Habit:** dense, pyramidal to rounded, deciduous tree **Height:** 25–80' **Spread:** 20–60' **Planting:** B & B, bare-root, container; spring or fall **Zones:** 2–8

THE NUMBER OF TIMES I'VE RECOMMENDED A LINDEN TO homeowners asking which shade tree to plant in the front yard of their newly constructed home must be up around 40. It's tough to beat *T. cordata* if what you're after is a well-proportioned, trouble-free lawn tree. Lindens are among the fastest growing of all large deciduous trees, and they grow more robustly in the north than in the south. They tolerate a wide range of soil types and do very well in clay soils. The fall leaf color (yellow) is not spectacular, but then the roots of a linden don't attack lawn mowers as do a maple's, and the trees don't trash the yard with buckets of acorns, mushy fruits, or seedpods.

Growing

Lindens grow best in **full sun.** The soil should be **average to fertile, moist** and **well drained.** These trees adapt to most pH levels but prefer an **alkaline** soil. *T. cordata* tolerates pollution and urban conditions better than the other lindens listed here.

Little pruning is required. Remove dead, damaged, diseased or awkward growth as needed. On multi-stemmed specimens, prune all but the strongest stems.

Tips

Lindens are useful and attractive street trees, shade trees and specimen trees. Their tolerance of pollution and their moderate size make them ideal for city gardens.

The flower clusters of all lindens are attached to long, lance-shaped bracts. The flowers exude a dripping honeydew that will coat anything underneath, so don't plant lindens near a driveway.

T. cordata (above & below)

Recommended

T. americana (basswood, American linden) grows 60–80' tall and 30–40' wide. Fragrant flowers appear in early to mid-summer. Native to most of the eastern half of the U.S., the species is hardy to Zone 2; its cultivars are less hardy. **'Boulevard'** is a narrow, pyramidal tree with upright branching. It grows 50–60' tall and 20–30' wide and makes a

great street tree. **'Redmond'** is a commonly grown cultivar with a pyramidal habit, dark green foliage and fragrant summer flowers. It grows 35–50' tall and 20–30' wide. 'Redmond' is sometimes attributed to *T. x euchlora.* **'Sentry'** has a very symmetrical, pyramidal form with upright branching. It grows 50–60' tall and 30–40' wide. **'Wandell'** (LEGEND) is a pyramidal tree, 50–60' tall and 30–40' wide, that has a strong main trunk and sturdy branching. The thick, dark green foliage holds its color well through summer. (Zones 3–7)

T. cordata (littleleaf linden) is a dense, pyramidal tree that may become rounded with age. It grows 60–70' tall, spreads 30–45' and bears small summer flowers with narrow, yellow-green bracts. **'Baileyi'** (SHAMROCK) has an open-topped habit and grows to 40' in height and 30' in width. GREENSPIRE ('PNI 6025') is a compact cultivar, 40–50' tall and 20–25' in spread. (Zones 3–7)

T. mongolica (Mongolian linden) is a small, elegant tree with a rounded crown. It grows 25–30' tall and wide. Fragrant yellow-white flowers appear in early summer. The deeply cut, shiny, dark green foliage develops a bright yellow fall color. This species is resistant to aphids, sunscald and leaf spot, but it is subject to storm, ice and snow damage. **'Harvest Gold'** is a hybrid of *T. cordata* and *T. mongolica.* This narrow, upright tree, which grows 30–40' tall and

T. cordata

25–30' wide and has an oval crown, is not as prone to damage as *T. mongolica*. It produces flowers in abundance and has bark that exfoliates as the tree ages. The deeply serrated, mid-green foliage becomes a golden yellow in fall. (Zones 3–6)

T. platyphyllos (bigleaf linden) is a large, broadly pyramidal to columnar tree that grows 60–80' tall and 40–60' wide and tolerates wind, salt, and air pollution. It has large, glossy, dark green leaves that, in spite of the common name, are not nearly as large as those of *T. americana*. In fall they turn an undistinguished yellow. The fragrant, creamy yellow-white flowers appear in early summer. (Zones 3–6)

T. tomentosa (silver linden) has a broadly pyramidal or rounded habit and can be grown as a multi-stemmed tree. It grows 50–70' tall, spreads 25–45' and bears small, fragrant flowers in summer. The glossy green leaves have fuzzy, silvery undersides. STERLING SILVER ('Sterling') is a broadly pyramidal tree that grows about 50' tall and 25' wide. The leaves are intensely silver on the undersides. This cultivar is resistant to Japanese beetle and gypsy moth larvae. (Zones 4–7)

T. americana

T. mongolica 'Harvest Gold'

Problems & Pests

Occasional problems can occur with aphids, borers, caterpillars, Japanese beetles, leaf miners, mites, anthracnose, canker, leaf spot or powdery mildew.

Picturesque shape, moderately fast growth and wide adaptability make lindens desirable shade and street trees.

Maackia
Amur Maackia
Maackia

Features: foliage, form, bark, flowers **Habit:** small, deciduous tree with a rounded crown **Height:** 20–30' **Spread:** 20–30' **Planting:** B & B, container; spring **Zones:** 3–7

AMUR MAACKIA MAY BE THE FINEST LITTLE-USED SMALL TREE in America, although expanding interest in this admirable gem has resulted in increased availability at nurseries. This species is excellent for urban lots and city streetscapes. Its loose, rounded crown forms early and is maintained throughout the life of the tree. Spring foliage emerges a soft, powdery gray before darkening to a lustrous green. Spires of soft, white flowers form in mid-summer. The bark is yet another great asset. Shiny and dark brown, it flakes and peels as the tree matures, adding strong winter interest.

The genus name, Maackia, *honors Richard Karlovich Maack (1825–86), the Russian explorer and naturalist who discovered the tree growing in the Amur River region near the border between Russia and China. The species name,* amurensis, *reflects the location of the discovery.*

Growing

This maackia grows well in **full sun** in **average to poor, slightly alkaline to acidic, well-drained** soil. It adapts to many different soils and is very drought tolerant. A member of the pea family, it can fix nitrogen in the soil.

Amur maackia needs little to no pruning. Any formative pruning should be done when the plant is young, in late winter to early spring, while the tree is still dormant. Mature trees resent being pruned, and the pruning wounds close slowly.

M. amurensis (above & below)

Amur maackia suffers from no serious pests and diseases, and the flowers have a fragrance like that of a freshly mown lawn.

Tips

Amur maackia is a great tree for use as a specimen, as a street tree and in parks. It is also useful for planting in containers.

Recommended

M. amurensis is a slow-growing small tree with a rounded crown and upright, slightly arching branches. In gardens it grows 20–30' tall and wide, but it can grow up to 45' tall in ideal conditions. The compound leaves, initially silvery gray-green, mature to dark green and produce no appreciable fall color. Erect clusters of fragrant, dull white flowers that appear in early to mid-summer are followed by flattened, pea-like pods. The mature bark, which exfoliates, is orange-brown to copper in color.

Magnolia
Magnolia

Features: flowers, fruit, foliage, habit, bark **Habit:** upright to spreading, deciduous shrub or tree **Height:** 8–40' **Spread:** 8–30' **Planting:** B & B, container; early spring **Zones:** 3–9

THAT WE CAN GROW MAGNOLIAS IN THE NORTH IS FINE TESTAMENT to the passion and devotion of our area's university and nursery experts, for it was not too long ago that the thought of growing these southern favorites in Zones 3 and 4 was merest whimsy. Today, planting magnolias in the Zone 3b–4 landscape is not only possible, it is highly recommended. With their lush, clean foliage and stately growth habits, these stunning shrubs and small trees lend an air of dignified elegance to the yard or garden. Most varieties produce large, fragrant flowers very early in spring, before the leaves have emerged.

Try training a magnolia as an espalier specimen along a bare wall.

Growing

Magnolias grow well in **full sun** or **partial shade.** The soil should be **fertile, humus rich, acidic, moist** and **well drained.** A summer mulch helps keep the roots cool and the soil moist.

Very little pruning is needed. When the plants are young, thin out a few branches to encourage an attractive habit. Avoid transplanting; if transplanting is necessary, do it in early spring.

Tips

Magnolias are commonly used as specimen trees. The small species can also be used in borders.

Consistent blooming is best achieved by planting magnolias in sunny, sheltered locations, such as near the house, along fencing or in corners of a mature landscape. Avoid sites where the morning sun will encourage the blooms to open too early in the season. The sensitive blossoms can be damaged by cold, wind and rain.

Recommended

M. acuminata (cucumber tree) is a vigorous, deciduous, pyramidal tree that grows up to 40' tall and 30' wide. Deceivingly narrow when young, it becomes quite broad with age. Small, cup-shaped, yellow-green flowers are borne in late spring to early summer. The cucumber-shaped fruit, green when immature, ripens a pink-red to brown-red. A spicy aroma emanates from the dark green foliage when it is bruised. The following two hybrids have *M. acuminata* as

M. stellata

Just one stunning magnolia flower display every few years will make up for any losses from frost damage in other years.

M. de Vos–Kosar hybrid 'Betty'

M. de Vos–Kosar hybrid 'Betty'

one of the parents. **'Butterflies'** is an upright tree that grows about 15–25' tall and spreads about 11–20'. In mid-spring it bears cup-shaped, yellow flowers with red stamens. **'Elizabeth'** bears mid-spring blooms of soft yellow. This well-proportioned, pyramidal tree grows 25–30' high and 15–25' wide. (Zones 4–8)

M. stellata

M. de Vos–Kosar hybrids (Little Girl hybrids, The Girl Magnolias) are largely crosses of *M. liliflora* 'Nigra' and *M. stellata* 'Rosea.' They grow 8–12' tall and wide, and because they flower later than many other magnolias, they are less likely to suffer frost damage. They will often survive in parts of Zone 3b. **'Ann'** bears purple-red flowers. **'Betty'** bears many-petaled white flowers that are dark purple on the outside. **'Jane'** has flowers that are red-purple on the outside and white inside. **'Ricki'** bears flowers that are pink to purple-pink on the outside and white to pink-purple on the inside. (Zones 4–7)

M. x *loebneri* (Loebner magnolia) was developed from a cross between *M. kobus* and *M. stellata*. This rounded, spreading tree grows 15–30' tall, with an equal or greater spread. It is one of the earliest magnolias to bloom, bearing white or pink flowers in early to mid-spring.

'**Leonard Messel**' bears flowers that are white on the inside and pink on the outside, with a darker pink or purple stripe down the center of each petal. '**Merrill**' bears abundant white flowers. This fast-growing cultivar is cold hardy to Zone 3. (Zones 4–9)

M. sieboldii (Oyama magnolia, Siebold's magnolia) is a spreading, deciduous shrub or tree. It generally grows 10–15' tall and wide, bearing dark green foliage. Fragrant, slightly nodding, white flowers with rose-pink to deep crimson stamens bloom in late spring and early summer, and then sporadically through summer. The carmine red fruit is somewhat showy when contrasted against the golden yellow fall foliage. (Zones 4–9)

M. stellata (star magnolia) is a compact, bushy or spreading shrub or small tree. It grows 10–20' tall and spreads 10–15'. Fragrant, many-petaled, white flowers appear in early to mid-spring. '**Centennial**' is a vigorous, upright cultivar that is cold hardy to Zone 3. Its white double flowers have 28 to 32 petals each. '**Royal Star**' is a vigorous cultivar with pink buds that open to white double flowers. '**Water Lily**' is a dense, upright shrub with fragrant white flowers arising from vibrant pink buds. It is often just starting to bloom when 'Royal Star' is in full bloom. (Zones 4–9)

Problems & Pests

Possible problems include scale insects, snails, thrips, treehoppers, weevils, canker, dieback, leaf spot, powdery mildew and *Verticillium* wilt.

M. de Vos–Kosar hybrid 'Ann'

Despite their often fuzzy coats, magnolia flower buds are frost sensitive.

M. stellata

Maple

Acer

Features: foliage, bark, fruit, fall color, habit, flowers **Habit:** small to large, single or multi-stemmed, deciduous tree or large shrub **Height:** 5–80' **Spread:** 5–70' **Planting:** B & B, container; preferably spring **Zones:** 2–9

IN THE NORTH, MAPLE TREES ARE SO COMMON IN THE WILD AND in the nursery trade that even people not much interested in trees can identify a maple by its distinctive leaf shape. The maples form a very large group of trees, affording extraordinary opportunity for use in the landscape. Many people think only of the largest maple varieties, with common names such as Norway maple, red maple, silver maple and sugar maple, but although these very tall and wide shade trees are glorious in large yards, don't overlook the smaller ornamental varieties discussed below. You don't need to grow huge maples to enjoy their wonderful foliage, stellar form and fiery fall color.

Growing

Maples do well in **full sun** or **light shade,** but their preference varies from species to species. The soil should be **fertile, moist,** high in **organic matter** and **well drained.**

If maples are allowed to grow naturally, you simply need to remove dead, damaged or diseased branches whenever necessary. For maples to be grown as hedges or bonsai, begin pruning when the plants are very young. All shaping pruning should take place when maples are fully leafed out, in early to mid-summer.

Tips

Maples can be used as specimen trees or as large elements in shrub or mixed borders. Some species work well as hedges, some are useful as understory plants bordering wooded areas, and others can be grown in containers on patios or terraces. Few Japanese gardens are without some attractive small maples. Almost all maples can be used to create bonsai specimens.

A. platanoides samaras

Maple fruits (samaras) have wings that act like miniature helicopter rotors and help in seed dispersal.

A. ginnala 'Bailey's Compact'

A. *platanoides* in fall color

A. *platanoides* 'Crimson King'

Recommended

A. campestre (hedge maple) forms a dense, rounded tree, 25–35' tall, with an equal spread. Its low-branching habit and tolerance of heavy pruning make it popular as a hedge plant. If the fall frosts are late, the foliage may turn an attractive yellow before it drops. (Zones 4–8)

A. x freemanii (Freeman maple) varies in habit and fall coloration. It can grow 75–80' tall and 45–50' wide. AUTUMN BLAZE ('Jeffersred') is more drought tolerant than *A. x freemanii* and has a consistently strong orange-red fall color. It grows 50–60' tall and 40–50' wide. **'Sieneca'** (Sienna maple) is similar in size and form to AUTUMN BLAZE, but with smaller leaves, finer branching and wonderful orange-red fall color. It is hardy to Zone 3. (Zones 4–7)

A. ginnala (Amur maple) can withstand temperatures as low as -50° F;
in cold climates it is often used in
place of *A. palmatum* or *A. japon-
icum* for Japanese-style gardens. It
adapts to many soil types and a
wide pH range. Growing 15–25' tall,
with an equal or greater spread, it
can be grown as a large, multi-
stemmed shrub or pruned to form a
small tree. It grows well in light
shade, but the fall foliage, often a
brilliant crimson, develops best in
full sun. Placed in a large planter, it
is a popular choice for patios and
terraces. **'Bailey's Compact'** ('Bailey
Compact,' 'Compactum') is a vigorous shrub with shiny, dark green
foliage. It grows 10–12' tall and
15–20' wide. It has good red-purple
fall color. **'Emerald Elf'** is a compact shrub, 5–6' tall and wide, with
shiny, dark green foliage that turns
scarlet to purple in fall. **'Flame'** is a
densely branched, seed-grown selection. It grows 15–20' tall and wide,
bears red fruit and has very reliable,
fiery red fall color. (Zones 2–8)

A. griseum (paperbark maple)
grows very slowly, reaching 20–35'
tall and wide. This tree adapts to
many conditions and is popular
because of its orange-brown bark,
which peels and curls in papery
strips. (Zones 4–8)

A. negundo (boxelder, Manitoba
maple) is a fast-growing, upright to
spreading, single or often multi-
stemmed, suckering tree that grows
30–50' tall and wide. Migrating birds
and squirrels consume the seeds
with gusto. Its suckering habit, abundance of viable seeds and ability to
handle tough conditions better than

A. ginnala

A. x freemanii AUTUMN BLAZE

A. saccharinum

A. saccharum *is the main source of sap for boiling down to make maple syrup, but other maples can also be tapped for their sweet sap.*

A. negundo cultivar

most maples has created a weedy reputation in many parts of the U.S. and Canada. The cultivars are better choices. **'Flamingo'** has light green foliage with wide, irregular pink margins that fade to white with age. **'Sensation'** is slower growing than the species and has better form. This nonsuckering, rounded tree grows 30–40' tall and 25–30' wide. The fall color is orange to red. (Zones 3–8)

A. nigrum (black maple) is a large tree, 60–80' tall and 40–60' wide, with an oval crown. The light green foliage turns yellow to red in fall. Similar to *A. saccharum* in form and function, it better tolerates heat and drought. (Zones 4–8)

A. palmatum (Japanese maple) is considered to be one of the most beautiful and versatile trees available. However, because it leafs out early in spring, this tree can be badly damaged or killed by a late-spring frost. **'Emperor 1'** is an upright plant, 10–15' tall, with an equal or slightly lesser spread. It leafs out later than other Japanese maples and very often avoids frost damage. The burgundy-purple foliage holds well through summer, turning red in fall. (Zones 5–8)

A. pensylvanicum (striped maple, moosewood) is a small, upright tree with a broad crown. It usually grows 20' tall and 15' wide, but it can easily reach a height of 40' and a width of 30' in ideal conditions. The large, bright green leaves, often tinged pink when young, turn bright yellow in fall. The most striking feature is the green-and-white-striped bark. (Zones 3–7)

A. platanoides (Norway maple) is a rounded or oval tree, 40–50' tall or taller, with an equal or slightly lesser spread. It has very dense growth, so grass may not grow well beneath it. Its yellow fall color can be good unless an early frost hits before the color develops. This maple is a tough city tree, but don't use it near natural wooded areas; the prolific seedlings can outcompete many native plants. **'Columnare'** is a narrow, columnar tree with short, horizontal branches. It grows 50–60' tall and 15–20' wide. The dark green foliage turns yellow in fall. **'Crimson King'** is a very common cultivar with dark purple foliage that casts heavy shade. **'Deborah'** has a strong central leader and is easy to grow. The wavy-margined, leathery, dark to bronze-green foliage is purple-red when young and orange-yellow in fall. EMERALD LUSTRE ('Pond') is a vigorous, well-branched selection that has excellent cold hardiness and will provide shade earlier than the other *A. platanoides* selections. The dark green foliage, tinged red when young, turns brilliant yellow in fall. (Zones 4–8)

A. palmatum 'Emperor 1'

A. ginnala 'Bailey's Compact'

A. pseudosieboldianum (Korean maple, purplebloom maple) is a small tree with a rounded crown. It grows 12–20' tall and wide and has red-orange fall color. An unusual feature is the purple flowers—most maples have yellow-green ones. This hardy species makes a wonderful *A. palmatum* substitute. (Zones 3–8)

A. rubrum (red maple) is pyramidal when young, becoming more rounded with age. Single- and

A. rubrum

branches and an oval to rounded crown. It grows 35–50' tall and 35' wide. Hardy to Zone 3, it has orange-red flowers and red fall color. RED SUNSET ('Franksred') boasts deep orange to red color early in fall and has good cold tolerance. (Zones 4–8)

A. saccharinum (silver maple) is a fast-growing, large, rounded tree with drooping branches. It grows 50–80' tall and spreads 30–50'. Because it has weak wood and tends to drop a lot of debris, this species is a poor choice close to buildings and on small properties. On a rural or large property this fast-growing native can be quite impressive, particularly when a light breeze stirs the leaves and reveals their silvery undersides. (Zones 3–9)

A. saccharum (sugar maple) is considered to be the most impressive and majestic of maples. It has a rounded to pyramidal outline, grows 60–80' tall and spreads 40–50'. Its brilliant fall color ranges from yellow to red. This large native of Minnesota and Wisconsin does not tolerate restricted, polluted, urban conditions but makes a spectacular addition to parks, golf courses and large properties. GREEN MOUNTAIN tolerates drought and small growing spaces. The dark green foliage may turn yellow, orange or scarlet in fall. 'Majesty' ('Flax Hill Majesty') is a densely branched cultivar with an upright oval habit and scarlet fall color. (Zones 3–8)

A. tataricum (Tatarian maple) is a large shrub or small tree. It can be multi-stemmed or trained to a single

multi-stemmed specimens are available. It grows 40–70' tall, with a variable spread of 20–70'. The cold tolerance depends on where the plant has been grown. Locally bred trees adapt best to the local climate. Fall color varies from tree to tree, with some developing no fall color and others turning bright yellow, orange or red. Named cultivars have the best fall color. **'Autumn Spire'** is an upright tree, 40–50' tall and 20–25' wide, with a narrow, oval crown. The red flowers appear before the foliage in spring. Hardy to Zone 3, it is one of the earliest *A. rubrum* cultivars to show bright red fall color. **'Northwood'** is a University of Minnesota selection with a straight trunk, sturdy, ascending trunk, and it grows 15–20' tall and wide. The shiny, mid- to dark green foliage yields yellow to red fall color. The ripening fruit stays red and showy for an extended period. (Zones 3–8)

A. triflorum (three-flower maple) is a rare, underused, slow-growing, small tree with ornamental, exfoliating, orange-brown bark. It eventually reaches a height and width of 20–30'. Its habit tends to be upright in shady conditions and more rounded in full sun. The fall color is vibrant orange to red, sometimes with purple and golden yellow mixed in, even when grown in shade. (Zones 4–8)

Problems & Pests

Aphids, borers, caterpillars, leafhoppers, scale insects, anthracnose, canker, leaf spot or *Verticillium* wilt can affect maples. Nutrient deficiency in alkaline soils can cause chlorosis (leaf yellowing). Prevent leaf scorch by watering young trees during hot, dry spells.

Hard and dense, maple wood is used for fine furniture construction and for some musical instruments.

A. platanoides

A. saccharinum

A. griseum

Mountain Ash

Sorbus

Features: form, flowers, foliage, fruit **Habit:** rounded to broadly pyramidal, single or multi-stemmed, deciduous trees **Height:** 15–40' **Spread:** 10–30'
Planting: B & B, container; spring, fall **Zones:** 2–8

NOW THE IMPORTANCE OF KNOWING THE PROPER BOTANICAL names for the plants we grow becomes hugely apparent—a mountain ash *(Sorbus)* is not an ash *(Fraxinus)*. Still, there is much to appreciate in the delightful (though erroneously named) mountain ashes. Of prime value are the wonderful flowers and fruits of all species. The fruits rarely despoil the yard, for they are enjoyed greatly by birds. These trees quickly develop extremely handsome, rounded-to-oval form and varied bark coloration; mountain ashes are very attractive in winter. They are susceptible to borer infestations and fire blight, however, but proper care when planting, ample water in the first three years and annual spring fertilization help minimize these occurrences.

Growing

Mountain ashes grow well in **full sun, partial shade** or **light shade** and in **humus-rich, average to fertile, moist, well-drained** soil. They prefer **neutral to slightly acidic** soil but tolerate a slightly alkaline situation. *S. aucuparia* tolerates pollution and urban conditions.

These plants need very little pruning. Remove damaged, diseased and awkward growth as needed.

Mountain ashes are susceptible to fire blight. If a plant contracts the disease, it will eventually die, so you might need to replace it after 12 to 15 years. Most people with mountain ashes agree that having them is worth the risk.

S. americana

Most mountain ashes, such as S. aucuparia, *have compound leaves with many leaflets per leaf. Two exceptions are* S. hybrida, *which has deeply lobed leaves, and* S. alnifolia, *which has simple leaves.*

S. aucuparia

S. aucuparia

Mountain ash berries, especially of S. aucuparia, *are a favorite food of birds, which often strip them from the trees before winter arrives.*

S. americana

Tips

Use mountain ashes as specimen trees in small gardens, or plant them in woodland and natural gardens. They can attract a variety of wildlife; many birds enjoy the fruit.

Recommended

S. alnifolia (Korean mountain ash) is a broad, pyramidal to rounded tree, 20–40' tall and 15–30' wide. More erect when young, this tree broadens with age. It has dark green, serrated foliage that turns golden yellow in fall. The clusters of white flowers produced in mid-spring are followed by persistent red to pink-red fruit. (Zones 4–8)

S. americana (American mountain ash) is an oval to rounded tree or large shrub that grows 15–30' tall and 10–22' wide. It has light green foliage that turns yellow to red in fall. In late spring and early summer it bears dense clusters of fragrant white flowers, which are followed by spherical orange to red fruit.

S. aucuparia (European mountain ash) is a single to multi-stemmed tree, 20–35' tall and 20–30' wide, with a low, rounded crown. It has mid- to dark green foliage that turns red to orange in fall. This floriferous tree produces its clusters of white flowers in late spring. The orange-red fruit is enjoyed by many birds. **'Asplenifolia'** has finely divided leaflets. **'Black Hawk'** grows 25–30' tall and 15–20' wide and is resistant to sunscald. It has orange fruit. **'Cardinal Royal'** is similar in size to 'Black Hawk,' but it has bright red fruit. **'Xanthocarpa'** has orange-yellow fruit. (Zones 3–7)

S. decora (showy mountain ash) is an upright tree or large shrub that grows to 20–25' tall and spreads 12–15'. The dark blue-green foliage turns a wonderful orange-red in fall. Clusters of white flowers appear in late spring. The spherical fruit is bright red.

S. hybrida is a cross between *S. aucuparia* and *S. aria*. Growing 20–35' tall and 15–25' wide, it is a vigorous, erect tree. When mature, it becomes broadly pyramidal, with wide, spreading branches. The deeply lobed, oak-like foliage is dark green to blue-green. (Zones 4–8)

Problems & Pests

In addition to fire blight, other potential problems include powdery mildew, anthracnose, rust, borers, sawflies, scale and aphids.

Delicious jams and jellies can be made from mountain ash berries, but wait for a few good frosts before harvesting the fruit clusters.

S. aucuparia cultivar with DIABOLO ninebark

Many parts of mountain ash trees have been used in herbal medicine. The ripe berries are made into a gargle for sore throats and inflamed tonsils. The berries have also been used to combat scurvy.

S. decora

Ninebark

Physocarpus

Features: mid-spring or early-summer flowers, fruit, bark, foliage **Habit:** upright, sometimes suckering, deciduous shrub **Height:** 2–10' **Spread:** 2–15'
Planting: container; spring or fall **Zones:** 2–8

NINEBARKS ARE AMONG MY FAVORITE SHRUBS, AND RARELY DO I fail to include one (or three) when designing a residential landscape. What's not to like? Ninebarks feature attractive foliage, ranging from green to gold to an amazing purple-bronze (DIABOLO), and they have eye-popping early-summer flowers. Tough as nails to Zone 2, they are perfect for use in foundation plantings and mixed shrub borders. These plants respond well to pruning and shearing, and they make a lovely, dense, clipped hedge in full sun. Both 'Dart's Gold' and DIABOLO look terrific placed to the rear of a mixed perennial and annual garden.

Ninebark is an easy-growing shrub that adapts to most garden conditions.

Growing

Ninebarks grow well in **full sun** or **partial shade,** but the best leaf coloring develops in a sunny location. The soil should be **fertile, moist** and **well drained,** and these shrubs adapt well to alkaline soil.

Little pruning is required. You can encourage vigorous new growth by removing one-third of the old stems each year after flowering finishes.

Tips

Ninebarks can be included in a shrub or mixed border or in a woodland or naturalistic garden.

Recommended

P. opulifolius (common ninebark) is a suckering shrub that has long, arching branches and exfoliating bark. It grows 5–10' tall and spreads 6–15'. Light pink flowers in early summer are followed by fruit that ripens to reddish green. **'Dart's Gold'** grows 5' in height and spread. The bright gold leaves hold their color well in summer. DIABOLO ('Monlo') has attractive purple foliage and grows 8–10' in height and spread. **'Nanus'** (var.

'Nugget'

nanus; dwarf ninebark) is a bushy shrub that grows about 24" (occasionally 48") tall and 24–36" wide, with small, dark green leaves. **'Nugget'** is a compact plant that grows 6' tall, with an equal spread. The bright yellow foliage matures to lime green over summer. **'Snowfall'** has more and larger clusters of flowers than the species. It grows 4–7' tall and wide or slightly wider. SUMMER WINE ('Seward') is a neat, compact plant, 5–6' in height and width. It has dark crimson foliage and pinkish white mid-summer flowers.

Problems & Pests

Occasional problems with leaf spot, fire blight and powdery mildew may occur.

DIABOLO

Oak

Quercus

Features: summer and fall foliage, bark, habit, acorns **Habit:** large, rounded, spreading, deciduous tree **Height:** 40–100' **Spread:** 15–100' **Planting:** B & B, container; spring, fall **Zones:** 2–9

THERE'S A WHITE OAK IN MY NEIGHBORHOOD WITH A TRUNK that's a good four feet in diameter. The tree could easily be 225 years old. All species and varieties of oaks mature into tall, formidable shade trees; such is the insurmountable power and majesty of these kings of the forest that nursery experts have never been able to cultivate any type of dwarf variety or even find a dwarf in the wild. *Q.* x *bimundorum* CRIMSON SPIRE is a wonderful hybrid that remains quite columnar while topping out at around 45'; it is the best oak for small lots. For people with ample room, it's tough to beat *Q. alba*, a popular native of Minnesota and Wisconsin.

Growing

Oaks grow well in **full sun** or **partial shade.** The soil should be **fertile, moist** and **well drained.** Most oaks prefer slightly acidic soils but (except for *Q. palustris*) adapt to alkaline conditions.

Oaks can be difficult to establish. Most species should be transplanted only when young, but *Q. bicolor* and *Q. palustris* tolerate transplanting when older. Do not disturb the ground around an oak's base—oaks are very sensitive to changes in grade.

No pruning is needed.

Q. macrocarpa

Tips

Oaks are large trees best suited to be grown as specimens or in groves in parks and large gardens.

Acorns are generally not edible, but some kinds can be eaten after the bitter tannins have been leached out.

Oaks have been held sacred by many cultures throughout history. The ancient Greeks believed these trees were the first ones created, and the Roman poet Virgil said that they gave birth to the human race.

Q. rubra

Q. REGAL PRINCE (above & below)

Recommended

Q. alba (white oak) is a rounded, spreading tree with peeling bark. It grows 50–100' tall, with an equal spread. The leaves turn purple-red in fall. (Zones 3–9)

Q. bicolor (swamp white oak) is a broad, spreading tree with peeling bark. It grows 50–70' tall, with an equal or greater spread, and develops orange or red fall color. (Zones 3–8)

Q.* x *bimundorum (*Q. alba* x *Q. robur;* Bimundors oak) is a vigorous hybrid, 60' tall and wide or wider, with a full, dense crown. The acorns, borne at a younger age than on most oaks, acquire a red tinge as they ripen. CRIMSON SPIRE ('Crimschmidt') is a narrow, columnar tree that grows 45' tall and 15' wide. The dark green to blue-green foliage turns red in fall. (Zones 4–8)

Q. coccinea (scarlet oak) is an open, rounded tree that grows 70–75' tall, with a spread of 40–50', sometimes more. The glossy, dark green leaves turn bright red in fall. (Zones 4–9)

Q. ellipsoidalis (northern pin oak, Hill's oak, jack oak) is a native tree, 40–60' tall and 30–50' wide, with an irregular, oval to rounded crown and low-hanging branches. The deeply cut foliage turns scarlet red in fall. This species likes full sun and is very drought tolerant. (Zones 3–6)

***Q.* x *macdanielli* 'Clemons'** (HERITAGE) has a broadly pyramidal to oval crown. It grows vigorously to 60–80' tall and 40–50' wide. The shiny green foliage, which resists powdery mildew and shredding in the wind, turns yellow-brown to bronze in fall. (Zones 4–7)

Q. macrocarpa (bur oak, mossycup oak) is a large, broad tree with furrowed bark. This species grows 50–80' tall, with an equal spread. The leaves turn shades of yellow in fall. (Zones 2–8)

Q. palustris (pin oak, swamp oak) is a fast-growing, pyramidal to columnar tree, 60–70' tall and 25–40' wide, with smooth bark. The fall foliage develops a good red to reddish brown color. (Zones 4–8)

Q. REGAL PRINCE (*Q.* x *warei* 'Long') grows 40–60' tall and 20–30' wide, forming an upright, oval shape. The mildew-resistant, glossy, dark green leaves with silvery undersides turn rusty red-orange in fall. (Zones 4–8)

Q. rubra (red oak) is a rounded, spreading tree, 60–75' tall, with an equal spread. The fall color ranges from yellow to red-brown. Be careful not to damage the shallow roots when cultivating near the tree. (Zones 4–9)

Problems & Pests

In spring 2004, 'sudden oak death,' caused by a fungus-like organism and first reported in California in 1995, was announced as having made a toehold in the Midwest. It is not yet clear how well this outbreak can be contained. *Q. rubra* is most susceptible. Other possible problems, rarely serious, are borers, gypsy moth caterpillars, leaf miners, leaf rollers, leaf skeletonizers, scale insects, canker, leaf gall, leaf spot, powdery mildew, rust, twig blight and wilt.

Q. bicolor

Oaks are important commercial trees. The wood is used for furniture, flooring, veneers, boatbuilding and casks for wine and whiskey.

Q. palustris

Pearl Bush

Exochorda

Features: spring flowers **Habit:** upright, vase-shaped shrub **Height:** 3–12'
Spread: 3–15' **Planting:** container, B & B (when very young); early spring
Zones: 4–9

AN EXTREMELY ATTRACTIVE AND EASY-TO-GROW ORNAMENTAL
shrub, the University of Minnesota selection *E. serratifolia* 'Northern Pearls'
will certainly do much to elevate the status of pearl bushes in the nursery
trade. Pea-like flower buds become pearl-like blossoms before opening fully
as bright, very showy, five-petaled, white flowers. 'Northern Pearls' is preferable to the broader, coarser and less hardy *E. racemosa*. Star-shaped, golden
brown seed capsules and an exfoliating bark habit give pearl bushes uncom-
mon winter interest.

Growing

Pearl bushes grow well in **full sun** and tolerate partial shade. They like soil of **average fertility** with **lots of organic matter** mixed in. It should be **slightly acidic, moist** and **well drained.** Pearl bushes tolerate heat and drought when mature. The foliage can be damaged by a late frost. *E. racemosa* may not perform well in shallow, alkaline soils, but most pearl bushes are pH adaptable.

E. racemosa

Pearl bushes respond well to renewal pruning after flowering. Large specimens can be trained as small trees.

Tips

Pearl bushes are low-maintenance, deciduous shrubs typically used in hedgerows and shrub beds.

E. x *macrantha* 'The Bride' (middle & below)

Recommended

E. **x *macrantha* 'The Bride'** is a compact, mounding shrub with arching branches. It grows 3–4' tall and wide or slightly wider. It bears abundant clusters of large white flowers in mid- to late spring. (Zones 5–9)

Exochorda bushes have flower buds that resemble pearls, hence the common name.

E. racemosa (common pearl bush) grows 12' tall and 12–15' wide. It is a rounded to spreading, multi-stemmed shrub with arching branches and medium green foliage. Clusters of large white flowers appear in early spring. Although this plant flourishes with little care, it can look scruffy with age, so prune regularly. It is hardy only to the warmer parts of Zone 4. (Zones 4–8)

E. serratifolia 'Northern Pearls' is an upright shrub that grows 6–10' tall and 4–6' wide or slightly wider. It produces plentiful clusters of white flowers in early spring. (Zones 4–7)

Peashrub

Caragana

Features: late-spring flowers, foliage, habit **Habit:** prickly, weeping (grafted) or upright to rounded, deciduous shrub **Height:** 2–20' **Spread:** 3–18'
Planting: container, B & B, bare-root; spring or fall **Zones:** 2–8

PERHAPS IT IS BECAUSE I HAVE SEEN ONE TOO MANY MISGUIDED plantings of *C. arborescens* 'Walker' in gardens that I have little exuberance for this increasingly popular variety of peashrub. Someone who can place this shaggy, dwarf oddity in a residential landscape so that it looks anything more than bewildered is a better designer than I. *C. frutex* 'Globosa,' however, is a fine small shrub, and although it cannot be counted on to flower each year, that's not a problem if the idea is to keep it clipped as a low hedge. In addition, the choice, bluish green foliage of 'Globosa' holds up well throughout the growing season, which cannot be said of all peashrubs.

Growing

Peashrubs prefer **full sun** and soil of **average to high fertility.** These plants adapt to just about any growing conditions, and they tolerate dry, exposed locations, especially *C. pygmaea. C. frutex* will grow in all but very wet soils.

Prune out awkward or damaged shoots as needed to maintain a neat shape. Rejuvenate unruly or overgrown plants by pruning them to within six inches of the ground. To control the spread of a weeping specimen that has been grafted, you can prune back to near the graft at the top of the main trunk; if you prune below the graft, the weeping habit will be lost.

C. arborescens (all photos)

Tips

Peashrubs are 'tough-as-nails' plants grown as windbreaks and as formal or informal hedges. They can be included in borders, and weeping forms are often used as specimen plants. *C. pygmaea* is an excellent low-barrier plant.

C. arborescens

Because peashrub roots fix nitrogen in the soil, these plants have been used in soil-improvement programs.

C. arborescens 'Walker'

Recommended

C. arborescens (Siberian peashrub) is a large, twiggy, thorny shrub that grows up to 20' tall and spreads up to 18'. The branches may be upright or arching. Yellow, pea-like flowers are borne in late spring. **'Lorbergii'** has fine, fern-like foliage with very narrow leaflets and narrower flowers than the species. **'Pendula'** has long, weeping branches. It is generally grafted to a standard that may be 3–6' in height; the spread is equal or greater. **'Sutherland'** is a narrow plant with many upright, unbranched stems. Weeping forms are often grafted onto it. **'Walker'** is a similar weeping form with fine, feathery foliage.

C. frutex (Russian peashrub) is an upright, spreading, suckering shrub, 6–9' tall and 4–7' wide. It rarely produces spines and has finer foliage than *C. arborescens*. It is not as attractive to pests as the other

peashrubs listed here. It bears yellow flowers in late spring and early summer. **'Globosa'** develops a rounded form that is branched to the base. It grows 36" tall and wide.

C. pygmaea (pygmy caragana) is a dense, mounding, very spiny plant, 24–36" tall and 4–6' wide. It displays yellow blooms in late spring and early summer. (Zones 3–8)

C. **'Roborovskyi'** *(C. roborovskyi)* develops a globe form that bears silver-green foliage and bright yellow late-spring flowers. It is available as a grafted standard that grows 4–8' tall and 3–4' wide.

C. rosea (red flower peashrub) is a compact, mounding plant that grows 36" tall and wide. It has sharp spines and bright green foliage that briefly turns yellow in fall. The bell-shaped, red-tinged, yellow-petaled flowers arise from brick red to purple-red buds; the brightest red occurs as the flowers are emerging and then fades with age. When mature, this species is very drought tolerant. (Zones 3–8)

Problems & Pests

The foliage can be somewhat prone to black spot, particularly during moist or humid summers. Aphids, spider mites and leafhoppers may disfigure young foliage but are generally not a problem.

Peashrubs bear pea-like pods that ripen to brown in summer. Hear them rattle in the wind in late summer, and listen for popping sounds as they burst.

C. arborescens 'Sutherland'

This plant is a good choice for difficult locations and regions, anywhere in our two states.

C. pygmaea

Persian Parrotia

Parrotia

Features: habit, summer and fall foliage, bark, early spring flowers **Habit:** single or multi-stemmed, rounded, deciduous tree **Height:** 10–40' **Spread:** 5–30' **Planting:** B & B, container; spring **Zones:** 4–8

WHY THIS EXTREMELY HANDSOME AND UNUSUAL TREE IS NOT AT all common in the northern nursery trade is a mystery. Spring frosts can sometimes thwart blooming, but so what? It happens with magnolias, and they are popular regardless. Hardy to Zone 4, Persian parrotia prefers cooler climates and nighttime relief from summer's heat. The species develops into a wide, mid-sized tree with a startling yet magnificent irregular form. Emerging bronze in spring, the oval, slightly ruffled, dark green leaves end the season as a mixed collage of chocolate brown, burnt orange and yellow-gold, and the spring flowers are raspberry red. The wonderfully mottled bark resembles a soldier's camouflage. 'Pendula' is a dense, broad, weeping cultivar that is even more difficult to find. If curious, consult specialty mail-order nurseries.

Growing

Persian parrotia prefers **full sun** and tolerates partial shade. The soil should be **average to fertile, slightly acidic, moist** and **well drained.** This plant tolerates alkaline soils, but the best fall color develops in acidic conditions.

Persian parrotia needs very little pruning. Remove damaged and awkward growth as needed.

Tips

This beautiful small tree deserves a place in any garden. It makes an attractive shade tree and can be used in borders and woodland gardens. Groups of Persian parrotia can be displayed to their best advantage in the expansive spaces of large gardens.

Recommended

P. persica is a small to medium-sized, single or multi-stemmed tree. It grows 20–40' tall and spreads 15–30' or more. As old, gray pieces of bark peel off to reveal newer, green bark, the mature tree develops a mottled appearance. It bears small red flowers in late winter or early spring. The glossy mid- to dark green summer foliage turns shades of yellow, orange, red and reddish purple in fall. **'Pendula'** has a weeping habit and grows about 10' tall, with a spread of 5–15'.

Problems & Pests

Persian parrotia rarely suffers from any problems, but Japanese beetles have been known to enjoy snacking on it.

P. persica (above & below)

A relative of witchhazel, Persian parrotia is native to the Caucasus Mountains and Iran.

Pine

Pinus

Features: foliage, bark, cones, habit **Habit:** upright, columnar or spreading, ever-green tree or shrub **Height:** 1–120' **Spread:** 2–50' **Planting:** B & B, container; spring or fall **Zones:** 2–8

PINES ARE ESSENTIAL TO NORTHERN LANDSCAPES, NOT JUST FOR their unmatched winter beauty, but also for their ability to serve as majestic, evergreen anchors. If you want a large stand or row of evergreens, select at least two pine species, and mix in spruce as well, to create a tapestry of con-trasting color, texture and form. Dwarf varieties of *Pinus* figure prominently in the wonderful new trend toward using small evergreens in foundation plantings, mixed shrub borders and perennial gardens. The consideration of *P. strobus* varieties such as 'Blue Shag,' 'Macopin,' 'Nana' and *P. resinosa* 'Morel' is heartily encouraged.

Growing

Pines grow best in **full sun.** They are not heavy feeders, but soil of **moderate fertility** is recommended. They adapt to most **well-drained** soils. *P. flexilis* tolerates partial shade and needs moist, well-drained soil.

Little or no pruning is required. Trim hedges in mid-summer. Pinch up to one-half the length of the 'candles,' the fully extended but still soft new growth, to shape the plant or to regulate growth.

Tips

Pines can be used as specimen trees, hedges or windbreaks. Smaller cultivars can be included in shrub or mixed borders to provide texture and interest year-round.

Austrian pine *(P. nigra)* is susceptible to diplodia tip blight. Provide good air circulation to help prevent the disease.

P. ponderosa

Pines are easy to distinguish from other needled evergreens. Their needles are borne in bundles of two, three or five, whereas spruce, fir and hemlock needles are borne singly.

P. sylvestris

Topgrafted *P. mugo* cultivar

Recommended

P. aristata (bristlecone pine) is a slow-growing, conical to shrubby tree that grows 8–30' tall and 6–20' wide. It doesn't tolerate pollution but survives in poor, dry, rocky soil. The needles may dry out if exposed to winter winds. (Zones 4–8)

P. banksiana (jack pine) is rounded to conical when young, becoming irregular with age. It grows 30–50' tall, with a variable but lesser spread. It is often considered too scruffy for areas where more attractive species thrive. **'Schoodic'** is a mat-forming, prostrate plant, 12–18" tall and 6–10' wide, with twisted branches and bright green needles. **'Uncle Fogy'** ('Uncle Fogey') is a prostrate plant, 12–24" tall and 12–15' wide, with wild, undulating branches. It is often found grafted as a standard.

P. bungeana (lacebark pine) is a slow-growing, bushy, multi-stemmed, pyramidal, columnar or rounded tree. It grows 30–50' tall and 15–35' wide. The smooth, reddish bark flakes off in scales to reveal creamy or pale green bark beneath. (Zones 4–8)

P. cembra (Swiss stone pine) is dense and columnar, growing slowly to 25–40' tall and 10–15' wide. It is resistant to white pine blister rust. **'Klein'** (SILVER WHISPERS) is narrow and upright, bearing dense, dark green needles with silvery white stripes and attractive, violet blue cones. It grows 10–12' tall and 5–6' wide. (Zones 3–7)

P. contorta var. *latifolia* (lodgepole pine) has a straight trunk and a narrow, open crown. Growing 60–80' tall and 20–30' wide, it has twisted, yellow-green to bright green needles and persistent cones. **'Taylor's Sunburst'** is broadly pyramidal, growing 12–15' tall and 8–10' wide. The new foliage is bright golden yellow, maturing to light yellow-green. (Zones 3–7)

P. flexilis (limber pine) is a broad, pyramidal tree, 50' tall and 15–35' wide, with flexible, wind-tolerant branches. **'Vanderwolf's Pyramid'** has blue-green needles and grows to 40' tall and 20' wide. (Zones 3–7)

P. koraiensis (Korean pine) is an open, columnar to pyramidal tree with long, blue-green needles, large, resinous cones and edible seeds. It usually grows 30–40' tall and 15–25' wide, but can get much taller in the wild. The crown becomes irregular with age. (Zones 3–7)

P. mugo (mugo pine) is a low, rounded, spreading shrub or tree, 10–20' tall and 15–20' wide. **'Big Tuna'** is a dense, upright, multi-stemmed shrub with dark green needles. It grows 6–8' tall and 4–6' wide. **Var. *pumilio*** is a dense, slow-growing, mounding variety, 2–8' tall and wide. **'Slowmound'** is a slow-growing, mounded shrub with dark green needles and white buds. It grows to 36" tall and wide. **'Tannenbaum'** is a uniquely (for this species) single-stemmed, small tree, 10–12' tall and 6' wide, with an upright, dense, pyramidal form. **'Teeny'** is a dense, upright globe that grows 24–36" tall and wide, with tiny, vibrant green needles. (Zones 2–7)

P. nigra (Austrian pine) is an upright tree with a broad, flat-topped to rounded crown. It grows 50–60' tall and 30–40' wide in gardens. It tolerates urban conditions, drought, heat, clay soils and alkaline soils. **'Arnold Sentinel'** is a narrow,

P. koraiensis

Pines are more diverse and widely adapted than any other conifers.

P. nigra

P. strobus cultivar

columnar form, 25' tall and 6–8' wide. (Zones 3–7)

P. parviflora (Japanese white pine) grows slowly to 20–50' tall and wide. Conical or columnar when young, this tree develops a spreading, irregular, flat-topped crown on maturity. **'Brevifolia'** has a narrow, columnar habit with distinctly horizontal branches. It grows to 8–10' in height and 4' in width in 15 years. (Zones 4–8)

P. flexilis

P. ponderosa (ponderosa pine, western yellow pine) is a conical, columnar or spreading tree, 80–120' tall and 20–30' wide. It has striking orange-brown bark with black fissures. It is extremely heat and drought tolerant. (Zones 5–8)

P. resinosa (red pine) is a conical to rounded tree with long, stiff needles. It grows 50–80' tall and 20–40' wide and is useful for creating windbreaks. **'Morel'** is a dense, rounded to broadly pyramidal shrub with soft, light green needles. It grows 4–6' tall and 4–8' wide. **'Norway Compact'** grows 30–40' tall and 15–20' wide. This upright tree has a broadly pyramidal crown and winterburn-resistant foliage. (Zones 3–7)

P. strobus (eastern white pine) is a slender, conical tree, 50–120' tall and 20–40' wide, with soft, plumy needles. It is sometimes grown as a hedge. Young trees can be killed by white pine blister rust, but mature trees are resistant. **'Blue Shag'** is a rounded, compact shrub, 6–8' tall and 4–6' wide, with blue-green to blue-gray foliage. **'Compacta'** is a dense, rounded, slow-growing cultivar that grows 6' tall and wide. It is wider than tall when young. **'Fastigiata'** is a narrow, columnar form that grows up to 40' tall and 15' wide. **'Macopin'** is a large, upright shrub growing 8–10' tall and wide, with an irregular, rounded crown, blue-green needles and a plethora of cones. **'Nana'** is a compact, rounded to flattened shrub with light green to blue-green foliage. It grows 6–8' tall and 6' wide. **'Pendula'** has long, ground-sweeping branches. It must be trained when young to form an upright leader to give it some height and shape; otherwise, it can be grown as a groundcover or left to spill over the top of a rock wall or slope. It develops an unusual soft, shaggy, droopy appearance with age. (Zones 3–8)

P. sylvestris (Scots pine) grows 30–70' tall and spreads 20–40'. It is rounded or conical when young and develops an irregular, flat-topped, spreading habit when mature. This species varies in size, habit, needle color and needle length. **'Albyn Prostrata'** is a mat-forming, prostrate plant growing 18–24" tall and 6' wide with mid- to dark green foliage. **'Bonna'** is a dense, upright tree with silver blue foliage and cinnamon-colored bark. **'Glauca Nana'** is a rounded to flattened shrub with dark green to blue-green needles. It grows 6–8' tall and wide. **'Globosa Viridis'** is a dense, upright shrub, 5–6' tall and 4–5' wide, with bright green foliage borne in tufts at the branch tips. **'Watereri'** is a rounded to broadly pyramidal tree with blue-gray needles. Typically growing 10–12' tall and wide or slightly wider, it may reach 25' in height and width. (Zones 2–7)

Problems & Pests

Borers, caterpillars, leaf miners, mealybugs, sawflies, scale insects, blight, blister rust, cone rust, pitch canker or tar spot can cause problems. European pine-shoot moths (minor pests) attack pines with needles in clusters of two or three.

P. ponderosa

P. cembra

Poplar and Aspen
Cottonwood
Populus

Features: fast, dense growth **Habit:** rounded, upright or narrow, deciduous trees
Height: 30–120' **Spread:** 6–75' **Planting:** bare-root, container; spring, fall
Zones: 1–9

ALTHOUGH SOME NOTED EXPERTS SUGGEST THAT *POPULUS* SPECIES
be left to have at it in the wild, their extremely fast growth rate makes them
worthy of some consideration. Many species and varieties have proven susceptible to a staggering range of diseases. The one variety most often available
in the trade that seems to hold up well—if properly watered and fertilized—is
P. deltoides 'Siouxland.' For quick shade and good summer
windbreaks in large, naturalized areas (where their
incessant leaf and twig drop can be ignored),
poplars have merit.

Growing

Poplars and aspens grow best in **full sun** in **deep, fertile, moist, well-drained** soil. They adapt to a wide range of soils, except constantly wet ones, and are quite tolerant of urban pollution.

Aspens and poplars need only minimal pruning to remove awkward and wayward growth and any diseased, damaged or dead wood. Pruning can be done in late summer to early fall to reduce bleeding.

Tips

Poplars and aspens are large, fast-growing trees useful for naturalizing, in shelterbelts, and on large, open properties. *P. tremuloides* is excellent for reclamation of disturbed sites; it looks best when planted in clumps. *P. nigra* 'Italica,' *P.* x 'Griffin' and *P. tremula* 'Erecta' are often used in tight spots and as screens.

P. alba

The flat leaf petioles of P. tremuloides *are easily moved by the wind. The leaves appear to tremble in the slightest breeze, hence the common names.*

P. tremula 'Erecta'

P. tremula 'Erecta'

Scientists Jeffrey B. Mitton and Michael C. Grant discovered a P. tremuloides *clone colony in Utah's Wasatch Mountains that occupies 17.2 acres and has in excess of 47,000 stems. The largest single organism in the world, it may be a million years old.*

P. nigra 'Italica'

These trees tend to drop their twigs and foliage, and the female plants often shed copious amounts of fluffy seed. Plant them well back from water pipes, drains and building foundations, which can be damaged by the often-invasive roots.

Recommended

P. alba (white poplar, silver-leaved poplar) is a large tree, 40–70' tall and wide, with a broad, irregular to flat-topped crown; the branches are subject to storm damage. It has shallow roots and produces a lot of suckers. The shiny, dark green leaves have silvery white undersides. (Zones 3–8)

P. deltoides (eastern poplar, cottonwood) is a large tree, 75–100' tall and 50–75' wide, with a broad, open, irregular crown and massive, spreading branches. The light to bright green foliage sometimes develops bright yellow fall color. **'Noreaster'** has thicker bark than the species and is resistant to canker. **'Siouxland'** (cottonless cottonwood) grows 60–80' tall and 30–40' wide. This seedless, rust-resistant selection has dark green foliage. (Zones 2–9)

P. x **'Griffin'** is a narrow, pyramidal, seedless clone, 30–60' tall and 10–15' wide, with ascending branches and dark green foliage. It is resistant to galls but susceptible to canker and borers. (Zones 3–8)

P. x *jackii* **'Northwest'** (northwest poplar) grows 50–80' tall and 40–50' wide. This upright, seedless selection with a broad, oval crown has dark green foliage (susceptible to rust) and golden yellow fall color. (Zones 2–6)

P. nigra (black poplar) is a large tree, 80–120' tall and 60–70' wide, with a spreading, rounded crown and thick, deeply fissured, almost black bark. Tinged bronze when young, the dark green foliage turns yellow in fall. **'Italica'** (var. *italica;* Lombardy poplar) is a short-lived male plant, 40–60' tall and 10–15' wide, with a narrow, columnar form and sharply ascending branches. (Zones 3–9)

P. tremula **'Erecta'** (Swedish columnar aspen, European columnar aspen) is a narrow, densely branched, spire-like, seedless tree growing 30–40' tall and 6–10' wide. The branches ascend sharply, and the upper ones are twisted. Fall turns the glossy green foliage yellow. (Zones 2–6)

P. tremuloides (trembling aspen, quaking aspen) is a widespread, native, colony-forming tree with an upright form, whitish bark and a dense, oval to rounded crown. Adapting to a wide range of soil conditions, it grows 30–60' tall and 20–30' wide. The glossy, light to bright green foliage turns bright yellow in fall. **'Pike's Bay'** is a selection from northern Minnesota that grows up to 70' tall and is hardy to Zone 2. It has lighter colored bark than the species, is resistant to black spot and may be more canker resistant. The fall color is bright golden yellow. (Zones 1–6)

P. tremuloides

Problems & Pests

Poplars and aspens are susceptible to a wide range of insects and diseases, including black spot, bacterial and fungal canker, leaf rust, powdery mildew, root rot, aphid-caused petiole gall, borers, caterpillars (especially forest tent caterpillars), leaf beetles, leaf miners, leaf hoppers and scale.

P. x jackii 'Northwest'

Potentilla
Shrubby Cinquefoil
Potentilla

Features: flowers, foliage, habit **Habit:** mounding, deciduous shrub **Height:** 1–4'
Spread: 2–5' **Planting:** bare-root, container; spring or fall **Zones:** 2–8

BEGINNING IN THE 1970S, LANDSCAPERS FELL IN LOVE WITH
Potentilla for some good and solid reasons. These shrubs are extremely winter hardy, shrug off all manner of meteorological abuse, and bloom for an
extended period from early summer through fall. Additionally, 'Potentilla'
was one proper botanical name that landscapers could not only pronounce
but remember. That you can't kill them with fire perhaps sealed their legacy
as the most overused shrub in the history of northern commercial and residential landscaping. They are, in a sense, too perfect: sheared into low
mounds, in bloom they look fake. Use these shrubs sparingly as singles.

Growing

Potentilla prefers **full sun** but tolerates partial or light shade. The soil should be of **poor to average fertility** and **well drained.** This plant tolerates most conditions, including sandy or clay soil and wet conditions, but not drought. Too much fertilizer or too rich a soil encourages weak, floppy, disease-prone growth.

If you wish to shape a potentilla, do so in late winter. For plant rejuvenation, either cut back all of the stems by one-third or do selective pruning by removing one or two of the oldest stems annually.

Tips

Potentilla is useful in a shrub or mixed border. Small cultivars can be included in rock gardens and on rock walls. On slopes that are steep or awkward to mow, potentilla can prevent soil erosion and reduce the time spent maintaining a lawn. Potentilla can even be used to create a low, informal hedge.

'Tangerine' (above & center)

In the scientific community, the plant we call 'potentilla' is now known as Dasiphora floribunda. *Botanists have changed the scientific name a number of times.*

'Abbotswood'

A potentilla's flowers may fade in bright sun or hot weather (yellow or white flowers are least affected). The colors should revive in fall as the weather cools, or try moving the plant to a more sheltered location. A cooler site that still gets lots of sun, or a spot with some shade from the hot afternoon sun, may be all your plant needs to keep its color.

Recommended

P. fruticosa is the yellow-flowered parent of many, many cultivars, of which the following are a few popular and interesting ones.
'**Abbotswood**' is one of the best white-flowered cultivars. It grows 30–36" tall and spreads up to 4'.
'**Coronation Triumph**' is a dense, mounding shrub that grows 3–4' tall and wide. One of the earliest potentillas to bloom, it bears a multitude of bright yellow flowers. DAKOTA

GOLDRUSH ('Absaraka') is a North Dakota State University introduction. It grows 36–42" tall and 4–5' wide and offers dark blue-green foliage and abundant large, golden yellow flowers. It blooms well late in the season. '**Dakota Sunrise**' has prostrate growth when young, becoming a dense mound, 24–36" tall and 2–4' wide. It has bright yellow flowers. '**Daydawn**' is a mounding shrub, 36" tall and wide, with creamy, peach pink flowers that fade to creamy yellow in the heat. '**Gold Drop**' ('Farreri') is a bushy dwarf cultivar with small leaves and bright yellow flowers. It grows 18–24" tall and spreads up to 36". '**Goldfinger**' has large, yellow flowers and a mounding habit. It grows up to 40" tall, with an equal spread. '**Jackmannii**' has good dark green foliage and yellow flowers; it finishes blooming earlier than 'Goldfinger.' It grows 3–4' tall and 3–5' wide. **'Katherine Dykes'** is a smaller cultivar, 24–36" tall, with an equal spread. Its arching branches bear yellow flowers. MANGO TANGO ('UMan') is a compact plant, up to 24" tall and wide, introduced by the University of Manitoba in Canada. Orange-red tinting emanates from the center of each deep yellow flower. In cool weather the flowers take on more red color. **'McKay's White'** bears creamy white flowers but doesn't develop seedheads. It grows 24–36" tall, with an equal spread. **'Pink Beauty'** bears pink semi-double flowers that stand up well in the heat and sun of summer. It grows 24–36" tall, with an equal spread. **'Snowbird'** bears large white semi-double flowers. This robust, somewhat spreading plant grows about 32" tall and spreads up to 4'. **'Tangerine'** has orange flowers that bleach to yellow in excessive direct sunlight, so place it in partial or light shade. This cultivar grows 18–24" tall and spreads 3–4'. **'Yellow Gem'** has bright yellow flowers. This low, mounding, spreading plant grows 12–18" tall and spreads up to 36".

Problems & Pests

Although infrequent, problems with spider mites, fungal leaf spot or mildew are possible.

Potentilla leaves make a pleasant tea that has been thought to relieve coughs and fevers.

'Abbotswood'

Potentilla tolerates excess lime in the soil and handles extreme cold very well. Try this small shrub as a low-maintenance alternative to turfgrass.

P. fruticosa

Redbud

Cercis

Features: spring flowers, fall foliage **Habit:** rounded or spreading, multi-stemmed, deciduous tree or shrub **Height:** 20–30' **Spread:** 25–35' **Planting:** B & B, container; spring **Zones:** 4–9

IF YOU'RE LOOKING FOR A SMALL TREE THAT PROVIDES GLORIOUS spring bloom, wonderful layered form and bold, unusual foliage, plant a redbud. This outstanding native is one of the most desirable ornamental trees for northern landscapes. Redbud is an understory tree, and, although it can grow in full sun (given excellent soil preparation and regular watering), its greatest function is as a main focal point in partial and even full (not dense) shade. In spring, step back and behold.

Select a redbud from a locally grown source. Plants grown from seeds produced in the south are not hardy in the north.

Growing

Redbud grows well in **full sun, partial shade** or **light shade.** The soil should be a **fertile, deep loam** that is **moist** and **well drained.** Mix organic matter such as compost into the soil in and around the planting area—up to 20% organic matter content. Water whenever the top two inches of soil has dried. Always mulch redbud with a three- to four-inch layer of pine needles or wood chips. Plant redbud in spring only.

Pruning is rarely required. The growth of young plants can be thinned to encourage an open habit at maturity. Remove awkward branches after the bloom. This plant has tender roots and does not like being transplanted.

Tips

Redbud can be used as a specimen tree, in a shrub or mixed border or in a woodland garden.

Recommended

C. canadensis (eastern redbud) is a spreading, multi-stemmed (sometimes single-stemmed) tree that bears red, purple or pink flowers in mid-spring before the leaves emerge. The young foliage is bronze, fading to green over summer and turning bright yellow in fall. Redbuds sold in Minnesota and Wisconsin are nearly always *C. canadensis* **Minnesota Strain** or *C. canadensis* **Wisconsin Strain,** both excellent varieties developed from seed strains. Some nurseries still use 'Northland' to mean the 'Minnesota Strain,' but the name has been officially withdrawn because the horticultural

C. canadensis (above & below)

experts who name trees decided that a seed strain did not qualify for a proper cultivar name.

Problems & Pests

Caterpillars, leafhoppers, scale insects, weevils, blight, canker, dieback, downy mildew, leaf spot and *Verticillium* wilt are potential problems for redbud.

Rhododendron
Azalea
Rhododendron

Features: late-winter to early-summer flowers, foliage, habit **Habit:** upright, mounding, rounded, evergreen or deciduous shrub **Height:** 1–10' **Spread:** 2–10' **Planting:** B & B, container; spring or fall **Zones:** 3–9

AMONG THE MOST BEAUTIFUL OF ALL FLOWERING SHRUBS, *Rhododendron* species grace the landscape with large, sensual blooms in spring and attractive form and foliage throughout the growing season. They include many varieties that retain their leaves—and charm—through winter. Plants in the azalea group within the *Rhododendron* genus are, with a few exceptions, deciduous and drop their leaves in fall. Key to the value of *Rhododendron* shrubs is that they flourish and bloom profusely in less than full sun. They are magnificent additions to foundation plantings and mixed shrub borders, and as backdrops in perennial gardens. They do require a bit of soil preparation and watering, so read the following Growing section with care, and you will enjoy great success.

Growing

Rhododendrons prefer **partial shade** or **light shade.** Deciduous azaleas typically perform best in **full sun** or **light shade,** whereas evergreen azaleas tend to appreciate **partial shade.** A location **sheltered** from strong winds is preferable. The soil should be **fertile, humus rich, acidic, moist** and **well drained.** These plants require a soil pH of around 4.5 to 6.0. They are very sensitive to salt. Regular watering is necessary during periods of drought.

Shallow planting with good mulching is essential, as is excellent drainage. In heavy soils, elevate the crown 1" above the soil level when planting to ensure surface drainage of excess water. Don't dig near rhododendrons and azaleas; they resent having their shallow roots disturbed.

Dead and damaged growth can be removed in mid-spring. Spent

flower clusters should be removed if possible. Grasp the base of the cluster between your thumb and forefinger and twist to remove the entire cluster. Be careful not to damage the new buds that form directly beneath the flower cluster.

R. 'Purple Gem'

Tips

A single placement of *Rhododendron* in a mixed shrub border can be stellar, but these plants grow and look better when planted in groups. Use them in shrub or mixed borders, in woodland gardens or in sheltered rock gardens. Take care to give them a suitable home, with protection from the wind and full sun. In a protected location they should not need a burlap wall in winter.

Rhododendrons and azaleas are grouped together in the genus *Rhododendron*. In general, rhododendrons are robust, evergreen shrubs whose flowers have 10 stamens. Azaleas tend to be smaller, evergreen or deciduous shrubs whose smaller flowers have five stamens. Hybridizing is tending to blur this distinction, however, and some people use the word 'rhododendron' to mean any *Rhododendron*.

Recommended

R. 'Anna H. Hall' is a dense, rounded, evergreen rhododendron with large leaves. This *R. yakushimanum* x *R. catawbiense* 'Album' hybrid grows 3–6' tall and 3–5' wide. Bright pink buds yield pale pink flowers that fade to white with age. (Zones 4–7)

R. carolinianum (Carolina rhododendron) is a rounded, evergreen rhododendron that grows 3–6' tall and wide or wider, often becoming open with age. In mid-spring it produces trusses of flowers ranging in

color from purple-pink to pink to white, with green or brown spots. The dark green foliage, which is aromatic when bruised or crushed, takes on purple highlights in winter. In sheltered sites it may survive in Zone 4. (Zones 5–8)

R. catawbiense (Catawba rhododendron, mountain rosebay) is a large, rounded, evergreen rhododendron. It grows 6–10' tall, with an equal spread. Clusters of reddish purple flowers appear in late spring. **'Nova Zembla'** has purple-hued red flowers. It is also heat tolerant. (Zones 4–8)

R. x *gandavense* (Ghent hybrids) are upright, deciduous azaleas, 6–10' tall and wide. The often-fragrant single or double flowers appear in mid- to late spring; they come in many colors, including white, yellow, pink, orange, purple-red and red. These plants often have excellent fall color. (Zones 5–8)

R. **'Ken Janeck'** (*R. yakushimanum* 'Ken Janeck') is vigorous, dense, mound-forming and evergreen.

R. PJM hybrid

It grows 24–36" tall and 2–5' wide. In mid-spring it produces dense trusses of deep pink flowers that fade to white with age. The large, dark green leaves have woolly undersides. (Zones 4–8)

R. x *kosteranum* (Mollis hybrids) are deciduous azaleas that grow 4–6' tall and wide, with trusses of flowers in yellow, orange, salmon, pink or

R. Northern Lights hybrid

R. Northern Lights hybrid 'Mandarin Lights'

red. They generally bloom in mid- to late spring. (Zones 4–8)

R. x *marjatta* (Marjatta hybrids) were developed at the University of Helsinki in Finland by Marjatta Uosukainen. These rhododendron hybrids have large, dark green, evergreen leaves and large showy flowers. '**Hellikki**' is a dense, spreading shrub that grows 5–6' tall and wide, with shiny foliage and dark violet red

R. PJM hybrid

flowers appearing in mid-spring. The buds and new growth are covered in yellowish fuzz. '**Helsinki University**' has bright pink mid-spring flowers with orange-red spots. The dense foliage is tinged red when young. This upright shrub grows to 5–7' tall and 4–5' wide. '**Mikkeli**' ('St. Michel') is the hardiest Marjatta hybrid (to Zone 3) and the last to bloom, usually in early to mid-summer. It is a rounded shrub growing 5–6' tall and wide, bearing pink-tinged white flowers with green spots. '**Pohjola's Daughter**' ('Pohjolan Tytär') is a low, dense, spreading shrub that grows 36" tall and 4' wide. The light pink flowers arising from the bright violet-red buds fade to white with green or brown spots. (Zones 4–8)

R. mucronulatum (Korean rhododendron) is a rounded to upright, deciduous azalea that grows 1–8' tall and spreads 3–8'. It bears pinky purple flowers in early spring. '**Cornell Pink**' bears bright pink flowers. (Zones 4–8)

R. **Northern Lights hybrids** are broad, rounded, deciduous azaleas developed by the University of Minnesota Landscape Arboretum. They grow about 5' tall and spread about 36". They are very cold hardy and are excellent choices for gardens in northern Wisconsin and Minnesota. '**Golden Lights**' has fragrant yellow flowers. '**Lemon Lights**' bears lemon yellow flowers. '**Mandarin Lights**' has bright orange flowers. '**Orchid Lights**' is a bushy, compact plant with light purple flowers. (Zones 3–7)

R. **'Northern Starburst'** is a rounded, evergreen rhododendron that grows 4–5' tall and 3–5' wide. Red buds in early spring produce thick, frilly, deep pink flowers that are lighter on the inside. Shiny green when new, the foliage takes on cinnamon brown highlights in summer, then turns purple-black in late fall and winter. (Zones 4–8)

R. **PJM hybrids** are compact, rounded, dwarf, evergreen rhododendrons. These weevil-resistant shrubs grow 3–6' tall, with an equal spread. They bloom in early to mid-spring. **'Aglo'** bears pink flowers with reddish throats. **'Black Satin'** is a semi-erect shrub with dark rose-pink to purple-pink flowers. In fall and winter the glossy foliage is dark purple-black to coal-black. **'Olga Mezitt'** bears peachy pink flowers. The leaves turn red in fall and winter. **'Regal'** has a more spreading habit than the original PJM hybrid and bears pink flowers. (Zones 4–8)

R. prinophyllum (*R. roseum*; rose-shell azalea) is a well-branched, spreading, deciduous azalea with dense trusses of fragrant (clove-scented) white to bright rose pink flowers in mid- to late spring. It grows 3–6' tall and 6' wide and tolerates a higher (more alkaline) pH than most other plants in this genus. The bright green foliage is tinted bronze in fall. *R. prinophyllum* is one of the parents of the Northern Lights hybrids. (Zones 3–8)

R. **'Purple Gem'** is a dwarf, rounded, evergreen rhododendron that grows 18–24" tall and 2–4' wide. It has small, dark green leaves and abundant trusses of small, light purple flowers. (Zones 4–8)

Problems & Pests

In good conditions with well-drained soil, rhododendrons and azaleas suffer few problems. Stressed plants may be troubled by aphids, black vine weevils, caterpillars, Japanese beetles, lace bugs, leafhoppers, scale insects, leaf gall, petal blight, powdery mildew, root rot or rust.

R. carolinianum cultivar

Russian Cypress
Russian Arborvitae, Siberian Cypress
Microbiota

Features: winter foliage, form **Habit:** wide-spreading, prostrate, evergreen shrub
Height: 12–18" **Spread:** 6–10' **Planting:** container; spring **Zones:** 2–8

OOH, NOW WE'RE TALKING! RUSSIAN CYPRESS IS AN EXQUISITE,
extremely cold-hardy, low-growing evergreen shrub that is finally getting the
attention—and nursery sales activity—it deserves. Too often,
when it comes to evergreen options for shady areas, the
first (and only) choice of homeowners and landscape
designers is the good old yew. Lovely as yews are, if what
you need is a beautifully textured, low-growing evergreen
in light to partial shade, give Russian cypress strong consideration. And don't freak out in fall when the entire plant turns
plum-colored. That's just a nice late-season bonus.

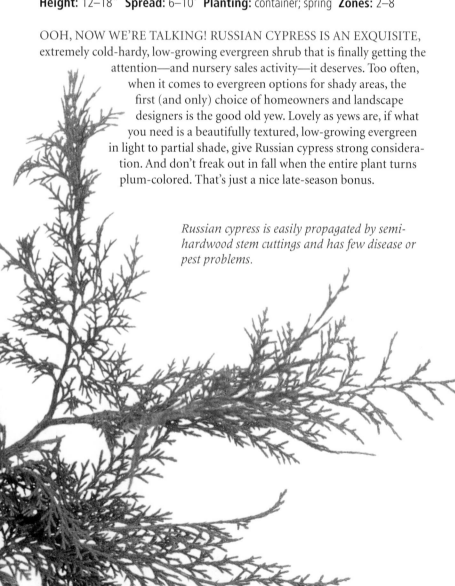

*Russian cypress is easily propagated by semi-
hardwood stem cuttings and has few disease or
pest problems.*

Growing

Russian cypress grows best in **partial to nearly full shade,** for it prefers life on the cool side, but it struggles in dense shade. If mulched and watered regularly, it does well in full sun. The soil should be of **moderate fertility** and must be **well drained** or the plant can die from root rot. Mulching around the base of the plant, and regular watering, help keep the soil cool. Russian cypress tolerates windy sites and can adapt to poor, dry soil if the drainage is good.

Russian cypress needs little to no pruning. Remove any wayward growth.

Tips

Russian cypress makes an excellent groundcover. It can be used for erosion control on slopes, and it cascades gracefully down walls and raised planters. It can be used in shrub beds and rock gardens, but some people might find it too large for that purpose. Russian cypress is a good substitute for the prostrate junipers and yews.

M. decussata

Recommended

M. decussata is an extremely cold-hardy, slow-growing evergreen shrub having wide-spreading, prostrate branches with pendent branch tips that radiate out from the crown of the plant. The flattened splays of bright green foliage gradually darken over summer and become an attractive reddish brown to bronze-purple in winter. In spring the green color returns very quickly. This shrub can grow a little taller and definitely much wider than it is reputed to. **'Northern Pride'** is a named selection available in nurseries. Likely the species with a different name, it has no apparent distinguishing features.

M. decussata

Serviceberry
Saskatoon, Juneberry, Shadberry
Amelanchier

Features: spring or early-summer flowers, edible fruit, fall color, habit, bark
Habit: single- or multi-stemmed, deciduous large shrub or small tree **Height:** 3–30'
Spread: 3–30' **Planting:** B & B, container; spring or fall **Zones:** 3–9

FEW LARGE SHRUBS ARE AS WELL SUITED FOR NATURALIZED AREAS as *Amelanchier*. These tough, easy-to-grow shrubs include a number of native varieties. They are splendid in informal mass plantings, although I've walked down the center of a formal *allée* of *A. canadensis* that was stunning. *Amelanchier* berries (which in truth are not berries, but pomes, similar to pears or apples) attract large numbers of birds; the fruits of *A. alnifolia* are edible and delicious. All serviceberries produce clusters of attractive white flowers in spring.

The alternative name 'shadberry' may have come about because the spring flowers appear about the time American shad spawn.

Growing

Most serviceberries grow well in **full sun;** any exceptions are noted by species. The soil should be **fertile, humus rich, moist** and **well drained.** *A. canadensis* tolerates boggy soil conditions.

Dead, damaged, diseased and awkward branches can be removed as needed. To encourage healthy growth and an attractive habit, you can prune young plants, particularly multi-stemmed ones, after flowering finishes. Keep only the strongest, healthiest stems.

Tips

Serviceberries make beautiful specimen plants or even shade trees in small gardens. Spring flowers, edible fruit, attractive fall color and an often artistic branching habit make them excellent ornamental trees all year long. The shrubbier forms can be grown along the edges of a woodland garden or in a border. In the wild, serviceberries are sometimes found growing near water sources, and they can make beautiful pondside or streamside plants.

Recommended

A. alnifolia (Saskatoon berry, alder-leaved serviceberry) is a large, rounded, suckering shrub, 3–12' tall, with an equal spread. This native bears clusters of white flowers in late spring and edible, dark purple fruit in summer. Shades of yellow, orange and red color the fall foliage. **'Regent'** is a compact plant, 4–6' tall, with an equal spread, featuring attractive flowers, delicious

A. laevis

A. alnifolia 'Regent'

fruit and good fall color. (Zones 3–8)

A. arborea (common serviceberry, Juneberry) is a small single- or multi-stemmed tree, native to Minnesota and Wisconsin, that grows 15–25' tall and spreads 15–30'. Spring brings clusters of fragrant white flowers. The edible fruit ripens to reddish purple in summer. Fall turns the foliage shades ranging from yellow to red. (Zones 4–9)

A. canadensis (shadblow serviceberry) forms a large, upright, suckering shrub, 6–20' tall and spreading 5–15'. Edible, dark purple summer fruit follows the white spring flowers. The foliage turns orange and red in fall. RAINBOW PILLAR ('**Glenn Form**') is a compact, columnar cultivar with strong fall color. Growing 8–15' tall and 5' wide, it is hardy only to Zone 4. (Zones 3–8)

A. x grandiflora (apple serviceberry) is a small, spreading, often multi-stemmed tree that prefers partial shade. It grows 20–30' tall, with an equal spread. The new foliage is often a bronze color, turning green in summer and bright orange or red in fall. Spring's white flowers are followed by edible purple summer fruit. AUTUMN BRILLIANCE is a fast-growing cultivar that grows to 25' in height and about 20' in spread. The leaves turn brilliant red in fall. This cultivar is hardy to Zone 3. '**Forest Prince**' and '**Princess Diana**' both flower prolifically in spring, bear foliage that turns brilliant red in fall, and may be single- or multi-stemmed. They are hardy to Zone 3. '**Robin Hill**' has pink buds that open to white flowers. It has an upright habit, spreading half as much as the species. (Zones 4–8)

A. laevis (Allegheny serviceberry) is a spreading tree that is native to Wisconsin and Minnesota. It prefers partial shade and grows about 25' tall, with an equal spread. The new leaves are reddish, turning green in summer; their fall color is scarlet. Sweet, dark blue fruit follows the white mid-spring flowers. **'Cumulus'** has an upright, oval habit. It grows to 15–25' in height and 15–20' in spread. This cultivar has white spring flowers and red-orange fall color. (Zones 4–8)

A. x lamarckii (Lamarck's serviceberry) is an erect, multi-stemmed shrub or small tree. Happy in full sun or partial shade, it grows 15–30' tall and 15–25' wide. The dark green foliage has bronze-red tinting; it turns bright orange to red in fall. Abundant pendent clusters of white flowers in spring are followed by sweet-tasting, vibrant purple-red fruit. (Zones 4–8)

Problems & Pests

Problems with borers, leaf miners, fire blight, leaf spot, powdery mildew or rust can occur but are generally not serious.

A. canadensis

A. x grandiflora 'Princess Diana'

With a similar but generally sweeter flavor, serviceberry fruit can be used in place of blueberries in any recipe.

A. arborea

Smokebush
Smoketree
Cotinus

Features: early-summer flowers, summer and fall foliage **Habit:** bushy, rounded, spreading, deciduous tree or shrub **Height:** 5–30' **Spread:** 5–30'
Planting: container; spring or fall **Zones:** 4–8

I'M TRYING TO RECALL IF I'VE EVER DESIGNED A RESIDENTIAL landscape in full sun where I didn't include a smokebush. Nope, I don't think I've missed an opportunity to place another *Cotinus* in the ground. I find little use for the varieties with green foliage, though. *C. obovatus*, which gets gangly and rather weedy-looking, is best used for naturalizing or in a corner of the back 40, but still visible enough so you can enjoy the fall color. The great joy is in growing the varieties with mesmerizing purple leaves. My favorite purple variety is *C. coggygria* 'Royal Purple.' It tends to die back in most Zone 4 winters, keeping the shrub at around 5' tall, with new annual foliage to maintain a rich color. 'Royal Purple' makes a magnificent addition to the formal and informal perennial garden. If the space calls for a taller, wider shrub, try 'Velvet Cloak.'

Growing

Smokebushes grow well in **full sun** or **partial shade,** but strongly purple foliage develops only in full sun. They prefer soil of **average fertility** that is **moist** and **well drained.** Established plants can adapt to dry conditions in sandy soils. Smokebushes are very tolerant of alkaline, gravelly soil.

Long, lanky growth develops from pruning cuts. Plants grown for their foliage are often pruned to the ground each spring, encouraging lush, colorful growth. Alternatively, to avoid lanky growth, shear or prune lightly when the plants are young, then leave them to develop and mature more naturally.

Tips

Smokebushes can be used in a shrub or mixed border, as single specimens or in groups. They are good choices for rocky hillsides.

C. coggygria

C. coggygria 'Royal Purple'

The many-branched flower clusters, usually dull purple and hairy, produce the effect of puffs of smoke over the foliage of smokebush.

C. coggygria cultivar

Smokebush is an easy-to-grow plant that adapts to poor, dry soils.

Recommended

C. coggygria (Eurasian smokebush) grows 10–15' tall and wide. It develops large, puffy plumes of flowers that start out green and gradually turn pinky gray in summer. The green foliage turns red, orange and yellow in fall. **'Grace'** is a hybrid of 'Velvet Cloak' and *C. obovatus*. Featuring large, pink flower panicles and purple-red foliage that fades to blue-green with age, it is the hardiest of the purple-leaved cultivars. **'Nordine'** ('Nordine Red') has pink flowers, showy red fruit and plum purple foliage that turns yellow-orange in fall. **'Royal Purple'** (purple smokebush) has purplish red flowers and dark purple foliage that turns reddish purple in fall. In Zone 4 it rarely grows taller than 5'. **'Velvet Cloak,'** which grows 10–12' tall and wide, also has deep purple foliage with a reddish purple fall color. Its flowers are purple.

C. obovatus (American smoketree, chittamwood) is a small tree or large, multi-stemmed shrub. It grows 20–30' tall and wide, forming an oval to rounded crown. The blue-green to dark green foliage turns shades of yellow, orange, red and purple in fall. The gray-brown bark flakes with age and is quite attractive. In late spring and early summer it produces large clusters of insignificant yellow-green flowers that turn smoke-pink to purple-pink over summer.

Problems & Pests

Verticillium wilt is a serious problem that excellent drainage helps prevent. Powdery mildew is also possible, especially on the purple-leaved forms.

C. coggygria 'Royal Purple' (above & below)

Try encouraging a clematis to wind its way through the spreading branches of a smokebush.

Spirea
Spiraea

Features: summer flowers, habit **Habit:** round, bushy, deciduous shrub **Height:** 6"–10'
Spread: 1–12' **Planting:** bare-root, container; spring or fall **Zones:** 3–9

NORTHERN GARDENERS HAVE BEEN IN LOVE WITH *SPIRAEA* FOR
many years, and with the ongoing introduction of beautiful new varieties,
the affair should last for many more. If you are looking for durable, easy-to-
grow, profusely blooming small shrubs to use in formal or semi-formal
foundation plantings, look no further. Depending on the variety, blooming
times range from spring to mid-summer. All spireas sport clean, striking
foliage, including yellow-, bronze- and lime-colored varieties. Many have a
naturally rounded form that can be maintained by shearing immediately
after blooming. Left to their own devices, these plants often develop an out-
ward-arching habit that fits well into the mixed shrub border.

Growing

Spireas prefer **full sun** but tolerate light shade. The soil should be **fertile, moist** and **well drained.**

Pruning is necessary to keep spireas tidy and graceful. The tight, shrubby types require less pruning than the larger, more open forms, which may require heavy renewal pruning in spring.

The correct pruning method varies with the species and depends on the flowering time. Plants that bloom in spring and early summer usually form their flower buds the previous year and should be pruned immediately after flowering is complete. Cut out one-third of the old stems to encourage new growth.

Plants that flower later in summer or in fall usually form their flower buds during the current year. Cut these plants to within a foot of the ground in early spring, as the buds begin to swell, to encourage lots of new growth and flowers later in the season.

S. japonica 'Shirobori'

Adapting to a variety of situations and requiring only minimal care once established, spireas have become popular as ornamental shrubs.

S. japonica 'Little Princess'

S. japonica 'Goldmound'

Spireas come in sizes, forms, flower colors and leaf colors (summer and fall) to suit almost any sunny area.

S. x vanhouttei

Tips

Spireas are used in shrub or mixed borders, in rock gardens and as informal screens and hedges.

Recommended

S. x arguta (*S.* 'Arguta'; garland spirea) is a dense, rounded shrub with arching stems and bright green foliage. It grows 5–8' tall and wide and bears dense clusters of snow white flowers at the branch tips in mid- to late spring. (Zones 4–7)

S. betulifolia (birchleaf spirea) is a dense, mound-forming shrub that grows 2–4' tall, with an equal spread. It bears clusters of small white flowers in early to mid-summer. The foliage turns golden yellow and bronze in fall and provides a long-lasting, colorful display. **'Tor'** has purple fall foliage.

S. x cinerea is covered with white blooms before the foliage emerges in early spring. It grows in a rounded

form that is 4–5' tall and wide.
'Grefsheim' has a mounding habit.
(Zones 4–7)

S. decumbens (white lace spirea,
Tyrolean spirea) is a prostrate shrub
with branches that ascend at the
tips. It grows 6–15" tall and 2–4'
wide and bears mint green foliage. It
produces an abundance of flat-
topped clusters of white flowers in
late spring. (Zones 5–8)

S. fritschiana (Korean spirea) is a
spreading shrub that grows 24–36"
tall and 4–5' wide. It has blue-green
to dark green foliage that turns
shades of yellow to purple in fall.
Flat-topped clusters of white flowers
appear in late spring to early summer. PINK PARASOLS ('Wilma') bears
abundant, large, parasol-like clusters of soft pink flowers and blue-
green foliage. This low, mounded
shrub, which grows 24–36" tall and
3–4' wide, is hardy only to Zone 4.
(Zones 3–8)

S. japonica (Japanese spirea) forms
a clump of erect stems. It grows 4–6'
tall and spreads up to 5'. Pink or
white flowers are borne in mid- and
late summer. Many cultivars and
hybrids are available—check your
local nursery. **Var. albiflora** (*S. albiflora*; Japanese white spirea) is a low,
dense, mounding shrub. It grows
24–36" tall, with an equal spread,
and bears white flowers in early
summer. **'Alpina'** (var. *alpina*;
'Nana') is a low-growing, spreading
shrub with dense, finely textured,
light blue-green foliage and light to
deep pink flowers. It grows 15–30"
tall and 3–5' wide. **'Anthony
Waterer'** grows 3–4' tall and spreads

S. nipponica

S. japonica 'Anthony Waterer'

S. thunbergii 'Mount Fuji'
S. japonica 'Little Princess'

3–5'. The foliage, reddish when new, turns blue-green over summer and then red again in fall. **'Goldflame'** grows 24–36" tall and 2–4' wide. The new foliage emerges red and matures to yellow-green, with red, orange and yellow fall colors. **'Goldmound'** has bright yellow foliage and bears pink flowers in late spring and early summer. **'Little Princess'** forms a dense mound, 18" tall and 3–6' wide. The flowers are rose pink. MAGIC CARPET ('Walbuma') grows 12–18" tall, with an equal spread. Its red new growth stands out above the gold and lime green of its older foliage. The flowers are dark pink. **'Neon Flash'** bears vivid pink flowers. It grows up to 36" tall and wide. **'Shirobori'** ('Shibori,' 'Shirobana') grows 24" tall and wide. Both pink and white flowers appear on the same plant.

S. nipponica (Nippon spirea) is an upright shrub with arching branches. It grows 3–8' tall, with an equal spread. White flowers appear in mid-summer. **'Halward's Silver'** is a compact, hardy shrub that grows 24–36" tall and 2–4' wide. **'Snowmound'** (snowmound Nippon spirea) has spreading, arching branches that are covered with flowers in early summer. Grown more commonly than the species, this cultivar grows 3–5' tall, with an equal spread. (Zones 4–8)

S. prunifolia (bridalwreath spirea) is an upright shrub, 5–8' tall and wide, with arching branches and shiny, dark green foliage. In late spring to early summer it produces a plethora of button-like, white double flowers.

The fall foliage ranges from yellow-orange to red to purple. (Zones 4–8)

S. thunbergii (Thunberg spirea) is a dense, arching shrub. It grows 3–5' tall and spreads 3–6'. Small clusters of white flowers appear along the stems in spring, before the leaves emerge. **'Mount Fuji'** has small, narrow leaves, each with a white stripe down the center. **'Ogon'** (MELLOW YELLOW) has narrow yellow leaves that turn bronzy in fall. (Zones 4–8)

S. trilobata (dwarf bridal wreath spirea, dwarf Vanhoutte spirea) is a dense, bushy shrub with arching branches. It grows 4–5' tall and wide. White flowers are borne in clusters in early summer. **'Swan Lake'** is a smaller plant with arching branches. It grows 3–4' tall and wide or slightly wider and bears abundant white flowers along its branches. (Zones 3–8)

S. x vanhouttei (bridal wreath spirea, Vanhoutte spirea) is a dense, bushy shrub with arching branches. It grows 6–10' tall and spreads 10–12'. White flowers are borne in clusters in late spring to early summer. **'Renaissance'** has disease-resistant foliage. It grows 5–8' tall and wide. (Zones 3–8)

Problems & Pests

Aphids, dieback, fire blight, leaf spot or powdery mildew can cause occasional problems.

Under a magnifying glass, the flowers of spireas, which are members of the rose family, indeed resemble tiny roses.

S. nipponica (above), *S. nipponica* 'Little Princess' (center)

S. thunbergii 'Ogon' (below)

Spruce
Picea

Features: foliage, cones, habit **Habit:** conical, columnar or globe-like, evergreen trees or shrubs **Height:** 1–80' **Spread:** 18"–30' **Planting:** B & B, container; spring or fall **Zones:** 2–8

PICEA IS A LARGE, INVALUABLE GENUS OF TREES THAT INCLUDES some of the most popular evergreens for Minnesota and Wisconsin gardeners. Looking for a tall, fast-growing, relatively narrow evergreen tree for a small lot? It's tough to beat a Norway spruce. How about broad, dense evergreens to protect your home from chilling northwest winds? Plant a swath of *P. glauca* 'Densata.' The attraction continues when one explores the wonderful dwarf varieties. *P. abies* 'Nidiformis' is spectacular in foundation plantings. *P. pungens* 'Globosa' features true blue needles and is breathtaking when planted near gold-tipped junipers, arborvitae, or *Chamaecyparis.*

Because spruce can maintain their lower branches right to the ground as they mature, they make excellent screens and windbreaks or graceful specimens.

Growing

Spruce grow best in **full sun.** *P. glauca* 'Conica' prefers **light shade** and a **sheltered** location. Spruce prefer **neutral to acidic, deep, well-drained** soil, but tolerate alkaline soil. *P. mariana* grows in boggy and wet areas and tolerates poor soil.

Spruce are best grown from young stock because they dislike being transplanted when larger or more mature. Pruning is rarely needed.

Tips

Spruce trees are used as specimens and windscreens. The dwarf and slow-growing cultivars can also be used in shrub or mixed borders and in containers. *P. mariana* is best used for reclamation and for naturalization.

Oil-based pesticides such as dormant oil can take the blue out of your blue-needled spruce.

P. abies

Antonio Stradivari used spruce to make his renowned violins. The resonant, lightweight but tough wood of spruce is still preferred for violins, guitars, harps and the sounding boards of pianos.

P. abies 'Mucronata'

P. pungens var. *glauca* 'Globosa'

Recommended

P. abies (Norway spruce) is a fast-growing, pyramidal tree with dark green needles. This wind-tolerant species grows 70–80' tall and spreads about 20'. **'Acrocona'** is a dense, pyramidal tree with slightly pendent branches that grows 6–15' tall and 4–9' wide. In spring it bears an abundance of bright red-purple cones at the branch tips. **'Mucronata'** has prominent brown buds and dark green needles. This slow-growing, irregular, mounding to broadly upright shrub grows 5–6' tall and 3–5' wide. **'Nidiformis'** (nest spruce) is a slow-growing, compact, low, mounding cultivar. It grows about 3–4' tall and spreads 3–5'. **'Pendula'** can be staked to a desired height to create a weeping form, or it can be left to sprawl along the ground. It spreads 10–15'. **'Pumila'** is a flattened globe, 3–4' tall and 4–6' wide, with dense branching and short, dark green needles.

P. glauca (white spruce) is a conical tree with blue-green needles. It grows 40–60' tall and spreads 10–20'. **'Conica'** (dwarf Alberta spruce) is a dense, conical, bushy shrub that grows 6–8' tall and spreads 24–36". 'Haal,' 'Jean's Dilly' and 'North Star' are branch sports of 'Conica.' **'Densata'** (var. *densata*; Black Hills spruce) is a slow-growing, dense tree, 30–40' tall and 20–30' wide, with dark green foliage. **'Haal'** grows 5–7' tall and 24" wide with silvery blue foliage. **'Jean's Dilly'** grows 4–6' tall and 18–24" wide, with shorter, thinner needles and twisted branch ends. New growth occurs later than on 'Conica.' **'North Star'** is a dense, compact, upright pyramid with green needles that resist winter windburn. It grows 8' tall and 5' wide. (Zones 2–6)

P. mariana (black spruce, bog spruce) is a narrow, spire-like, conical tree that typically grows 30–40' tall and 6–10' wide. It has dull, blue-green to blue-gray foliage and small purple cones that mature to brown. '**Eri-coides**' (blue nest spruce) is a flat-topped mound that grows 12–18" tall and 30–36" wide. It has short, blue-gray foliage and heath-like stems. '**Golden**' is a broad, upright tree with blue-gray foliage frosted with golden yellow. It grows 20–30' tall and 12–15' wide. (Zones 2–5)

P. omorika (Serbian spruce) is a slow-growing, spire-like tree with upward-arching branches and drooping branchlets. Two white stripes run the length of each needle. It grows 30–50' tall and spreads 10–15'. It is best planted in spring. '**Pendula**' grows 30' tall and 10–15' wide, with pendent, slightly twisted branches that ascend at the tips. '**Pendula Bruns**' has more pronounced weeping branches than 'Pendula.' '**Pimoko**' is a dense, low-growing, irregular shrub that is globe-shaped when young. It grows 2–4' tall and wide. (Zones 4–8)

P. pungens (Colorado spruce) is a conical or columnar tree with stiff, blue-green needles and dense growth. This drought-tolerant tree grows 30–60' tall and 10–20' wide. Var. *glauca* (Colorado blue spruce) is similar to the species but has blue-gray needles. The following cultivars arise from this variety. '**Fat Albert**' is a dense, cone-shaped tree with ascending branches and steel blue needles. It typically grows 10–15' tall and 7–10' wide, but can grow 40' tall and 15' wide in perfect conditions. '**Globosa**' forms a flattened globe, 3–5' tall and 4–6' wide, with blue foliage. It is often grown as a standard. '**Hoopsii**' is a dense, pyramidal tree, 60' tall and 20' wide,

with foliage even more blue-white than var. *glauca*. '**Mission Blue**' is a dense form, up to 40' tall and 20–25' wide, with bold blue foliage. '**Montgomery**' has silvery blue-gray foliage. It grows 3–5' tall and wide and is rounded when young and broadly pyramidal with age. '**Pendula**' has graceful, weeping branches and silver-blue foliage. Stake when young to develop a small, weeping tree, or leave it alone to become a prostrate groundcover. '**Procumbens**' is a prostrate groundcover with bright blue foliage, 18" tall and 3–6' wide.

Problems & Pests

Aphids, caterpillars, gall insects, nematodes, sawflies, scale insects, spider mites, needle cast, rust or wood rot are potential problems.

P. abies 'Nidiformis'

P. glauca

Sumac

Rhus

Features: summer and fall foliage, summer flowers, late-summer to fall fruit, habit
Habit: bushy, suckering, colony-forming, deciduous shrub **Height:** 2–25' **Spread:** 5–25'
or more; often exceeds height **Planting:** container; spring or fall **Zones:** 2–9

MUCH NURSERY RESEARCH AND EXPERIMENTATION HAVE BEEN
invested in this native genus, and the resulting plants are excellent additions
to the northern landscape. Sumacs are long-lived, often spreading and
always easy to grow. The season-long foliage displays outstanding form and
color, with many varieties putting forth a stellar fall show of brilliant yellows, oranges and reds. Sumacs bear male and female flowers on different
plants, and both produce interesting, greenish-yellow, catkin-like flowers.
If pollinated from a nearby male plant, the female flowers develop into
dense, pyramidal clusters of small red fruits that attract birds. *R. aromatica*
'Gro-Low' is a great groundcover for hills and banks near water. An exciting,
new, compact variety to look for is the yellow-leaved *R. typhina* 'Bailtiger.'

Growing

Sumacs develop the best fall color in **full sun** but tolerate partial shade. The soil should be of **average fertility, moist** and **well drained.** Once established, sumacs are very drought tolerant.

These plants can become invasive. Remove suckers that come up where you don't want them; a lawnmower works well for suckers in lawns. Cut out some of the oldest growth each year and allow some replacement suckers to grow in.

Tips

Sumacs can be used to form a specimen group in a shrub or mixed border, in a woodland garden or on a sloping bank. Both male and female plants are needed for fruit to form.

When pulling up suckers, be sure to wear gloves to avoid getting the unusual, onion-like odor all over your hands.

R. typhina

The fruit of the recommended sumac species is edible. For a refreshing beverage that tastes like pink lemonade, soak the ripe fruit in cold water overnight and then strain and sweeten to taste. The species R. coriaria, *also edible, is the source of the important Middle Eastern spice sumac.*

R. glabra

R. typhina

Recommended

R. aromatica (fragrant sumac) forms a low mound of suckering stems, 2–6' tall and 5–10' wide. Clusters of inconspicuous yellow flowers appear in spring, followed in late summer by fuzzy fruit that ripens to red. The aromatic foliage turns red or purple in fall. This species tolerates hot, dry, exposed conditions. It can be used to prevent erosion on hills too steep for mowing. **'Green Globe'** is a rounded, dense shrub that grows 6' tall and wide. **'Gro-Low'** is a groundcover

R. aromatica 'Gro-Low'

growing about 24" tall and spreading up to 8'. (Zones 3–9)

R. copallina (shining sumac, flame-leaf sumac) has exotic, shiny foliage with 'wings' on the leaf stalks between the leaflets. In fall the foliage turns crimson. Fuzzy red fruit appears in mid-fall. This species grows 12' tall and wide. Use it as a spreading shrub in a mass planting. PRAIRIE FLAME (var. *latifolia* 'Morton') has a compact habit, glossy foliage, yellowish white August flowers and brilliant red-orange fall color. It grows 5–7' in height and width. (Zones 4–9)

R. glabra (smooth sumac) grows 8–12' tall, with an equal or greater spread, and forms a bushy, suckering colony. Green summer flower spikes are followed, on female plants, by fuzzy red fruit. The foliage turns brilliant shades of orange, red and purple in fall. (Zones 2–8)

R. trilobata (skunkbush sumac, lemonade sumac) is an upright, vase-like shrub that forms colonies by suckering. It grows 3–6' tall and 6–8' wide, producing yellow-green flowers in late spring to early summer, followed by spherical red fruit. Foul smelling when bruised, the dark green foliage turns shades of yellow to red in fall. This plant is very closely related to *R. aromatica* but has smaller leaves, flowers and fruit. (Zones 3–8)

R. typhina (*R. hirta;* staghorn sumac) is a suckering, colony-forming shrub whose branches are covered with velvety fuzz. This species grows 15–25' tall and spreads 25' or more. Fuzzy, yellow, early-summer blooms are followed by hairy red fruit. The leaves turn stunning shades of yellow, orange and red in fall. **'Bailtiger'** (TIGER EYES) has finely cut, burn-resistant, golden yellow foliage that is bright yellow-green when new and bright red in fall. This open, low-branched shrub grows 6–10' tall and 10–12' wide. **'Laciniata'** (cutleaf staghorn sumac) has finely cut, lace-like leaves and lace-like bracts that give the plant a graceful appearance. (Zones 3–8)

Problems & Pests

Caterpillars, scale insects, canker, dieback, leaf spot, powdery mildew, wood rot or *Verticillium* wilt can afflict sumacs.

R. glabra

R. typhina 'Laciniata' (above & below)

Summersweet Clethra
Sweet Pepperbush, Sweetspire
Clethra

Features: fragrant summer flowers, habit, fall foliage **Habit:** rounded, suckering, deciduous shrub **Height:** 2–8' **Spread:** 3–8' **Planting:** B & B, container; spring **Zones:** 3–9

WHAT WOULD A SHADE GARDENER DO WITHOUT *CLETHRA*? HE OR she would certainly see a lot less bloom. This relatively small, charming shrub has a wide variety of uses and isn't planted nearly enough by northern garden-ers. Its mid-summer bloom is a riotous show featuring long spires of white, pink or reddish-pink flowers. The foliage is a clean, rich green. I plant *Clethra* as singles, pop-ping one here, one there, wherever a compact shrub is needed, be it the foun-dation planting, in front of the mixed shrub border or for extra structure in the perennial garden. *Clethra* doesn't like it dry, so give it a little extra watering time, and then be prepared to fall in love.

Summersweet clethra's late-season flowers are much appreciated in damp, shaded gardens.

Growing

Summersweet clethra grows best in **light shade** or **partial shade.** The soil should be **fertile, humus rich, acidic** and **moist;** it tolerates poor drainage in organic soils.

Deadhead, if possible, to keep the shrub looking neat. Summersweet clethra does best with minimal pruning; dwarf cultivars typically require little if any. One to three of the oldest unproductive stems can be removed every second or third year if the growth seems congested.

Tips

This shrub tends to sucker, although not aggressively, forming a colony of stems. Use it in a border or in a woodland garden. The light shade of a woodland edge is ideal.

Recommended

C. alnifolia is a large, rounded, upright, colony-forming shrub. It grows 3–8' tall, spreads 3–6' and bears attractive spikes of white, highly fragrant flowers in mid- to late summer. The foliage turns yellow in fall. **'Compacta'** ('Nana') is a compact shrub, 3–4' tall and wide, that is hardier than 'Hummingbird.' It has shiny, dark green foliage and abundant clusters of fragrant, creamy white flowers. **'Hummingbird'** is a compact plant that grows 24–40" tall, with a spread of about 3–6'. The very dark green foliage turns yellow in fall. **'Paniculata'** produces large, intensely fragrant flowers. It grows 5–8' tall and wide. **'Pink Spires'** ('Rosea') bears pink flowers and grows up to 8' tall and wide. **'Ruby Spice'** bears fade-resistant, deep pink flowers.

C. alnifolia cultivars (above & below)

Problems & Pests

Although generally trouble free, this plant may suffer some fungal infections, such as root rot.

Tree Peony

Paeonia

Features: flowers, foliage **Habit:** upright, deciduous shrub **Height:** 3–6'
Spread: 3–4' **Planting:** container; spring **Zones:** 4–8

TREE PEONIES ARE DIVAS OF THE PLANT WORLD—SOMEWHAT
fussy and fairly high-maintenance, but when it comes time to put on a show,
boy, do they deliver. The blossoms are enormous, and the foliage is heavily
lobed and supremely attractive. Tree peonies serve well as main focal points
in the formal or semi-formal landscape. This is the type of plant you place in
a line—three spaced evenly along a four-foot iron fence, or two across from
each other at the broad entrance to a formal stone path. I have on occasion
seen them used to good effect as singles, placed where they can be readily
seen on the point of a curving garden bed.

Growing

Tree peonies prefer **full sun** but toler-ate some shade. They like **moderately fertile, humus-rich, neutral to slightly alkaline, moist, very well-drained** soil; add ample compost, up to 25%. *P. delavayi* tolerates clay soils. Too much fertilizer, particularly nitrogen, causes floppy growth and retards blooming. Provide **shelter** from strong winds.

Remove unwanted suckers and deadwood in late winter or early spring. Rejuvenate unkempt plants by cutting back to just above ground level in fall.

Remove and discard or destroy all leaf litter in fall, before snowfall, to reduce disease potential.

Tips

Use tree peonies as specimens or put them in a mixed or shrub bor-der with other early-flowering plants. Avoid sites under other trees to reduce competition for moisture and nutrients.

Plant grafted shrubs with the graft union 5–10" underground to encourage the grafted portion to develop roots.

Recommended

P. delavayi is an upright, minimally branched, deciduous shrub, 3–6' tall and 3–4' wide, that spreads by stolons. The large compound leaves have deeply cut, dark green leaflets. Large, nodding, cup-shaped, dark red to purple-red single flowers appear in mid- to late spring. (Zones 4–7)

P. suffruticosa cultivars

P. suffruticosa (Moutan) is similar to *P. delavayi*. It grows 3–5' tall and 3–4' wide, with large, mid- to dark green leaves. The large, cup-shaped flowers come in red, pink, white, yellow or purple. **Subsp.** *rockii* (*P. rockii;* 'Rock's Variety,' 'Joseph Rock') has white semi-double flow-ers marked with maroon to deep purple at the petal bases.

Problems & Pests

Tree peonies may have trouble with scale, canker, leaf blight, stem wilt or tip blight.

P. suffruticosa

Trumpetcreeper
Trumpet Vine
Campsis

Features: habit, summer flowers **Habit:** clinging, deciduous vine **Height:** 10–60'
Spread: 10–60' **Planting:** container; any time **Zones:** 4–9

ONE OF THE BEST—AND ONLY—FREELY FLOWERING, LARGE VINES
for partial shade, trumpetcreeper is a chugging locomotive of a plant that
will cover, entwine and ascend anything and everything in its path. It's a
great choice for covering an unsightly chain-link
fence, provided no unsuspecting dogs are sleep-
ing nearby. Decent flowering occurs in partial
shade if the plant is fertilized in spring, but
keep a sharp eye on the other end—the
added nutrients will intensify this vine's
already vigorous growth.

*Hummingbirds are
attracted to the long,
tube-like flowers of
trumpetcreepers.*

C. radicans (above & below)

Growing

These heat-tolerant vines grow well in **full sun, partial shade** or **light shade,** but they flower best in full sun. Any soil is fine, but the richer the soil, the more invasive trumpet-creepers can be.

These vines are perfect for people who love to do a lot of pruning. They grow very fast and can quickly take over entire gardens if not kept in check. Prune them back hard each spring to encourage lots of new growth, which is where the summer flowers appear.

Tips

Trumpetcreepers cling to any surface—a wall, a tree, a fence or a telephone pole. Once you have one of these vines, you will probably never get rid of it. One plant can provide a privacy screen very quickly, or it can be grown up an exterior wall or over the porch of a house. Trumpet-creepers can be used on arbors and trellises but need frequent pruning to stay attractive and within bounds.

Recommended

C. x *tagliabuana* INDIAN SUMMER ('Kudian') grows 10–13' tall and wide, producing prominently veined, light salmon orange flowers with darker orange-red throats throughout summer. (Zones 4–8)

C. radicans is valued for its fast growth and for the attractive, trumpet-shaped, dark orange to orange-red flowers it bears for a long period over summer. It can reach 30–60' in height and spread. **'Crimson Trumpet'** has bright red flowers. **'Flava'** bears yellow flowers.

Problems & Pests

Powdery mildew, scale insects, leaf spot or whiteflies can cause problems, but rarely serious ones.

Viburnum

Viburnum

Features: flowers, summer and fall foliage, fruit, habit **Habit:** bushy or spreading, deciduous shrub **Height:** 2–20' **Spread:** 2–15' **Planting:** bare-root, B & B, container; spring or fall **Zones:** 2–9

VIBURNUMS HAVE BEEN HEAVILY USED IN NORTHERN LANDSCAPES for generations, and the many splendid, recently developed varieties available at nurseries today keep them as popular as ever. All manner of fungal disease problems I encountered during my early attempts at growing viburnums soured my opinion of these shrubs, but a decade later many of these problems have been assuaged by hard-working plant hybridizers. Today I couldn't imagine planting a mixed shrub border that did not include several varieties. Take some time deciding. Viburnums feature a wide assortment of attractive foliage choices and ornate, often fragrant flowers. Many produce large clusters of decorative black, blue or red berries in addition to splendid fall color.

Growing

Viburnums grow well in **full sun, partial shade** or **light shade.** The soil should be of **average fertility, moist** and **well drained.** Viburnums tolerate both alkaline and acidic soils.

Little pruning is needed. Remove awkward, dead, damaged or diseased branches as needed.

Tips

Viburnums can be used in borders and woodland gardens. They are a good choice for plantings near patios, decks and swimming pools.

Viburnum fruit varies in its palatability. The very tart fruits of *V. opulus* and *V. trilobum* are popular for making jellies, pies and wine. They can be sweetened somewhat by freezing or by gathering after the first frost or two.

Fruiting is generally better when more than one plant of a species is present, provided they flower at the same time, to allow for cross-pollination.

V. sargentii 'Onondaga' (above)

V. plicatum cultivar (above), *V. opulus* (below)

V. opulus

Recommended

V. cassinoides (withe-rod viburnum) is a compact, dense, rounded, suckering shrub with slightly arching branches. Typically growing 5–6' tall and wide, it can reach a height of 15' and a width of 12' in ideal conditions. Tinted chocolate-bronze when new, the dull, dark green foliage turns dull orange-red to purple in fall. Late

V. plicatum

spring to early summer brings flat-topped clusters of white flowers; the yellow stamens give them a creamy yellow appearance. As the fruit ripens, it changes from green to pink to red to blue to black, often with all the colors present at once in the same fruit cluster. (Zones 3–8)

V. dentatum (arrowwood) is an upright, arching shrub that grows 6–15' tall, with an equal spread. Clusters of white flowers appear in late spring or early summer, followed by dark blue fruit in fall. This hardy, durable shrub adapts to almost any soil conditions. AUTUMN JAZZ ('Ralph Senior') has creamy white flowers followed by blue-black fruit in fall. The fall foliage features many shades of yellow through red. This Chicagoland Grows selection reaches a height and spread of 10–15'. BLUE MUFFIN ('Christom') is a compact cultivar that flowers prolifically and bears clusters of bright blue fruit. It grows 5–7' tall, with an equal spread. CHICAGO LUSTRE ('Synnestvedt') is another Chicagoland Grows selection. The foliage is a glossy dark green. NORTHERN BURGUNDY ('Morton') is a Chicagoland Grows selection that achieves 10–12' in height and 6–8' in width. It offers burgundy fall color and a dense growth pattern. (Zones 2–8)

V. dilatatum (linden viburnum) is an open, upright shrub that grows 8–10' tall and spreads 6–10'. Late-spring or early-summer clusters of white flowers are followed by bright red berries in fall, and the fall foliage is bronze, red or burgundy. CARDINAL CANDY ('Henneke') bears plentiful flowers and fruit. It grows 5–6' tall, with an equal spread, and is hardy to Zone 4. (Zones 5–7)

V. x **'Emerald Triumph'** is a compact hybrid developed through complex breeding. It grows 6–8' tall and wide and bears flat-topped clusters of white flowers in late spring and early summer. The following bright red fruit ripens to black. The shiny, dark green foliage is disease resistant. (Zones 4–7)

V. x *juddii* features dark, leathery foliage and a rounded habit. It grows 6–8' in height and width. Slightly fragrant, the May flowers are pink in bud but open to white. The red fruit turns black, providing a contrast with the red fall foliage. (Zones 4–8)

V. lantana (wayfaring tree) is a large, multi-stemmed shrub or small tree that grows 10–20' tall and

V. lantana

10–15' wide. Clusters of white flowers are borne in late spring and early summer, followed by green fruit that ripens to orange and red before finally turning black in fall. **'Mohican'** is a compact cultivar that grows 8–12' tall and wide. The fruit of this cultivar stays red longer than that of the species. (Zones 3–8)

V. lentago (nannyberry, sheepberry) is an upright, suckering, large shrub or small tree with arching branches. It grows 12–20' tall and 8–10' wide, with shiny, dark green leaves that

V. lantana 'Mohican'

V. dentatum BLUE MUFFIN ('Christom')

V. plicatum cultivar

turn purple-red in fall. It produces flattened clusters of fragrant, cream white flowers in spring. The pinkish red fruit ripens to blue-black. (Zones 2–8)

V. opulus (*V. opulus* var. *opulus;* European cranberrybush, guelder-rose) is a rounded, spreading shrub that grows 8–15' tall and spreads 8–12'. The white flower clusters consist of an outer ring of showy sterile flowers surrounding the inner fertile flowers, giving the plant a lacy look when in bloom in late spring. The fall foliage and bitter, inedible fruit are red. **'Nanum'** ('Compactum') is dense and slow growing, reaching 2–5' in height and spread. **'Roseum'** ('Sterilis,' European snowball bush) bears large clusters of white flowers but does not form fruit. **'Xanthocarpum'** bears bright golden yellow fruit. (Zones 3–8)

V. plicatum (Japanese snowball viburnum) is a bushy, upright shrub with arching stems, reaching 10–15' in height and 12–15' in spread. Ball-like clusters of white flowers appear in late spring, followed by ovoid, bright red fruit that turns black as it ripens. The fall foliage color is reddish purple. (Zones 5–8)

V. prunifolium (blackhaw viburnum) features reddish purple fall color on a horizontally branched, tree-like form that grows 8–15' tall and 8–12' wide. It grows in sun or shade and tolerates dry soil. The May blooms are white and the fruit is pink before turning black. (Zones 3–9)

V. sargentii (Sargent viburnum) is a large, bushy shrub that grows 10–15' tall, with an equal spread. The white early-spring blossoms consist of clusters of inconspicuous fertile flowers surrounded by showy sterile flowers. Red fruit follows in summer and early fall. In fall the foliage is yellow, orange and red. **'Onondaga'** has purple stems and red to pink fertile flowers ringed with showy, pinkish white sterile flowers. The purple-green foliage turns red in fall. (Zones 3–7)

V. trilobum (*V. opulus* var. *americanum;* American cranberrybush, highbush cranberry) is a dense, rounded shrub that is native to much of central North America. It grows 8–15' tall, with a spread of 8–12'. White clusters of showy sterile and inconspicuous fertile flowers appear in early summer, followed by edible red fruit. The fall color is red. This species is resistant to aphids. **'Bailey Compact'** is a compact plant, 5–6' tall and wide, with bright red fall foliage. **'Hahs'** is an upright to rounded shrub, 6–8' tall and wide, that is distinguished by its heavy fruiting. REDWING ('J.N. Select') has red-tinged new foliage that turns bright red to wine red in fall. It grows 8–10' tall and 6–8' wide. The bright red fruit persists as late as early winter. **'Wentworth'** has bright red fall color and abundant yellow-red fruit that ripens to bright red. It grows 10–12' tall and wide. (Zones 2–7)

Problems & Pests

Aphids, borers, mealybugs, scale insects, treehoppers, weevils, dieback, downy mildew, gray mold, leaf spot, powdery mildew, *Verticillium* wilt or wood rot can affect viburnums.

V. opulus 'Xanthocarpum' (above)

V. dilatatum CARDINAL CANDY 'Henneke' (center)

V. plicatum cultivar (below)

Virginia Creeper

Boston Ivy

Parthenocissus

Features: summer and fall foliage, habit **Habit:** clinging, woody, deciduous climber **Height:** 1–70' **Spread:** 30–70' **Planting:** container; spring or fall **Zones:** 3–9

WHEN WE PURCHASED OUR HOME, MY wife told me she had always wanted to live in a house covered with ivy, so I planted five *P. tricuspidata* plants along the front of the two-story structure. Nearly 20 years later, I believe one of them has died, but no matter. Ivy covered it is, and each spring, summer and fall the plants, and the house, look wonderful. Four or five times a summer I scale a ladder in order to keep things tidy, clear the windows and halt growth where I don't want it, but the chore seems a small price to pay. Even in our somewhat shady yard, the large, maple-like leaves remain clean and healthy all season, then turn a rich scarlet in fall.

Growing

These vines grow well in any light from **full sun to full shade.** The soil should preferably be **fertile** and **well drained.** The plants adapt to clay or sandy soils.

Trim back these vigorous growers frequently to keep them where you want them.

Virginia creeper and Boston ivy can cover the sides of buildings, helping keep them cool in summer. Cut the plants back to ensure windows and doors are accessible.

Tips

Given enough time, these vines can cover an entire building, wall, fence or arbor. With clinging rootlets that can adhere to just about any surface—even smooth wood, vinyl, glass or metal—they need no support. The little marks left where a vine is pulled off can be hard to remove or even paint over, though. As groundcovers, these plants spread 50' but grow only up to 12" tall.

The fruit is poisonous.

Recommended

P. quinquefolia (Virginia creeper, woodbine) is a clinging, woody climber that can grow 30–50' tall. The dark green foliage turns flame red in fall. **'Engelmanii'** (var. *engelmanii*) clings better and spreads less rapidly than the species. The rich, deep green leaves turn crimson in fall. Birds relish the bluish black berries.

P. tricuspidata (Boston ivy, Japanese creeper), also a clinging, woody climber, grows 50–70' tall. The three-lobed leaves turn red in fall.

P. tricuspidata 'Lowii'

'Fenway Park' has new yellow foliage that matures to green in summer, then turns red in fall. **'Lowii'** has dainty leaves and brilliant red fall color. (Zones 4–8)

Problems & Pests

Aphids, grape-leaf beetles, leafhoppers, leaf skeletonizers, scale insects, bacterial leaf scorch, canker, dieback, downy mildew, leaf spot, powdery mildew or scab can cause trouble.

P. quinquefolia

Weigela
Weigela

Features: flowers, foliage, habit **Habit:** upright or low, spreading, deciduous shrub **Height:** 18"–6' **Spread:** 18"–6' **Planting:** bare-root, container; spring or fall **Zones:** 3–8

ANY HOT SPOT IN FULL SUN CALLS FOR *WEIGELA*, FOR YOU WILL never tire of the dazzling fireworks display created by its hearty, early summer bloom. Blooming is noticeably reduced in partial shade, enough so that placement in shade seems a disservice to the shrub (plant *Clethra* instead). The listed varieties vary greatly in size, from rounded, compact cultivars such as 'Minuet' to the upright and broad 'Red Prince.' WINE & ROSES is a fine mid-sized variety, with intensely rose pink flowers that contrast magically with the plant's dark burgundy-purple foliage. *Weigela* is unsurpassed in sunny foundation plantings or when grouped to form a mid-sized informal hedge.

Growing

Weigela prefers **full sun** but tolerates partial shade. For the best leaf
color, grow purple-leaved plants in
full sun and yellow-leaved plants in
partial shade. The soil should be
both **fertile** and **well drained,** but
this shrub adapts to most well-
drained soils.

Once flowering is finished, cut the
flowering shoots back to strong
buds or branch junctions. Up to
one-third of the old growth can be
cut back to the ground at the same
time.

Tips

Weigela can be used in a shrub or
mixed border, in an open woodland
garden or as an informal barrier
planting.

Recommended

W. florida is a spreading shrub with
arching branches. Dark pink flower
clusters appear in late spring and
early summer. The species is rarely

'Polka'

*Plant breeders have given us weigela
cultivars with yellow, purple or
variegated foliage and pink, red,
purple or white flowers.*

W. florida MIDNIGHT WINE ('Elvera')

W. florida WINE & ROSES ('Alexandra')

grown; its many wonderful cultivars are preferred. 'Polka,' 'Rumba,' 'Samba' and 'Tango' are hardy in Zones 4–8. **'Carnaval'** ('Courtalor') bears red, pink and white flowers on the same plant. It grows 3–4' tall and wide. FRENCH LACE ('Brigela') grows 4–5' tall and wide and has lime green to yellow leaf margins. The flowers are dark reddish pink. **'Java Red'** has pale lavender pink flowers and purple-frosted, deep green foliage. It grows 3–4' tall and 4–5' wide. MIDNIGHT WINE ('Elvera') is a

W. florida variegated cultivar

dwarf plant that grows up to 18" tall and spreads 18–24". The foliage is purple and the flowers are pink. **'Minuet'** is a compact, spreading shrub, 24–36" tall and about 3–4' wide. The dark pink flowers have yellow throats. The purplish green foliage matures to dark green over summer. This cultivar is hardy in Zones 3–7. **'Pink Princess'** is a spreading shrub with an open habit and lavender pink flowers. It grows 5–6' tall and 4–6' wide. **'Polka'** is a hardy selection that grows 3–4' tall and 4–5' wide. Its large, two-tone flowers are pink with yellow throats. **'Red Prince'** is an upright shrub. It grows 5–6' tall, spreads about 5' and is hardy in Zones 4–7. Bright red flowers appear in early summer, with a second flush in late summer. **'Rumba'** is a compact, spreading plant, 36–42" tall and wide. It has purple-edged, yellow-green foliage and produces abundant dark red flowers with yellow throats from early summer to early fall. **'Samba'** is a vigorous, spreading shrub, 36" tall and wide, with yellow-throated red flowers. It has purple-edged, dark green leaves. **'Tango'** is a hardy selection that grows 24–30" tall and wide. Its dark purple-green foliage has some bronze tinges. The deep red flowers have yellow throats. **'Variegata'** is a compact plant about 5' tall and wide. The flowers are pale pink and the leaves have creamy white margins. This cultivar is hardy to Zone 5. WINE & ROSES ('Alexandra') has dark purple foliage and vivid pink flowers. It grows 4–5' tall and 3–5' wide.

Problems & Pests

Foliar nematodes, scale insects, twig dieback and *Verticillium* wilt are possible problems, but usually not serious ones.

'Rumba'

Weigelas are among the longest-blooming shrubs—the main flush of blooms lasts six weeks, and sporadic flowers appear all summer.

W. florida cultivar

Willow

Salix

Features: form, foliage, catkins, young stem color **Habit:** deciduous; small tree with oval to rounded crown, or small to large, oval to rounded shrub **Height:** 6"–40'
Spread: 3–25' **Planting:** B & B, container; spring or fall **Zones:** 2–8

INTEREST IN WILLOWS HAS RISEN STEADILY IN THE PAST FEW YEARS as more gardeners become familiar with the splendid varieties only recently available in the north. They are star performers in moist areas and are ideal for naturalizing in low, marshy areas. Most varieties have curling branches that add sculptural interest in winter. *S. purpurea* 'Nana' features blue-green, finely textured foliage and deep purple stems and has rapidly become a favorite of landscape designers. *S.* 'Flame' is a magnificent variety, with intense orange-red winter bark, that was discovered by chance in Fertile, Minnesota. Sporting salmon pink stems and light green leaves mottled with pink and cream, the extremely striking *S. integra* 'Hakuro Nishiki' is marvelous as an accent plant in foundation plantings.

Growing

Willows generally grow best in **full sun** in **deep, moist, well-drained** soil. *S.* 'Flame' and *S. integra* 'Hakuro Nishiki' grow well in **light shade.** *S. caprea, S. discolor, S. elaeagnos* and *S. purpurea* are suitable for wet areas. The large *Salix* species and cultivars should not be planted near water supply and drainage lines, because the roots may invade the pipes and cause expensive blockages.

Prune in early spring before new growth begins. For all willows, remove dead, diseased and damaged branches and any branches that spoil the form. *S. caprea* 'Pendula' requires annual removal of up to one-half of the existing branches so the crown does not become congested. For grafted standards, remove all suckers below the graft union.

Young growth has the best stem color. Shrubs grown for this feature need regular rejuvenation pruning. *S.* 'Flame,' *S. elaeagnos* and *S. integra* 'Hakuro Nishiki' look best when cut to within six inches of the ground in early spring every few years. *S. purpurea* can be pruned lightly in early spring if needed. For rejuvenation, *S. purpurea* and *S. caprea* can also be cut back hard to within two to three buds above the ground.

Tips

Willows make excellent specimen plants. The small species look great when used in shrub and mixed borders. Many willows are very effective next to water features.

S. elaeagnos

Willow bark contains salicin, the original source of aspirin (acetylsalicylic acid).

S. matsudana

S. integra 'Hakuro Nishiki'

Recommended

S. caprea (goat willow, pussy willow) is a fast-growing, upright tree or large shrub that grows 15–25' tall and 12–15' wide. The dark green foliage turns yellow in fall. Large, showy, gray catkins appear in late winter to early spring. **'Pendula'** ('Kilmarnock') is a strongly weeping form, growing 18–24" tall and 4–6' wide, that can be used as a sprawling ground cover. It is often sold as a standard of varying height and a 4–6' width. The female form of 'Pendula' is also known as 'Weeping Sally.' (Zones 4–8)

S. discolor (common pussy willow) is a small, upright tree or large shrub that grows 12–18' tall and 6–12' wide. The wonderfully soft, fuzzy, gray catkins are produced in mid- to late spring. (Zones 2–7)

S. elaeagnos (rosemary willow, hoary willow) is a delicate, arching shrub that grows about 10–12' tall and 12–15' wide. It shows off the white, woolly undersides of its long, shiny, narrow leaves in a breeze. Fall color is yellow. (Zones 4–7)

S. **'Flame'** is a large, densely branched shrub, about 15–20' tall and 15' wide, with an oval crown. The young stems are bright orange-red, and the fall color is golden yellow.

S. integra **'Hakuro Nishiki'** (dappled willow) is a somewhat weeping shrub that grows 3–5' tall and wide. Its stems and flower buds are tinged orange-pink, and its light green foliage is mottled with white and pink. This shrub is often grafted onto a stem to create a standard form. (Zones 5–8)

S. matsudana (Hankow willow, Peking willow) is an upright tree, 30–40' tall and 15–25' wide, with an oval to rounded crown. The bright green young foliage darkens in summer and turns yellow-green in fall. **'Golden Curls'** is a hardy, large shrub or small tree with golden-hued, arching, mildly contorted stems and slightly contorted foliage. It grows 30' tall and 15–20' wide. **'Tortuosa'** (corkscrew willow, dragon's claw willow) has contorted and twisted stems and grows 20–30' tall and 15–20' wide. (Zones 4–7)

S. nakamurana var. *yezoalpina* (*S. n.* 'Yezo Alpina,' *S. jezo-alpina;* alpine willow) is a prostrate shrub with thick, trailing stems and large, woolly, silver-green leaves. It has silver catkins and yellow fall color. It grows 6–12" tall and 3–5' wide. (Zones 3–7)

S. purpurea (purple willow, basket willow, purple osier willow) is a large, spreading shrub or small, upright tree with arching branches. It grows 10–15' tall and wide. The foliage is dark green to blue-green, and the young stems are purple. The silvery green catkins appear before the foliage. **'Gracilis'** is a mounding shrub, 4–6' tall and 4–8' wide, with thin, upright, unbranched stems arising from a central crown. The fine foliage is blue-green to gray-green. **'Nana'** is a compact shrub, 3–5' tall and wide, with blue-green to gray-green foliage. (Zones 4–7)

Problems & Pests

Possible problems include aphids, borers, caterpillars, leaf beetles, nematodes, scale insects, canker, crown gall, heart and root rot, powdery mildew and rust. When willows are grown in appropriate conditions, problems are unlikely.

S. purpurea weeping cultivar

During the American Revolution, willow wood was reduced to a fine charcoal that was used to make gunpowder.

S. purpurea 'Nana'

Witchhazel

Hamamelis

Features: flowers, foliage, habit **Habit:** wide-spreading, deciduous shrub or small tree **Height:** 6–20' or more **Spread:** 6–20' or more **Planting:** B & B, container; spring or fall **Zones:** 3–9

WITCHHAZELS WORK WELL AS TRANSITION PLANTS BETWEEN YARD and woods. Most of them bloom in late winter or spring, but *H. virginiana* is a delightful oddity in that it is often the final shrub to bloom in fall. In Zones 3 and 4, *H. virginiana* is usually the only witchhazel available at nurseries. This large, native shrub is found in the wild across Wisconsin and Minnesota, always an indication that the same plant purchased at the nursery likely requires little special care in your home landscape. Wisconsin gardeners in Zone 5 have more choices to explore, including the wonderful varieties found below under *H.* x *intermedia*.

Cut some branches of H. vernalis *or* H. x intermedia *in winter for forcing into bloom indoors.*

Growing

Witchhazels grow well in **full sun** or **light shade.** The soil should be of **average fertility, neutral to acidic, moist** and **well drained.**

Pruning is rarely required. Remove awkward shoots once flowering is complete.

Tips

Witchhazels work well individually or in groups. They can be used as specimen plants, in shrub or mixed borders or in woodland gardens. As small trees, they are ideal for space-limited gardens.

The unusual flowers have long, narrow, crinkled petals that give the plant a spidery appearance when in bloom. If the weather gets too cold, the petals roll up, protecting the flowers and extending the flowering season.

H. virginiana

Early-blooming witchhazels are a welcome sight in late winter and early spring, signaling that a long winter is coming to an end.

H. virginiana with hydrangea

H. virginiana (above & below)

Recommended

H. x *intermedia* is a vase-shaped, spreading shrub that grows 10–20' tall, with an equal spread. Clusters of fragrant flowers in yellow, orange or red appear in late winter. The leaves turn attractive shades of orange, red and bronze in fall. **'Arnold Promise'** has large, fragrant, bright yellow or yellow-orange flowers. **'Diane'** ('Diana') bears dark red flowers, and its fall foliage is yellow, orange and red. **'Jelena'** ('Copper Beauty') has a horizontal branching habit. The fragrant flowers are coppery orange, and the fall color is orange-red. **'Pallida'** is a more compact plant, growing up to 12' tall and wide. It bears very fragrant, bright yellow flowers. **'Ruby Glow'** is a vigorous, upright shrub with deep orange flowers. (Zones 5–9)

H. vernalis (vernal witchhazel) is a rounded, upright, often suckering shrub. It grows 6–15' tall, with an equal spread. The very fragrant flowers of early spring are yellow, orange or red. The foliage turns bright yellow in fall. **'Autumn Embers'** ('Klmnineteen') has fragrant yellow-orange flowers and burgundy red fall foliage. It has an upright to rounded habit and grows to 6' in height and spread. **'Sandra'** has purplish young foliage that turns to purple-tinged green in summer and to yellow, orange or red in fall.

It has dark yellow flowers.
(Zones 4–8)

H. virginiana (common witch-hazel) is a large, rounded, spreading shrub or small tree, 12–20' or more in height, with an equal spread. The yellow fall flowers are often hidden by the foliage, which turns yellow at the same time, but this Minnesota and Wisconsin native is attractive nonetheless. (Zones 3–8)

H. virginiana

Problems & Pests

Aphids, leaf rollers, scale insects, leaf spot, powdery mildew and wood rot are possible problems, but rarely serious ones.

Witchhazel branches have been used as divining rods to find water and gold.

H. vernalis

Yew

Taxus

Features: foliage, habit, red seed cups **Habit:** evergreen; conical or columnar tree, or bushy or spreading shrub **Height:** 1–70' **Spread:** 2–30' **Planting:** B & B, container; spring or fall **Zones:** 2–7

I CAN THINK OF AT LEAST A DOZEN OCCASIONS WHEN I HAVE suggested planting yews to homeowners during design consultations, only to be met with a quick, "Oh, isn't there anything else?" I understand why. For decades, landscapers and homeowners alike have planted yews in tight rings around houses, making yews perhaps the most common evergreen shrubs in America. My advice is, snap out of it. Evergreens are essential for winter interest. For shady places where evergreens 3–15' tall are needed, only yews will do. Boring? Let the spreading varieties spread and don't be so quick with the clippers. Take a look at recent varieties, such as the upright, golden-yellow *T. cuspidata* 'Dwarf Bright Gold' and the sublime *T. c.* 'Nana Aurescens.'

Growing

Most yews grow well in any light conditions from **full sun to full shade.** The soil should be **fertile, moist** and **well drained.** They generally tolerate soils of any acidity, most urban pollution and windy or dry conditions. Avoid very wet soil, such as near downspouts, and areas contaminated with road salt. *T. canadensis* prefers a **cool** site in **partial to full shade,** with **shelter** from strong winds.

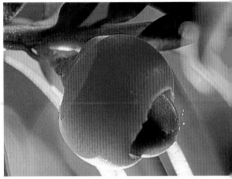

T. baccata

All parts of yews are poisonous, except the pleasant-tasting, fleshy red cup that surrounds the hard, toxic seed.

T. x media cultivar

Because new growth will sprout from old wood, yews can be cut back very hard to reduce their size or for rejuvenation. Hedges and topiary can be trimmed back in summer and fall.

Tips

Use yews in borders or as specimens, hedges, topiary or groundcovers. Male plants must be present for most females to bear the attractive red arils (seed cups).

T. cuspidata

T. baccata

Recommended

T. baccata (English yew) is a broad, conical tree, typically 30–70' tall and 15–30' wide, with attractive flaking bark. Some specimens in Britain are huge trees thousands of years old. To prevent winter foliage discoloration and rotten roots, wind protection and excellent drainage are musts. **'Repandens'** is a spreading, mounding shrub, 2–4' tall and 12–15' wide. (Zones 5–7)

T. x *media* cultivar

T. canadensis (Canadian yew, American yew, ground-hemlock) is a low-growing, spreading, native shrub with prostrate branches that root at the nodes. Usually growing 12–36" tall and spreading 6–8' wide, it sometimes reaches 6' tall and 12' wide. Mostly self-fertile, it produces light red to orange-red fruits. The dense, shiny, dark green foliage is tinged red in winter. (Zones 2–6)

T. cuspidata (Japanese yew) is a slow-growing, broad, columnar or conical tree. It grows 30–50' tall and spreads 20–30'. **'Capitata'** is a pyramidal form that can grow to 30' tall and 20' wide if left unpruned. **'Dwarf Bright Gold'** is an upright, spreading shrub with an irregular form, growing slowly to 6–8' tall and wide. The striped, green-and-gold foliage produces an overall gold cast. **'Green Wave'** is a spreading, mound-forming plant, 3–4' tall, that spreads up to 5'. **'Monloo'** (EMERALD

SPREADER) is a low-growing, flat-topped shrub, 18–30" tall and 8–10' wide, with shiny, emerald to dark green foliage that holds its color through winter. **'Nana Aurescens'** grows slowly to 24–36" tall and 4–6' wide. The burn-resistant foliage, golden yellow when young, turns green with age. **'Nova'** develops a columnar form, 4–6' tall and 24–36" wide, with year-round, dark green foliage. (Zones 4–7)

T.* x *media (English Japanese yew, Anglo-Japanese yew) is a cross between *T. baccata* and *T. cuspidata*, with the vigor of English yew and the cold hardiness of Japanese yew. It forms a rounded, upright tree or shrub of variable height and spread. **'Brownii'** is globe-shaped and about 5' in height and spread. **'Dark Green Pyramidalis'** is a narrow, pyramidal shrub, 12–15' tall and 6–8' wide. It appreciates protection from intense winter sun. **'Densiformis'** is a dense, rounded shrub, 6–8' tall and wide. **'Nigra'** is a mounding shrub, 4–5' tall and wide, with very dark green foliage. **'Tauntonii'** is a spreading cultivar, 3–4' tall and up to 6' wide. It suffers very little foliage browning in either heat or cold. (Zones 4–7)

Problems & Pests

Black vine weevils, mealybugs, mites, scale insects, dieback, needle blight or root rot are possible problems, but not serious ones. A wash with soapy water during hot weather can help control mites; be sure to rinse well. Deer browsing can be a concern in some areas.

T. cuspidata cultivar

Taxol, a drug for treating ovarian, breast and other cancers, was originally derived from the bark of T. brevifolia *(western yew).*

T. x *media* 'Green Wave'

TREE HEIGHT LEGEND: Tall: > 50' • Medium: 25–50' • Short: < 25'

SPECIES by Common Name	Tall Tree	Med. Tree	Short Tree	Shrub	Groundcover	Climber	Evergreen	Deciduous	Variegated	Blue/White	Purple/Red	Yellow/Gold	Dark Green	Light Green
American Bittersweet					•	•		•					•	
Aralia		•	•	•				•	•		•	•	•	
Arborvitae		•	•				•			•		•	•	
Ash	•	•	•					•					•	•
Barberry				•				•	•		•	•	•	•
Beech	•	•						•	•		•	•	•	
Birch	•	•	•					•			•		•	•
Blueberry				•				•					•	
Bog Rosemary				•			•			•			•	
Boxwood				•			•					•	•	•
Bush Honeysuckle				•				•				•	•	
Butterfly Bush				•				•					•	•
Cherry, Plum, Almond	•	•	•	•				•			•		•	•
Chokeberry				•				•					•	
Cotoneaster				•	•			•					•	
Crabapple		•	•					•			•		•	
Currant				•				•	•				•	•
Daphne				•			•	•	•	•		•	•	
Deutzia				•				•					•	•
Dogwood		•	•	•				•	•				•	•
Douglas-Fir	•	•	•				•			•			•	
Elderberry				•				•	•		•	•	•	•
Elm	•	•						•				•	•	
Euonymus			•	•	•	•	•	•	•			•	•	
False Cypress	•	•	•	•			•			•	•	•	•	
False Spirea				•				•					•	
Fir	•	•	•	•			•			•			•	
Forsythia				•				•					•	•
Fringe Tree			•	•				•					•	

Form	Flowers	Foliage	Bark	Fruit/Cones	Scent	Spines	Fall Colour	Winter Interest	Spring	Summer	Fall	Zones	Page Number	SPECIES by Common Name
				•			•		•			2-8	76	American Bittersweet
	•	•		•	•					•		4-8	78	Aralia
•		•	•						•			2-9	80	Arborvitae
							•		•	•		2-9	84	Ash
	•	•		•		•	•		•			4-8	88	Barberry
•		•	•				•		•			4-9	92	Beech
•		•	•				•	•	•			2-10	96	Birch
	•	•		•			•		•	•		2-7	100	Blueberry
	•	•							•	•		2-6	104	Bog Rosemary
•		•							•			4-8	106	Boxwood
•	•	•					•		•	•		3-8	110	Bush Honeysuckle
•	•	•			•				•	•	•	4-9	112	Butterfly Bush
	•		•	•	•		•		•	•		2-9	114	Cherry, Plum, Almond
	•			•	•		•		•	•		3-8	120	Chokeberry
•	•	•		•			•		•			2-8	122	Cotoneaster
•	•		•	•			•		•			2-8	126	Crabapple
	•	•		•					•			2-7	132	Currant
	•	•			•				•		•	4-7	134	Daphne
	•						•		•	•		4-9	138	Deutzia
•	•			•			•		•	•		2-9	140	Dogwood
•		•						•				4-9	146	Douglas-Fir
	•	•		•	•				•	•		3-9	148	Elderberry
•			•				•		•			2-9	152	Elm
•		•	•	•			•		•	•		3-8	156	Euonymus
•		•		•								3-8	160	False Cypress
	•	•								•		2-8	164	False Spirea
•		•		•								3-7	166	Fir
	•						•		•			4-9	170	Forsythia
•	•	•		•	•	•					•	4-9	174	Fringe Tree

TREE HEIGHT LEGEND: Tall: > 50' • Medium: 25–50' • Short: < 25'

SPECIES by Common Name	FORM							FOLIAGE							
	Tall Tree	Med. Tree	Short Tree	Shrub	Groundcover	Climber		Evergreen	Deciduous	Variegated	Blue/White	Purple/Red	Yellow/Gold	Dark Green	Light Green
Ginkgo	•	•							•				•		•
Hawthorn		•	•						•					•	
Hazelnut		•	•	•					•			•	•	•	
Heather					•			•		•	•	•	•	•	
Hemlock	•		•	•				•						•	
Holly			•	•				•	•		•	•		•	•
Honeylocust		•							•				•	•	
Honeysuckle				•		•			•	•			•	•	
Hornbeam		•	•						•					•	
Horsechestnut	•	•	•						•					•	
Hydrangea			•	•		•			•					•	
Juniper	•	•	•	•	•			•			•		•	•	•
Kentucky Coffee Tree	•	•							•					•	
Kerria				•					•	•					
Kiwi						•			•	•	•				
Lilac		•	•	•					•					•	•
Linden	•	•							•					•	
Maackia		•	•						•						
Magnolia		•	•	•					•					•	
Maple	•	•	•	•					•	•		•		•	•
Mountain Ash		•	•						•					•	•
Ninebark				•					•			•	•	•	•
Oak	•	•							•			•			
Pearl Bush				•					•						•
Peashrub				•					•		•			•	•
Persian Parrotia		•	•						•					•	
Pine	•	•	•	•				•				•	•	•	•
Poplar	•	•							•		•			•	•
Potentilla				•					•			•		•	

Form	Flowers	Foliage	Bark	Fruit/Cones	Scent	Spines	Fall Colour	Winter Interest	Spring	Summer	Fall	Zones	Page Number	SPECIES by Common Name
•		•	•				•		•			3-9	176	Ginkgo
	•	•		•		•	•		•	•		3-7	178	Hawthorn
•	•	•		•			•	•	•			3-9	182	Hazelnut
	•	•								•	•	3-7	186	Heather
•		•		•								3-8	188	Hemlock
•		•		•				•	•	•		3-9	190	Holly
•		•				•	•		•			4-8	194	Honeylocust
•	•			•	•				•	•		3-9	196	Honeysuckle
•							•		•			3-9	200	Hornbeam
	•	•		•			•		•	•		3-9	202	Horsechestnut
•	•						•			•	•	3-9	206	Hydrangea
•		•										2-9	212	Juniper
•		•	•	•			•	•	•	•		3-8	218	Kentucky Coffee Tree
•	•								•			4-9	220	Kerria
•	•	•		•	•					•		3-8	222	Kiwi
•	•				•				•	•	•	2-8	224	Lilac
•	•			•			•			•		2-8	230	Linden
•	•	•	•	•						•		3-7	234	Maackia
•	•	•	•	•	•		•		•	•		3-9	236	Magnolia
•	•	•	•	•			•		•			2-9	240	Maple
•	•	•		•			•	•	•	•		2-8	248	Mountain Ash
	•	•	•	•					•	•		2-8	252	Ninebark
•		•	•	•			•		•	•		2-9	254	Oak
	•		•	•				•	•			4-9	258	Pearl Bush
•	•	•				•			•	•		2-8	260	Peashrub
•	•	•	•				•		•			4-8	264	Persian Parrotia
•		•	•	•								2-8	266	Pine
							•		•			1-9	272	Poplar
•	•	•							•	•	•	2-8	276	Potentilla

TREE HEIGHT LEGEND: Tall: > 50' • Medium: 25–50' • Short: < 25'

SPECIES by Common Name	Tall Tree	Med. Tree	Short Tree	Shrub	Groundcover	Climber	Evergreen	Deciduous	Variegated	Blue/White	Purple/Red	Yellow/Gold	Dark Green	Light Green
Redbud		•	•	•				•			•		•	•
Rhododendron				•			•	•			•		•	•
Russian Cypress				•			•				•		•	
Serviceberry		•	•	•				•			•		•	•
Smokebush			•	•				•			•		•	•
Spirea				•				•		•	•	•	•	•
Spruce	•	•	•	•	•	•	•			•			•	•
Sumac			•	•	•			•				•	•	
Summersweet Clethra				•				•					•	•
Tree Peony				•				•					•	
Trumpetcreeper						•		•					•	
Viburnum				•				•					•	
Virginia Creeper						•		•				•	•	
Weigela				•				•	•		•	•	•	•
Willow		•	•	•				•	•	•			•	•
Witchhazel			•	•				•			•		•	
Yew	•	•	•	•			•			•	•	•	•	•

	FEATURES								BLOOMING					SPECIES by Common Name
Form	Flowers	Foliage	Bark	Fruit/Cones	Scent	Spines	Fall Colour	Winter Interest	Spring	Summer	Fall	Zones	Page Number	
	•						•		•			4-9	280	Redbud
•	•	•			•		•	•	•	•		3-9	282	Rhododendron
•								•				2-8	288	Russian Cypress
•	•		•	•	•		•		•	•		3-9	290	Serviceberry
	•	•					•		•	•		4-8	294	Smokebush
•	•	•					•		•	•		3-9	298	Spirea
•		•		•								2-8	304	Spruce
•	•	•		•	•		•		•	•		2-9	308	Sumac
•	•				•		•			•		3-9	312	Summersweet Clethra
	•	•							•			4-8	314	Tree Peony
•	•									•		4-9	316	Trumpetcreeper
•	•	•		•	•		•		•	•		2-9	318	Viburnum
•		•		•			•			•		3-9	324	Virginia Creeper
•	•	•							•	•		3-8	326	Weigela
•	•	•	•						•			2-8	330	Willow
•	•	•			•		•		•		•	3-9	334	Witchhazel
•		•		•	•							2-7	338	Yew

Glossary

B & B: abbreviation for balled-and-burlapped stock, i.e., plants that have been dug out of the ground and have had their rootballs wrapped in burlap

Bonsai: the art of training plants into miniature trees and landscapes

Bract: a modified leaf at the base of a flower or flower cluster; bracts can be showy, as in flowering dogwood blossoms

Candles: the new, soft spring growth of needle-leaved evergreens such as pine, spruce and fir

Crown: the part of a plant at or just below the soil where the stems meet the roots; also, the top of a tree, including the branches and leaves

Cultivar: a cultivated plant variety with one or more distinct differences from the species; e.g., *Hedera helix* is a botanical species, of which 'Gold Heart' is a cultivar distinguished by leaf variegation

Deadhead: to remove spent flowers in order to maintain a neat appearance, encourage a longer blooming period and prevent the plant from expending energy on producing fruit

Dieback: death of a branch from the tip inwards; usually used to describe winter damage.

Dormancy: an inactive stage, often coinciding with the onset of winter

Double flower: a flower with an unusually large number of petals, often caused by mutation of the stamens into petals

Dripline: the area around the bottom of a tree, directly under the tips of the farthest-extending branches

Dwarf: a plant that is small compared to the normal growth of the species; dwarf growth is often cultivated by plant breeders

Espalier: the training of a tree or shrub to grow in two dimensions

Forma (f.): a naturally occurring variant of a species; below the level of subspecies in biological classification and similar to variety

Gall: an abnormal outgrowth or swelling produced as a reaction to sucking insects, other pests or diseases

Genus: a category of biological classification between the species and family levels; the first word in a scientific name indicates the genus, e.g., *Pinus* in *Pinus mugo*

Girdling: a restricted flow of water and nutrients in a plant caused by something tied tightly around a trunk or branch, or by an encircling cut or root

Habit: The growth form of a plant, comprising its size, shape, texture and orientation

Heartwood: the wood in the center of a stem or branch consisting of old, dense, nonfunctional conducting tissue

Hybrid: any plant that results from natural or human-induced cross-breeding between varieties, species or genera; hybrids are often sterile but may be more vigorous than either parent and have attributes of both. Hybrids are indicated in scientific names by an x, e.g., *Forsythia* x *intermedia*

Inflorescence: a flower cluster

Leader: the dominant upward growth at the top of a tree; may be erect or drooping

Nodes: the places on the stem from where leaves grow; when cuttings are planted, new roots grow from the nodes under the soil

pH: a measure of acidity or alkalinity (the lower the pH below 7, the greater the acidity; the higher the pH between 7 and 14, the greater the alkalinity); soil pH influences nutrient availability for plants

Pollarding: a severe form of pruning in which all younger branches of a tree are cut back virtually to the trunk to encourage bushy new growth

Procumbent, prostrate: terms used to describe plants that grow along the ground

Rhizome: a modified stem that grows horizontally underground

Rootball: the root mass and surrounding soil of a container-grown or dug-out plant

Semi-evergreen: describes evergreen plants that in cold climates lose some or all of their leaves over winter

Single flower: a flower with a single ring of typically four or five petals

Species: the original plant from which cultivars are derived; the fundamental unit of biological classification, indicated by a two-part scientific name, e.g., *Pinus mugo* (*mugo* is the specific epithet)

Sport: an atypical plant or flower that arises through mutation; some sports are horticulturally desirable and propagated as new cultivars

Standard: a shrub or small tree grown with an erect main stem; accomplished either through pruning and training or by grafting the plant onto a tall, straight stock

Subspecies (subsp.): a naturally occurring, regional form of a species, often geographically isolated from other subspecies but still potentially able to interbreed with them

Sucker: a shoot that comes up from a root, often some distance from the plant; it can be separated to form a new plant once it develops its own roots

Topiary: the training of plants into geometric, animal or other unique shapes

Variegation: describes foliage that has more than one color, often patched or striped or bearing differently colored leaf margins

Variety (var.): a naturally occurring variant of a species; below the level of subspecies in biological classification

Lilac

Blueberry

Index of Plant Names

Entries in **bold** type indicate the main plant headings.

Pine

Poplar

Potentilla

Redbud

Rhododendron

Serviceberry

Smokebush

Spirea

Spruce

Sumac

Tree Peony

Trumpetcreeper